BALANCED LITERACY INSTRUCTION:

A TEACHER'S RESOURCE BOOK

2nd Edition

BALANCED LITERACY INSTRUCTION: A TEACHER'S RESOURCE BOOK

2nd Edition

Kathryn H. Au
Jacquelin H. Carroll
Judith A. Scheu

Christopher-Gordon Publishers, Inc.
Norwood, Massachusetts

0377666

Credits

Every effort has been made to contact copyright holders for permission to reproduce borrowed material where necessary. We apologize for any oversights and would be happy to rectify them in future prints.

Au, K. H. (1998). Constructivist approaches, phonics, and the literacy learning of students of diverse backgrounds. In T. Shanahan & F. V. Rodriguez-Brown (Eds.), Forty-seventh yearbook of the National Reading Conference (pp. 1-21). Chicago, IL: Used with the permission of National Reading Conference.

Excerpt from *The American Heritage Word Frequency Book*, copyright 1971, used with permission of Houghton Mifflin Company.

Figure from Wylie and Durrell, *Elementary English,* 47, 1970. Used with permission of National Council of Teachers of English.

Figure from Raphael, T. E., & McMahon, S. (October 1994). Book Club: An alternative framework for reading instruction. *The Reading Teacher,* 38(2), reprinted with permission of Taffy E. Raphael and the International Reading Association. All rights reserved.

Au, Kathryn Hu-Pei, Scheu, Judith A., Kawakami, Alice J., & Herman, Patricia A., (1990 April). Assessment and accountability in a whole literacy curriculum. *The Reading Teacher*, 43(8). Used with permission of International Reading Association.

Forms from; *Together is Better: Collaborative Assessment, Evaluation & Reporting* by A. Davies, C.Cameron, C. Politano, & K. Gregory, 1992. Reprinted with permission of Peguis Publishers.

Christopher-Gordon Publishers, Inc.
1502 Providence Highway, Suite 12
Norwood, MA 02062
1-800-934-8322
781-762-5577

Copyright © 2001 by Christopher-Gordon Publishers, Inc.

Printed in the United States of America

10 9 8 7 6 5 4 3 2   05 04 03 02

Library of Congress Catalog Card Number:00-110841

ISBN: 1-929024-26-6

Table of Contents

PREFACE

Since the first edition of this book was published, reading instruction has become an even more hotly debated topic. In this contentious atmosphere, we think the message of balance in literacy instruction needs to come through loud and clear. In this second edition, we have expanded our treatment of the more controversial issues: beginning reading and standards-based assessment. Our overall message remains the same: Learning to read is not a simple process and cannot adequately be addressed through simple solutions to instruction. Teachers need a repertoire of strategies in order to adjust instruction to meet the needs of every child. It is this repertoire that we have described here.

The authors of this book—Kathy, Jackie, and Judy—worked together as teacher educators for more than a decade, assisting classroom teachers in grades K through 6 in the implementation of readers' and writers' workshops. We wrote this book to make available, in one place, the ideas and instructional approaches we and these teachers found most valuable and effective in improving literacy instruction and students' achievement.

These ideas and instructional approaches fall under the heading of *balanced literacy instruction.* In this type of instruction, we acknowledge that it is necessary and essential to consider both (a) children's interests and processes of meaning-making and (b) systematic instruction in the skills and strategies required for effective reading and writing. Literacy instruction is organized in two workshops: one focusing on reading and one focusing on writing.

The audience for this book is educators, particularly inservice and preservice teachers, interested in a sound introduction to balanced literacy instruction. We wrote this book to serve as a resource for teachers. While comprehensive in terms of the topics and issues addressed, the book consists entirely of short articles that can be read in a brief period of time, from 5 to 10 minutes. As teacher educators working with inservice teachers, we often found ourselves looking for readings that could fit into after-school workshops of 45 minutes or an hour. We developed these articles to meet the needs of staff developers and teachers who find themselves in a similar time crunch. For those who want to do in-depth reading, reference information is provided.

About 85% of the more than 90 articles in this book are practical in nature. Most articles describe particular instructional approaches or strategies, such as scheduling in the readers' workshop or how to teach spelling. Some articles are vignettes of particular classrooms, showing how instruction or assessment is actually carried out by teachers at different grade levels. Most chapters include a "troubleshooting" article addressing a challenging or controversial topic, such as phonics, grading, or the instruction of struggling readers. Most chapters also include an article on making connections to the home and community.

The remaining 15% of the articles feature the thinking of experts ranging from the Russian psychologist Lev Vygotsky to children's literature expert Violet Harris. We wrote these articles as a way of presenting theories and key concepts in as painless a manner as possible. It is only through theory that the reasons for teaching in one way rather than another become clear. We know, however, that most teachers prefer to start with practice rather than theory, and many may choose to read these "expert" articles last. Many teachers told us that the theory made sense to them only after they had become comfortable with teaching the readers' and writers' workshops. Then the theory became highly valuable, as a way of guiding their instructional decision-making.

Each article, chapter, and section can be read on its own. We designed the book to be used as a resource that teachers might dip into from time to time, reading as much or as little as time and interest permit.

Nevertheless, a few words about the overall structure of the book might be helpful to readers. The book is organized into five parts. The first part, which consists of just one chapter, is an introduction to balanced literacy instruction. It opens with classroom vignettes, followed by an article presenting a curriculum framework for balanced literacy instruction. The rest of the section features the ideas of some of the key figures in the field. Don't be alarmed. This is the only section that consists largely of the "expert" articles mentioned earlier.

Section I, on the readers' workshop, opens with a chapter showing how the readers' workshop operates in sample classrooms at grades K, 2, and 4. The next chapter explores the structure and organization of the readers' workshop. The last two chapters in this section look at teacher-directed activities and at student-directed activities in the readers' workshop.

Section II, on the writers' workshop, is organized in the same manner as the section about the readers' workshop, so that the reader can see parallels between the two. In our experience, teachers find it best to begin by implementing just one of the workshops, usually the writers' workshop. Once the first workshop has been implemented, they find it easier to put the second workshop in place, because many of the same principles can be applied.

Section III addresses the all-important topic of assessment and evaluation. States, districts, and schools are attempting to promote students' literacy achievement through the implementation of standards, outcomes, or benchmarks. Our treatment of assessment provides practical advice for teachers working with standards-based assessment. This section gives an overview of assessment procedures in sample classrooms, then presents chapters on the procedures teachers can follow to make standards-based assessment straightforward, manageable, and beneficial to students.

Section IV, the conclusion, is entitled "Keeping It Going" and deals with the process of change. We begin this section with vignettes of teachers engaged in the change process. Then we discuss specific steps that staff developers and groups of teachers might follow to initiate and sustain the process of moving toward balanced literacy instruction. This section might be particularly useful to staff developers, instructional leaders, and others working with the change process. This chapter also provides guidance to teachers who wish to direct their own professional development.

In short, we believe this book brings together the theoretical and practical information teachers need to make balanced literacy instruction a reality in their classrooms. We believe that the systematic application of this knowledge will lead us closer to the goal of helping all students reach high levels of literacy.

Kathy Au
Jackie Carroll
Judy Scheu
Honolulu, Hawai'i
October, 2000

Chapter 1

PERSPECTIVES

Classroom Vignettes

You are about to read three vignettes that will give you an idea of the kinds of learning experiences students have in classrooms with balanced literacy instruction. The vignettes provide a quick look at the major approaches to be discussed in detail in this book: the process approach to writing and the writers' workshop and literature-based instruction and the readers' workshop. As you read the vignettes, notice how the students are learning to use reading and writing in purposeful ways. Notice also how reading and writing are social experiences that allow students to learn from classmates as well as from the teacher.

A Kindergarten Writer Gains Independence

One day in March, Debbie couldn't wait for the writers' workshop to begin, because she had something important to write about. She wrote independently, pronouncing each word and recording letters for the sounds she heard. When she conferred with her teacher, Sally O'Brien, she read the exciting news, pointing to each word:

> I WNT TO SE MY BE nES
> [I went to see my baby niece]

> AT MY ANTE RNAS HS.
> [at my Aunty Renee's house.]

> After sharing her writing with her teacher, Debbie exclaimed, "Dasherez is her name. I better add that to my story." She returned to her draft and wrote:

> DCRACWZ is r NM
> [Dasherez is her name.]

In the days that followed, Debbie added to this draft. When she was finished, Mrs. O'Brien helped her spell the words correctly. Debbie published her story as an illustrated book. She shared her book in the author's chair, and Mrs. O'Brien placed the book in the classroom library so it would be available for the other children to read.

The kindergarten children in this class functioned with remarkable independence during the writers' workshop, because Mrs. Brien developed and fostered that independence. For example, she modeled a strategy for sounding out and writing words by leaving spaces in the middle for unknown letters, and she told her students they could do the same in their writing. When Debbie wanted to write *were,* Mrs. O'Brien asked her how she could do that. Debbie wrote the letters *w* and *r*, leaving a space between them. "I'm going to fill it in," she told her teacher. Then she put an *e* between the other two letters. Mrs. O'Brien showed the class how to use print resources around the room to find the words they needed for their stories. When Debbie needed the word *monster*, Nathan led her to the word charts and began looking through the *m* page with her. Debbie told Nathan, "I can do it myself. I know where to find it."

A Second Grader Makes Reading-Writing Connections

During the writers' workshop, Elaine and Kanani went to an area designated for peer conferences to talk about a piece Elaine had written, a 3 1/4 page text inspired by the story of Goldilocks and the three bears. Elaine's draft reflected revisions she had made earlier when working on her own. She and Kanani left the area to get a sticker from the table at the front of the room. They returned to the conference table and Elaine wrote the date and their names, then placed the sticker at the bottom of her story as a record of their conference. The children pulled a card from the tub containing guides for conferences and read, "Read story." Elaine began, "Once upon a time…" Soon she stopped and said, "No," crossed out a word and added another. She continued to revise her writing as she read aloud. Kanani played with a sticker but listened attentively. When Elaine occasionally hesitated on a word, he said one aloud that made sense.

Kanani had no questions for Elaine, so they decided their conference was complete. Kanani went to the publishing center and continued working on illustrations for his latest book. Elaine got a copy of *The Three Bears* from the classroom library and took it to her desk. She used it to correct words she had circled in her story, words she thought were spelled incorrectly. She changed *samill* (small) to *wee* and *bag* (big) to *great*.

Elaine said to herself, "Now what I got to do? O.k. I know what to do." She went to the front table and wrote her name in the notebook to show that she was ready for a teacher conference.

During the readers' workshop, Marcus Jamal, Elaine's teacher, had had the students read an assortment of traditional tales. These included stories from the European tradition (such as *Cinderella*), as well as those from Africa (such as *Mufaro's Beautiful Daughters*) and Asia (*Yeh-Shen*). After the students had read and enjoyed these stories, Mr. Jamal had them prepare illustrations to add to a story matrix. This activity allowed the students to see similarities and differences among the tales. Mr. Jamal suggested that students might like to try writing their own versions of familiar tales during the writers' workshop. Elaine was one of the students who chose to do so.

A Fourth Grader Responds to Literature

During the readers' workshop, Sol joined a group of five classmates in a circle on the carpet for a literature discussion group. The students were reading *A Taste of Blackberries*, and today it was his turn to lead the discussion. The students began to take turns reading aloud the latest entries written in their literature response logs. Halfway around the circle, Sol stopped the group.

"Do you see what we're doing?" he asked. The others didn't understand what he meant. Sol explained, "We're just reading aloud and we're not talking about anything. Like when Jamie just read, nobody said anything. We're supposed to tell her what we think about what she wrote." Following Sol's suggestion, the students commented on Jamie's written response, saying what they liked about it and whether they had written something similar or different. Gradually, what had begun as a stilted display of reading aloud turned into an animated conversation about the novel.

Sol and the other students in Brenda DeRego's class were given many opportunities to lead their own literature discussion groups. At the beginning of the year, Ms. DeRego taught her students standards for good discussions, so that they learned to value a diversity of ideas and respect each other's opinions. One day, Ms. DeRego spoke with Sol's group about how they could improve their discussions of literature.

"No arguing," Kurt said.

"Yeah, but what if you don't agree with what that person is saying?" Sol wondered.

"If you disagree with someone, how can you say it?" Ms. DeRego asked the group.

"Excuse me, I have another idea," Jamie suggested. Ms. DeRego nodded and emphasized the importance of being able to express a different opinion without hurting someone's feelings.

The Six Aspects of Literacy:
A Curriculum Framework

The vignettes in the previous section gave you a glimpse of balanced literacy instruction from the perspective of students. We turn now to the perspective of teachers such as Sally O'Brien, Marcus Jamal, and Brenda DeRego. How do they view balanced literacy instruction? The starting point for these teachers is a curriculum framework specifying the important areas of literacy to be addressed in classroom instruction.

In this curriculum framework, reading and writing have equal status. The framework addresses both the cognitive and affective dimensions of literacy. It recognizes that literacy is a process of meaning-making, and that the meaning-making process is made easier when students learn the strategies and skills used by proficient readers and writers.

The framework for a balanced literacy curriculum is presented in Figure 1.1. This framework can also be called a *whole literacy* curriculum (Au, Scheu, Kawakami, & Herman, 1990). The *whole* part of this label recognizes the importance of students' engagement in the full processes of reading and writing in the authentic contexts for learning provided by the readers' and writers' workshops. The *literacy* part of the label refers to the curriculum's emphasis on reading and writing. Of course, speaking and listening are central to the development of literacy and to activities in the readers' and writers' workshops. Oral language and listening comprehension are fully integrated with reading and writing, since students at all grade levels are expected to share their own ideas and respond to the ideas of others. This approach is consistent with research in emergent literacy, which supports the view that literacy does not wait on oral language development (Teale, 1987).

As shown in Figure 1.1, the overall goal of the curriculum is to promote students' ownership of literacy (see Student Ownership, chapter 5). Students who have ownership of literacy value it so much that they use reading and writing at home as well as at

FIGURE 1.1   THE SIX ASPECTS OF LITERACY

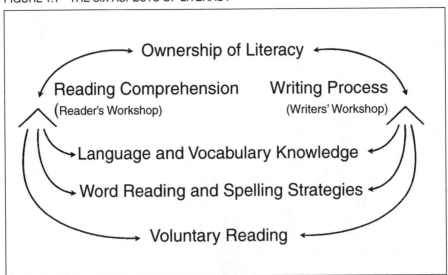

school, for purposes they set for themselves. For example, students choose to read a book in their spare time or to write a letter to a grandparent. Ownership develops best in classrooms in which students and teachers form a community of learners and support one another's literacy learning (Cairney & Langbien, 1989; see also Dudley-Marling & Searle, 1995).

The next two aspects of literacy, reading comprehension and the writing process, are listed below ownership in Figure 1.1. Reading comprehension is at the heart of the readers' workshop, while the writing process serves as the focus for the writers' workshop. The remaining three aspects of literacy—language and vocabulary knowledge, word reading and spelling strategies, and voluntary reading—are all developed within both the readers' and the writers' workshops.

Reading Comprehension

Reading comprehension involves the ability to construct meaning from and to respond to text, using background knowledge as well as printed information. Reading is viewed as the dynamic interaction among the reader, the text, and the situation or social context in which reading takes place (Wixson, Peters, Weber, & Roeber, 1987). In this perspective, a text may have different interpretations, depending on the background knowledge the reader brings to it (Anderson & Pearson, 1984). The social context also influences the process of constructing meaning from text. For example, a reader's interpretation of a novel might differ depending on whether she will be discussing the novel in class or is reading purely for her own enjoyment (Purves, 1985).

Reader response theory (see The Impact of Louise Rosenblatt: Reader Response Theory, chapter 2) plays an important part in a balanced approach to literacy instruction. According to Rosenblatt (1978), more emphasis needs to be placed on the enjoyment of the reading experience, rather than on reading to gather facts or details from the text. Traditional instruction in reading comprehension was largely based on quizzing students about details in the text. Rosenblatt and others argue that an overemphasis on low-level questions detracts from students' efforts to appreciate the novel or other text as a whole and to draw relationships between the text and their own lives. In keeping with reader response theory, teachers might ask students to discuss their feelings about a text, its possible themes, and connections between the text and their own lives (see chapter 4).

Writing Process

Writing involves a process of using print (or for younger children, drawing) to construct meaning and communicate a message. Students experience ownership of writing when they write on self-selected topics and come to see themselves as authors. In a balanced literacy curriculum, writing is viewed as a dynamic, nonlinear process. This process includes planning, drafting, revising, editing, and publishing (Graves, 1983; see The Impact of Donald Graves: The Process Approach to Writing, chapter 6).

Typically, writers go back and forth among these different activities. While drafting, for example, the writer may decide to abandon the piece and begin planning a new one. This thoughtful and deliberate shifting from one activity to another is characteristic of good writers. Good writers pay attention mainly to the overall shape and message of the piece. In contrast, poor writers often become overly concerned with the mechanics of writing, such as spelling and punctuation, rather than with the flow of ideas.

Language and Vocabulary Knowledge

This aspect of literacy concerns students' ability to understand and use appropriate terms and structures in both spoken and printed English. The approach to language development in a balanced literacy curriculum is based on the idea that children learn language by using it for real purposes in social situations (Pinnell & Jaggar, 1991). For example, children can develop oral language through small group, teacher-guided discussions in which they share their responses to an interesting book. Teachers foster children's language development by providing them with many opportunities for authentic communication. Through these opportunities, children gain communicative competence, the ability to use language to express themselves appropriately in a variety of social contexts, and the ability to use language as a tool for learning.

The approach to vocabulary taken in a balanced literacy approach is based on the knowledge hypothesis (Mezynski, 1983), the idea that vocabulary represents the knowledge a person has of particular topics, not just dictionary definitions. The meaning of a new word is acquired gradually, through repeated encounters with that word (Nagy, Herman, & Anderson, 1985). Teachers can build students' vocabulary knowledge by heightening their interest in words, by teaching them strategies for inferring word meanings from text, and by encouraging them to do wide independent reading (see Vocabulary Development, chapter 4).

Word Reading and Spelling Strategies

Many children first learn to deal with print through home experiences with literacy (Taylor, 1983), especially storybook reading. Through storybook reading, children learn concepts about print, for example, that the left page is read before the right and that words run from left to right. Learning concepts about print gives children the foundation for developing word reading and spelling strategies.

Students need to have word reading and spelling strategies if they are to read words accurately and quickly. Fluent readers, those who experience a smooth and easy flow through the text, integrate knowledge of meaning, structure, and visual cues (Clay, 1993) and decode by analogy (by comparing the unknown word to known words with the same spelling patterns) (Gaskins, Gaskins, & Gaskins, 1991; see Decoding by Analogy, chapter 4). Instruction in word reading strategies involves helping students to use the three cue systems mentioned above in a balanced manner. Students must learn to check their guesses about words by using not just one but all three cue systems, and then to correct their guesses. Once students learn to use the three cue systems in a balanced manner, they usually stumble only over multisyllabic words. At this point, they can benefit from learning about base words and affixes, including plural endings, prefixes, and suffixes.

Teachers can help students to develop word reading strategies by teaching them to apply knowledge of the three cue systems when reading (see The Impact of Marie Clay: Cue Systems, chapter 4). Many students benefit from specific instruction in word reading strategies, including phonics (see Troubleshooting: What About Phonics?, chapter 4). In addition to teaching word reading strategies, teachers can make sure children receive ample opportunity to read and reread favorite books. Through reading and rereading, students learn to apply knowledge of the three cue systems in a fluent, coordinated manner. Writing, especially invented spelling, provides children with an excellent opportunity to learn about sound-symbol relationships (see Troubleshooting: What About Conventional Spelling?, chapter 8).

Voluntary Reading

In voluntary reading, students select the materials they want to read, either for information or for pleasure (Spiegel, 1981). Students read to fulfill their own goals, not just to meet the expectations of the teacher and other adults. Ideally, students choose the times when they will read. Voluntary reading is one way that students demonstrate their ownership of literacy (see Voluntary and Independent Reading, chapter 5).

Students' voluntary reading is promoted if they become part of a community of readers. In a community of readers, students and teachers give book talks and otherwise share their reading with one another. Students' voluntary reading is supported because they receive recognition and support for their reading and gain ideas about what they would like to read next. Of course, students must also have ready access to books, preferably through an inviting and well stocked classroom library (Morrow & Weinstein, 1986).

Conclusion

In a balanced literacy curriculum, teachers attend to all six aspects of literacy. Two aspects, ownership and voluntary reading, are affective, while the others are cognitive. Two aspects, reading comprehension and the writing process, focus on complex, higher level thinking and meaning-making. The final two aspects, language and vocabulary knowledge and word reading and spelling strategies, attend to the supporting skills students need to become proficient readers and writers.

References

Anderson, R. C., & Pearson, P. D. (1984). A schema-theoretic view of basic processes in reading comprehension. In P. D. Pearson (Ed.), *Handbook of reading research.* New York: Longman.

Au, K. H., Scheu, J. A., Kawakami, A. J., & Herman, P. A. (1990). Assessment and accountability in a whole literacy curriculum. *The Reading Teacher, 43* (8), 574–578.

Cairney, T., & Langbien, S. (1989). Building communities of readers and writers. *The Reading Teacher, 42* (8), 560–567.

Clay, M. M. (1993). *Reading recovery: A guidebook for teachers in training.* Portsmouth, NH: Heinemann.

Dudley-Marling, C., & Searle, D. (Eds.). (1995). *Who owns learning: Questions of autonomy, choice, and control.* Portsmouth, NH: Heinemann.

Gaskins, R. W., Gaskins, J. C., & Gaskins, I. W. (1991). A decoding program for poor readers—and the rest of the class, too! *Language Arts, 68* (3), 213–225.

Graves, D. (1983). *Writing: Teachers and children at work.* Exeter, NH: Heinemann.

Mezynski, K. (1983). Issues concerning the acquisition of knowledge: Effects of vocabulary training on reading comprehension. *Review of Educational Research, 53* (253–279).

Morrow, L. M., & Weinstein, C. S. (1986). Encouraging voluntary reading: The impact of a literature program on children's use of library centers. *Reading Research Quarterly, 21* (3), 330–346.

Nagy, W. E., Herman, P., & Anderson, R. C. (1985). Learning words from context. *Reading Research Quarterly, 20,* 233–253.

Pinnell, G. S., & Jaggar, A. M. (1991). Oral language: Speaking and listening in the classroom. In J. Flood, J. M. Jensen, D. Lapp, & J. R. Squire (Eds.), *Handbook of research on teaching the English language arts* (pp. 691–720). New York: Macmillan.

Purves, A. C. (1985). That sunny dome: Those caves of ice. In C. R. Cooper (Ed.), *Researching response to literature and the teaching of literature: Points of departure* (pp. 54–69). Norwood, NJ: Ablex.

Rosenblatt, L. (1978). *The reader, the text, the poem: The transactional theory of the literary work.* Carbondale, IL: Southern Illinois University Press.

Spiegel, D. L. (1981). *Reading for pleasure: Guidelines.* Newark, DE: International Reading Association.

Taylor, D. (1983). *Family literacy: Young children learning to read and write.* Portsmouth, NH: Heinemann.

Teale, W. H. (1987). Emergent literacy: Reading and writing development in early childhood. In J. E. Readence & R. S. Baldwin (Eds.), *Research in literacy: Merging perspectives (Thirty-sixth yearbook of the National Reading Conference)* (pp. 45–74). Rochester, NY: National Reading Conference.

Wixson, K. K., Peters, C. W., Weber, E. M., & Roeber, E. D. (1987). New directions in statewide reading assessment. *The Reading Teacher, 40* (8), 479–754.

The Impact of Dorothy Strickland: Balance in Literacy Instruction

You are about to read the first of several articles, placed throughout this book, addressing the work of a prominent researcher whose ideas have had a major influence on the way educators think about literacy instruction. These articles are intended to acquaint you with the theory and concepts underlying balanced literacy instruction.

Dorothy Strickland has worked with many districts, schools, and teachers seeking to make changes in their programs of literacy instruction (Strickland, 1994, 1994–1995). She notes that most teachers are at some point along a continuum of change. They find the process of change challenging, because certain topics in literacy instruction, such as literature-based instruction and phonics, are hotly debated. Many teachers want to come to terms with the issues in order to improve their instruction. Strickland (1994–1995) advises these teachers to

> Get in touch with what you believe about teaching and learning. Your belief system provides the foundation for everything you do. Examine it and give it care and nurturing. But always keep the door open for new ideas and insights. (p. 301)

Skills Versus Meaningful Activities

Achieving a balance in literacy instruction sometimes requires that teachers think about both sides of an emotional conflict. An example of such a conflict is that between advocates of skills and advocates of meaningful literacy activities (Strickland, 1994). Advocates of skills believe that phonics, spelling, punctuation, grammar, and other language conventions must be the focus of the literacy curriculum. They argue that these skills must be taught through direct instruction, in a process that involves students in drill and practice. Advocates of meaningful activities think that literacy curriculum should focus on the full processes of reading and writing. They contend that students gain an understanding of these full processes as they engage in meaningful activities such as reading literature and writing about topics of their own choosing.

Teachers striving for a balanced approach recognize the value in both points of view. They realize that many students, particularly those who do not speak standard English as their first language, may benefit from direct instruction in the conventions (Delpit, 1986). However, they also recognize that skill activities in and of themselves are seldom intrinsically motivating to students. To help students see the purposes of skills, teachers have skill instruction grow out of meaningful literacy activities. For example, a phonics lesson on the sound of *w* can follow the reading of *Whistle for Willie* (Keats, 1964). Similarly, a lesson on beginning sentences with capital letters can occur when students are ready to edit the drafts of the stories they have written. Strickland (1994–95) advises:

> *Don't waste time debating whether or not to teach phonics, spelling, grammar, and other "skills" of literacy.* Obviously, young children cannot read or write without encountering the use of phonics, grammar, spelling, and other

conventions of written language. Do spend time discussing how to teach them in a way that contributes to the learners' self-improvement. Keep in mind that these conventions and enablers to reading and writing are not reading and writing nor are they precursors to involvement in reading and writing as meaningful acts. (p. 299; italics in original)

Strickland asks educators to rethink the whole issue of ability grouping. In her opinion, the disadvantages of fixed ability groups far outnumber the advantages. Ability grouping lowers the self-esteem of struggling readers and results in these students receiving far less instruction than they need. In contrast to fixed ability groups, flexible skills groups (see Troubleshooting: What About Phonics?, chapter 4) give teachers the opportunity to provide intensive skill instruction to those who need it, without creating a permanent "low group" in the classroom.

In balanced literacy instruction, students are given the chance to learn through both direct and indirect instruction. Direct instruction occurs in mini-lessons during the Readers' and Writers' Workshops (see Mini-lessons, chapters 4 and 8). Indirect instruction and opportunities for discovery occur as students are involved in the full processes of reading and writing, and teachers respond to "teachable moments" in small group and individual instruction. With both direct and indirect instruction, Strickland points out, it is important to recognize the difference between what teachers teach and what students learn.

The Curriculum Versus Students' Needs

Strickland (1994-1995) considers the tension between the set curriculum versus students' needs and interests. Teachers may be directed to follow a curriculum from the district, school, or basal reading program. Yet the curriculum may not match teachers' knowledge of their students and what it makes sense to teach at a given moment. Strickland advises teachers to refer to curriculum guides to understand the expectations at their grade level, but not to feel obligated to teach the skills in the exact order in which they appear in the guides. In balanced literacy instruction, skills are developed in an ongoing way. As Strickland points out, it is not a matter of checking off a skill such as "sequence of events" and moving on to the next skill. A skill such as identifying the sequence of events may be taught, applied, and reviewed on a number of occasions, with increasingly complex texts.

Structures for Literacy Instruction

Strickland makes the following suggestions to teachers engaged in changing the way they teach literacy. First, she suggests, teachers should work together to establish structures for planning and organizing instruction. Skillful teachers, Strickland writes, establish predictable schedules and routines with their students. Within the structure set by the teacher, children have experiences with whole group, small group, and individual instruction. Groups are formed on the basis of children's needs for instruction in a particular area, and there are no permanent ability groups.

In Strickland's experience, the first step toward change occurs when teachers can conceptualize an instructional framework for the readers'/writers' workshops. Once teachers have put an overall structure is place, they have a sense of how to move forward with planning and instruction, because new activities build upon the previous ones (see Structuring the Readers' Workshop, chapter 3, and Structuring the Writers' Workshop, chapter 7). Strickland finds that content area activities soon become integrated into the readers'/writers' workshops, and artificial separations between parts of the school day begin to disappear.

Second, Strickland recommends that teachers make good use of both direct and indirect instruction. Excellent teachers, Strickland finds, plan activities so that students have the opportunity to make discoveries about literacy throughout the school day, both with and without teacher guidance. Even during direct instruction these teachers do not rely on the lecture method alone but constantly interact with students, demonstrating, modeling, and helping students rehearse the strategies and skills they will be expected to carry out independently.

Third, Strickland believes that teachers need to evaluate critically the kinds of assessments they have in place. Many school districts are in the process of decreasing norm-referenced testing and increasing performance assessement (see The Impact of P. David Pearson: Standards-Based Assessment, chapter 10). These changes are taking place because performance assessment is closely tied to the curriculum, and the results of these assessments can indicate students' progress toward the outcomes specified by a particular curriculum. Making changes in assessment requires extensive professional development for teachers and administrators and communication among teachers, administrators, school boards, and parents.

As Strickland implies, many teachers find that achieving a balance in literacy instruction involves a process of exploration in which the pros and cons of various theories and teaching approaches must be weighed. There is no recipe for balanced literacy instruction, and the process of change can be difficult. Yet, Strickland (1994) concludes, educators now have the opportunity to provide excellent, learner-centered literacy instruction to all students.

> The knowledge is available. It is time we demonstrated the commitment to seek a better way. (p. 335)

For further discussion of the concept of balance, see Pearson and Raphael (1999).

References

Delpit, L. D. (1986). Skills and other dilemmas of a progressive Black educator. *Harvard Educational Review, 56* (4), 379–385.

Keats, E. J. (1964). *Whistle for Willie.* New York: Viking.

Pearson, P. D., & Raphael, T. E. (1999). Toward a more complex view of balance in the literacy curriculum. In W. D. Hammond & T. E. Raphael (Eds.), *Early literacy instruction for the new millennium* (pp. 1–21). Grand Rapids, MI: Michigan Reading Association and Center for the Improvement of Early Reading Achievement.

Strickland, D. S. (1994). Educating African American learners at risk: Finding a better way. *Language Arts, 71* (5), 328–336.

Stickland, D. S. (1994–1995). Reinventing our literacy programs: Books, basics, and balance. *The Reading Teacher, 48* (4), 294–306.

The Impact of Lev Vygotsky: Social Constructivism

An important question in discussions of literacy instruction is that of how people learn to read and write, or of how people learn in general. Constructivism and social constructivism are philosophical views that challenge traditional views about learning. The ideas of the Russian psychologist Lev Vygotsky (1896–1934) have had a profound influence on the thinking of literacy researchers working from a constructivist perspective.

The significance of Vygotsky's ideas can perhaps best be understood in contrast to the traditional view of learning. The traditional view is that the learner is a passive recipient of knowledge. In this view, the learner may be compared to a blank tablet, and the teacher's job may be compared to filling the tablet with writing. The constructivist view is quite different. According to this view, learners actively construct or create their own understandings. Students do not learn simply because teachers tell them something (for example, that plants need light to grow). They learn when they have the opportunity to engage with the new ideas and make them their own (for example, by seeing for themselves what happens when plants are kept in the closet).

As its name suggests, social constructivism differs from "just plain" constructivism in emphasizing the social world surrounding the learner. Earlier forms of constructivism (for example, as seen in the work of the famous developmental psychologist Jean Piaget) tended to see learning mainly as a matter of changes that took place within the the learner. In social constructivism, learning is not seen only in terms of the individual. Rather, learning is seen in terms of the interactions of the individual with other people.

Importance of the Social World

Vygotsky's work has done much to bring the social aspect of social constructivism to the attention of educators. One of the major themes in Vygotsky's work is the idea that complex types of human activity, such as language and literacy, begin in the social world (Wertsch, 1990). Vygotsky argues that the individual's first attempts at complex types of activity, such as speech, are carried out with social support from other people. When a baby babbles, "Wah-wah," her mother may help by saying, "Water, do you want water?" Over time, the child takes over more and more responsibility for speaking, until she can speak independently. As the child does more, the adult can do less. There is a gradual release of responsibility from the adult to the child.

In the same way, literacy begins as a social activity between the child and adult. For example, a child may be able to write at first only when an adult guides him with questions, helps him to phrase his ideas, and assists him in putting the words down on paper. Gradually, as the child learns the strategies and skills of planning and drafting his writing independently, less and less adult help is required.

In Vygotsky's view, the key to learning does not lie in the child's innate ability (Moll, 1990). Rather, the key to learning is the social support the child receives from adults or peers. Differences in literacy achievement are not simply the result of some children having more ability than others. Children's success or failure in learning to read and write, Vygotsky's thinking suggests, can best be understood by examining the social world in which their learning is taking place. Differences in achievement have probably come about because of differences in the literacy instruction and experiences students have received.

Zone of Proximal Development

In Vygotsky's thinking about how people learn, the zone of proximal development is a central concept. Vygotsky (1978) states that the zone represents the "difference between the child's actual level of development and the level of performance that he achieves in collaboration with the adult" (p. 209). The zone is the region of sensitivity to instruction.

The learning the child is doing, or the new level of performance the child is attempting, must be in the zone of proximal development. Below the zone, the child will not learn anything new, because the level of performance is too easy. For example, a kindergarten child who already can read simple, predictable books will not benefit from prolonged instruction in reading more of the same kind of books. Beyond the zone, the child will not benefit either, because the level of performance demanded is beyond the child's capacity. Thus, the same kindergarten child will not benefit from instruction in reading a wordy chapter book with few pictures, because these books are much too difficult.

To help the child learn, the teacher or peer must engage him in a performance of just the right degree of difficulty. In this case, the teacher may make the decision to work with the child on picture books that do not have such predictable text. This decision takes the child to a higher level of performance. However, the child can be successful at this level with the teacher's assistance.

In Vygotsky's view, if children are to learn, they must have the opportunity to try out the new level of performance with the assistance of someone who knows more than they do. This "more knowledgeable other" may be an adult, or it may be a capable peer. The teacher or peer must provide the proper degree of help. More help is needed at first, and less help is needed later, when the child has become more proficient. When the amount of help changes in this way, to match the needs of the learner, the process is called *scaffolding*. Scaffolding is a temporary kind of help, to be removed when the learner no longer needs it.

Full Processes

Vygotsky's approach to learning is a holistic one. He believed that complex forms of thinking, such as reading and writing, needed to be viewed in a holistic manner, in terms of the full processes involved. Reading and writing and complex forms of thinking involve much more than the accumulation of many simple skills. The skills have to be used in their proper time and place, as part of a complicated process. It is this whole complicated process that children must learn. This view implies that students will learn literacy best by engaging in authentic literacy activities, not isolated skill activities (Moll, 1990). Literacy learning activities should involve the full processes of reading and writing, and skills can be taught as part of students' involvement in these full processes.

The terms sociocultural or sociohistorical are sometimes used to describe Vygotsky's view, because he believed that culture and history both play a role in learning. When we look at children's literacy learning, Vygotsky's thinking suggests, we have to consider the broader cultural and historical context surrounding their learning. For example, children from some cultural groups grow up speaking standard English at home. Children from other cultural groups grow up speaking Spanish or a nonmainstream variety of English, such as Black English. These cultural groups have unique histories within the United States that may affect their present relationship to schools and to literacy learning in school.

Research conducted from a social constructivist perspective highlights the fact that schools present children who speak different languages or come from different cultural backgrounds with different opportunities for learning. In general, schools are more successful with mainstream students who speak standard English as a first language than with other students. Vygotsky's thinking implies that teachers should be aware of the cultural and historical factors that affect students' opportunity to learn, and of ways to adjust the classroom environment and systems of instruction to enable students to be successful in learning to read and write.

In Vygotsky's view, language and literacy are not fixed entities. Instead, Vygotsky saw language and literacy as human inventions. These inventions developed over time to help people coordinate their interactions with the physical world and with each other (Cole, 1990). Language and literacy, like other human inventions, change to meet different purposes at different times. For example, over the past decade people have invented and brought into common English usage terms for the computer's many parts and accessories. In connection with the computer, people have begun to develop new forms of literacy, such as writing messages for electronic mail.

In short, the social constructivist perspective, and the work of Vygotsky, present literacy educators with many new ideas. Perhaps most importantly, this perspective suggests that children of all linguistic and cultural backgrounds can achieve high levels of literacy, if educators understand how to adjust the classroom environment to support their learning.

References

Cole, M. (1990). Cognitive development and schooling: The evidence from cross-cultural research. In L. C. Moll (Ed.), *Vygotsky and education: Instructional implications and applications of sociohistorical psychology* (pp. 89–110). Cambridge: Cambridge University Press.

Moll, L. C. (1990). Introduction. In L. C. Moll (Ed.), *Vygotsky and education: Instructional implications and applications of sociohistorical psychology* (pp. 1–27). Cambridge: Cambridge University Press.

Vygotsky, L. S. (1978). *Mind in society.* Cambridge, MA: Harvard University Press.

Wertsch, J. V. (1990). The voice of rationality in a sociocultural approach to mind. In L. C. Moll (Ed.), *Vygotsky and education: Instructional implications and applications of sociohistorical psychology* (pp. 111–126). Cambridge: Cambridge University Press.

The Impact of Ken Goodman: Whole Language

Ken Goodman, like Dorothy Strickland, believes that the teacher's own philosophy plays a key role in literacy instruction. Goodman is perhaps the best known advocate of whole language, an educational philosophy that deals with the nature of language and learning. In addition to being a school of thought, whole language is a grassroots movement of teachers interested in improving their practice.

Although Goodman (1992) argues that he did not found whole language, he is widely recognized for his contributions to this philosophy. In research beginning in the 1960s, Goodman challenges the idea that reading involves little more than the decoding of letters and words. He argues instead that reading is best understood as a process of meaning-making.

Miscue Analysis

In studies of children's reading, Goodman (1969) introduced the term *miscue* for a departure from the text that others would call an oral reading error. He suggested that miscues be seen as children's efforts at meaning-making. By looking at the strategies underlying children's miscues, teachers can understand children's existing strategies and help them learn more effective new strategies.

For example, take the sentence *Sue went to school.* Suppose that a child makes a miscue in reading this sentence, substituting the word *some* for *school.* On the basis of this miscue, the teacher can infer that the child is relying heavily on letter-sound information, having noticed that the word began with *s*. However, the child has created a nonsense sentence, indicating that she can benefit from instruction in attending to the meaning of sentences.

Goodman's studies led him to the conclusion that reading and language should be viewed in a broad, holistic manner, in which meaning takes precedence over letters, words, and skills. Goodman's position is referred to as a top-down view of reading, because it begins with meaning and moves down to letters and sounds. It may be contrasted with a bottom-up view, which begins with letters and sounds and moves up to meaning.

Successive Approximation

Advocates of whole language believe that children will learn to read and write by engaging in the full processes of reading and writing, not skill activities. They suggest that children can learn to read and write naturally, in much the same way that they learned to speak.

Holdaway (1979) describes the process of learning in the whole language approach as one of successive approximation. When learning to speak, young children try to communicate messages to those around them. Parents and others encourage children by responding to their messages, engaging them in conversation, and modeling conventional patterns of speech. Gradually, through repeated encounters, children's speech becomes more and more like that of adults. Children learn to speak by speaking and receiving social support for their learning. Similarly, children learn to read by reading and to write by writing.

Goodman (1986) notes that both oral and written language are most easily learned in the context of use. This is the idea of authenticity, or reading and writing for real purposes that occur in the world outside as well as in the classroom. For example, reading can be taught through the reading of good books, because in the real world, people can and do read good books. This approach may be contrasted with the traditional view that reading should be taught through practice activities and texts written for the purpose of teaching reading.

Choices Offered to Students

In whole language, learners are offered choices and take control of their own learning. For example, children often choose their own topics for writing and make decisions about the organization and content of their pieces. In traditional classrooms the teacher assigns children topics and often determines the form of the piece as well (for example, a three-paragraph essay). Goodman believes that learners who have the ability to make decisions become invested in their own learning. This is the idea of ownership, in this case, students' valuing of language and language learning (see Student Ownership, chapter 5). Language and literacy learning can be empowering to students if activities make sense to them and they feel in control of the process.

Goodman, Weaver (1990), and others tend to emphasize the child's efforts to learn rather than the teachers' efforts to teach. In the classroom, children are given ample time to use language, to read, and to write. Within this time they have many opportunities to make their own discoveries about how language and literacy work. For example, young children are placed in print-rich classroom environments that let them see how print is used: in poetry charts, picture books, labels, signs, attendance forms, and so on. They are encouraged to engage with this print and use print in these same ways themselves.

While children are engaged in these activities, for example, writing their own picture books, teachers provide encouragement and look for teachable moments when children's knowledge can be extended. For example, if a child is writing about a conversation with her brother, the teacher may show the child how to use dialogue and quotation marks.

Teachers look for patterns in children's reading and writing and provide mini-lessons on concepts, strategies, and skills that will prove useful to many in the class (see Mini-lessons, chapters 4 and 8). For example, the teacher may notice that children's stories begin in a boring way and decide to present a mini-lesson on writing an exciting lead. Notice that the teaching of skills occurs in the context of children's involvement with an authentic and meaningful literacy activity. In whole language, skills are not taught or practiced in isolation.

Integration of the Language Arts

Whole language includes the idea that reading, writing, and oral language are not separate entities but should be taught and used together. For example, in a whole language classroom there may be time scheduled daily for a writers' workshop when children write on topics of their choice. Although writing is emphasized, the teacher will be aware of developing children's oral language through discussion and peer conferences, and of developing their reading through the rereading of their own pieces and the reading of others students' pieces. The teacher will also make connections to literature, for example, to show students examples of interesting leads.

Reading, writing, and oral language are integrated with instruction in the content areas, including math, science, and social studies, as well as with instruction in the arts (Weaver, 1990). Children may write their own word problems, discuss their observations of insects, and read historical novels. They may write and perform their own plays and compose their own songs.

With guidance from the teacher, students in a whole language classroom form a community of learners. Teachers show students that they too are learners, for example by sharing their writing and asking students for ideas. In a community of learners, students support one another's efforts. Risk-taking is encouraged and miscues or mistakes are not punished but seen as part of the learning process.

Goodman (1997) highlights the importance of teachers using the best knowledge available to them, from research and from their own professional experience. He sees teachers as researchers in their own classrooms. Teachers, like their students, form communities of learners for the purpose of improving their practice (see chapter 13).

References

Goodman, K. (1969). Analysis of oral reading miscues: Applied psycholinguistics. *Reading Research Quarterly, 5*, 9–30.

Goodman, K. (1986). *What's whole in whole language?* Portsmouth, NH: Heinemann.

Goodman, K. S. (1992). I didn't found whole language. *The Reading Teacher, 46* (3), 188–199.

Goodman, K. (1997). Putting theory and research in the context of history. *Language Arts, 74* (8), 595–599.

Holdaway, D. (1979). *The foundations of literacy.* Sydney, Australia: Ashton Scholastic (distributed in the United States by Heinemann).

Weaver, C. (1990). *Understanding whole language: Principles and practices.* Portsmouth, NH: Heinemann.

The Impact of Luis Moll: Second-Language Learners

One of the challenges teachers face is providing effective literacy instruction to students of diverse cultural and linguistic backgrounds. Luis Moll has been an advocate for improved instruction, especially for Spanish-speaking students, and he has studied the approaches used by highly effective teachers of Latino students. In one study, Moll (1988) looked at the teaching practices of two fifth-grade teachers, one a Spanish-English bilingual and the other a monolingual English speaker. In keeping with the ideas of Vygotsky (see article in this chapter and Moll, 1990), Moll focused on the teachers' social mediations or the ways in which they arranged social situations to promote the students' learning.

Moll notes that many Latino students, in common with other second language learners, are from working-class backgrounds. He cites studies indicating that these students generally receive a different quality of instruction from middle-class students. Working-class students often receive rote instruction with few opportunities for choice, while middle-class students tend to receive instruction oriented toward higher-level thinking and conceptual understanding with some opportunities for choice.

The situation worsens, Moll asserts, when working-class students speak a first language other than English. The tendency in schools is to reduce the complexity of the curriculum to match the level of the students' ability to speak English. This approach ignores the fact that students may understand far more than they can express in English and that they may already be literate in Spanish or another language (Moll & Diaz, 1985). Students' achievement may be hampered because they are prevented from participating in challenging activities, such as the writing of research reports.

In contrast, the effective teachers in Moll's (1988) study believed that literacy instruction should center on developing students' ability to make meaning, gain understanding, and communicate ideas. The teachers created environments in which they worked collaboratively with students on purposeful, meaningful activities involving varied uses of language and literacy. Readers' and writers' workshops (see chapters 2–9), in which students read and discuss literature and write on topics of their own choice, provide this type of environment.

Moll's research led to five findings, which he believes apply whether students are in a bilingual classroom or in a classroom where English is the only language of instruction. First, the effective teachers of second-language learners maintained a high intellectual level in the classroom. As Moll (1988) puts it, "the students were as smart as allowed by the curriculum" (p. 467). The teachers firmly believed the students could deal with a rich and rigorous curriculum. Moll did not observe any rote teaching of skills in isolation. Instead, the teachers stressed students' active engagement in language and literacy activities.

Rich Content

Second, Moll found that the teachers saw the content of the curriculum as highly important. The teachers believed that rich content allowed students more opportunities to make connections between academic learning and real life. Moll (1992; Moll & Gonzalez, 1994) found that second-language learners come from families that possess "funds of knowledge." These funds of knowledge encompass fields such as agriculture, marketing, religion, the arts, and medicine. Moll discovered that teachers could successfully tap these funds of knowledge by involving parents as resources in the classroom and by designing activities that drew on these funds. For example, a sixth-grade teacher had her students conduct library research on home building. As homework, students made models of houses or other structures. A parent familiar with construction techniques served as a guest speaker.

Rich content extends to the idea that students should read excellent literature, including multicultural works (see The Impact of Violet Harris: Multicultural Children's Literature, chapter 3). When the text holds interest for students, Moll (1988) states, they will want to comprehend it. Once the text has captured students' attention, the teacher can address comprehension strategies. These may include building awareness of strategies students are already using, such as prediction, or providing instruction in strategies new to students, such as interpreting the author's message.

Meaningful content, Moll (1988) argues, facilitates students' learning of English. As one of the teachers in the study stated, "The richer the content, the more the students had something they connected to" (p. 468). Students' interest in content motivates them to learn English or to improve their proficiency in their home language.

Diversity of Instruction

Moll's third finding highlights the diversity observed in the different social arrangements for learning. Students engaged in many forms of reading and writing, usually within a broader activity. For example, the teachers had students participate in creative drama (see chapter 4) as a means of exploring character development in a story. The students acted as tutors for younger children. In addition to serving as a learning experience, tutoring gave teachers a chance to assess students' understandings of literacy. The teacher in the bilingual classroom allowed students to write their responses in Spanish, even when the text read was in English, and vice versa. Students in both classes kept journals and logs. In short, students gained a wide variety of experiences with language and literacy.

Drawing on Students' Experiences

Fourth, the teachers encouraged students to use their personal experiences to make sense of academic content. Students frequently referred to experiences in the home and community during lessons, and the teachers built upon these experiences to reinforce students' academic learning (see Experience-Text-Relationship Lessons, chapter 4). The following example occurred when a group was reading a novel about the American revolution. The students discussed how relationships became strained when members of the same family took different sides in the conflict. One of the students related a personal experience similar to that faced by a character in the novel, and other students shared their ideas. Adding to the foundation provided by the students' experiences, the teacher made the point that learning about history through a novel often provides insights about how past events affected people's lives.

Moll's final finding was that the teachers needed political and social support in order to create effective curricula for their students. The teachers felt the need to develop their own curricula rather than adhere strictly to preset curricula imposed from the outside. They needed to feel a sense of autonomy in order to promote a sense of autonomy or ownership of learning by students (see Student Ownership, chapter 5). The teachers offered the students choices, for example, in the projects and assignments to be completed and books to be read. They encouraged students to help one another with their work. Moll (1988) argues that "it was the teachers' freedom to select or create their own curricular activities that afforded the students the opportunity to be selective and independent in their work" (p. 470).

Moll noted several factors that contributed to the teachers' ability to develop effective curricula. The teachers had a good understanding of the theory behind their work; they could explain exactly why they taught as they did. They saw themselves as active thinkers rather than as passive recipients of knowledge, and they saw their students in the same light. In order to build on students' backgrounds and make learning meaningful, they needed the freedom to exercise their professional judgment. The teachers did not proceed alone but relied on the support of colleagues who shared their views about language, literacy, and instruction (see chapter 13). They held regular meetings with other teachers and university professors from whom they received both advice and moral support.

In short, Moll's research suggests guidelines that teachers can follow to be effective in developing the literacy of second language learners, either in bilingual or English-language classrooms. Moll's work points to the importance of presenting second-language learners with a wealth of opportunities to engage in reading and writing in meaningful contexts. Effective teachers work from students' strengths by building on background experiences and encouraging students to make connections between academic concepts and their own lives.

References

Moll, L. C. (1988). Some key issues in teaching Latino students. *Language Arts, 65* (5), 465–472.

Moll, L. C. (Ed.) (1990). *Vygotsky and education: Instructional implications and applications of sociohistorical psychology.* Cambridge: Cambridge University Press.

Moll, L. (1992). Bilingual classroom studies and community analysis. *Educational Researcher, 21* (2), 20–24.

Moll, L. C., & Diaz, S. (1985). Ethnographic pedagogy: Promoting effective bilingual instruction. In E. Garcia and R.V. Padilla (Eds.), *Advances in bilingual education research.* Tucson: University of Arizona Press, pp. 127–149.

Moll, L. C., & Gonzalez, N. (1994). Critical issues: Lessons from research with language-minority children. *Journal of Literacy Research, 26* (4), 429–456.

Resources

Freeman, D. E., & Freeman, Y. S. (1994). *Between worlds: Access to second language acquisition.* Portsmouth, NH: Heinemann.

Rigg, P., & Allen, V. G. (Eds.) (1989). *When they don't all speak English: Integrating the ESL student into the regular classroom.* Urbana, IL: National Council of Teachers of English.

Spangenberg-Urbschat, K., & Pritchard, R. (Eds.) (1994). *Kids come in all languages: Reading instruction for ESL students.* Newark, DE: International Reading Association.

SECTION 1:

THE READERS' WORKSHOP

Chapter 2

OVERVIEW OF THE
READERS' WORKSHOP

Reader's Workshop in
Mrs. Sally O'Brien's Kindergarten Class

Mrs. Sally O'Brien's kindergarten class is learning about farms and farm animals. The thematic unit gives the teacher and students a focus for reading, sharing their ideas, follow-up assignments, activities, and projects. Earlier the class visited a farm where the students saw chickens laying eggs. Currently the class has been eagerly observing an incubator with eggs nearly ready to hatch, and that is how this morning began.

Now the class has gathered together on the carpet. Mrs. O'Brien begins the reading instruction by writing a message on the whiteboard.

> Good morning boys and girls,
>
> The chicks have started to hatch! Two eggs have little cracks. Soon we will see the baby chicks.

As the children observe her writing, they spontaneously try to read along. Then Mrs. O'Brien and the students read the message together. They discuss the news and share the excitement. Leanne exclaims, "I think I heard a little peep." The children help Mrs. O'Brien add that sentence to the message by listening for the sounds in the words and suggesting letters for the sounds. The children can supply most of the consonants and a few of the vowels. Brian notices the word "little" is already in the message and Mrs. O'Brien praises him for "having good eyes."

She then focuses their attention on the whole message and asks the children what they see. They note, among other things, the exclamation point and several words ending with *s*. She uses their observations for brief mini-lessons on this special punctuation and how *s* makes these words mean more than one.

Next Mrs. O'Brien presents a large-text version of the traditional rhyme *Five Little Ducks* (Paparone, 1995), as a shared reading. She props the big book on a stand so the students can see the large print and colorful illustrations. She reads the story using a pointer to mark each word as she reads. Occasionally she pauses to ask a question about the story or to allow the children to chime in.

Then Mrs. O'Brien begins an activity using the familiar children's song, "Old Mac Donald." The words to the song are printed on chart paper and hang on the chart stand which Mrs. O'Brien brings from the poetry center. As the children sing Mrs.

O'Brien points to the words. Today they add another verse and the students decide to include a hen. The students chant the new verse as Mrs. O'Brien adds the words to the chart paper. Later the students will use the pointer to reread when they visit the poetry center.

Then Mrs. O'Brien invites a small group of students to meet with her for small group instruction. The other students begin a variety of literacy activities throughout the classroom. Mrs. O'Brien has organized the students into three groups based upon their levels of development. Students in one group read beginning books quite easily. Another group knows some words and is using simple pattern books. The third group is focusing on text awareness, distinguishing letters and words, and working on initial letter sounds. Mrs. O'Brien meets daily with each group for 20 minutes.

Today the group reading *The Little Red Hen* by Byron Barton (1993) will finish the book. Using the Experience-Text-Relationship approach for guided discussion, Mrs. O'Brien begins by asking the students to recall the story thus far. The students share story events from their previous meetings. She asks them what they think might happen next. The children open their books to page 26 and talk briefly about the illustrations. Mrs. O'Brien says, "You had some good ideas about what Little Red Hen will do. Let's read to see what she does." The students, as well as Mrs. O'Brien, read quietly. After everyone has read, the teacher talks with the children about their predictions. They continue in this way to the end of the story. Mrs. O'Brien then asks the students to think of how the *Little Red Hen* and the mother of the *Five Little Ducks* are similar and how they are different. She continues to ask questions to encourage comparison of the two texts. For their independent follow-up assignment the students will draw a picture and write to show how the stories are similar.

Another group is reading *Farm Concert* by Joy Cowley (1998). This is their second reading and Mrs. O'Brien is focusing on story language, drawing attention to what each animal says. For their follow-up assignment the students will create an innovation by adding more farm animals to the farm concert. They will write what the animals say and draw a picture. (See Figure 2.1 for an example of an earlier response written by children in this group.)

The third group is reading a pattern book, *Yuk Soup* by Joy Cowley (1986). Mrs. O'Brien uses a big book and positions it so everyone in the reading group can see. She draws attention to the cover, the cover illustration, and the title. She turns to the title page and reads the title again. The group discusses the picture, pointing out some of the details, and then makes predictions about what might go in the soup. Mrs. O'Brien begins reading, pointing to each word as she reads. The students recognize the pattern and read along. For their follow-up assignment the students will draw and label some things they saw growing on the farm that could be used to make soup.

The classroom activities support the farm theme and provide other literacy opportunities. The library center has lots of trade books and a special collection of books about farm animals and life on a farm. There are stories published by students and books the class published together. The block area has toy farm animals for use with block construction. There is a box with construction paper and markers for the students to make labels and signs. The housekeeping area has been converted into a roadside restaurant featuring home-cooked meals with fresh produce (in this case, plastic replicas) from the farm. There are menus to read and paper and pencils to write orders. The science center (where the incubator resides) has both fiction and nonfiction picture books related to the unit of study, along with materials the children use to record their observations and new ideas. The listening post has a tape of *Pigs in the Mud in the*

FIGURE 2.1   KINDERGARTEN STUDENT'S RESPONSE TO LITERATURE

Response to Literature (K)

Name **Anela**

Date **3-15**

Title **The Farm Concert**

Draw and write about your favorite part of the story.

the frmr is laing it the
The   farmer   yelling   at   the

shnamoc.   nao the frmr kuncep
animals.   Now   the farmer   can sleep.

Middle of the Rud and copies of the book by Lynn Plourde (1997) so students can follow along as they listen to the story.

Before the end of readers' workshop, Mrs. O'Brien tells the class she will read aloud Paul Galdone's *The Little Red Hen* (1973). This is a more sophisticated version of the story than the one she chose for small group instruction. After reading the story Mrs. O'Brien allows time for the students to talk about story ideas and events and to ask and respond to questions.

Children's Books Cited

Barton, B. (1993). *The little red hen*. New York: HarperCollins.

Cowley, J. (1986). *Yuk soup*. Ill. by R. McRae. Bothel, WA: The Wright Group.

Cowley, J. (1998). *Farm concert*. Bothel, WA: The Wright Group.

Galdone, P. (1973). *The little red hen*. Jefferson City, MO: Scholastic.

Paparone, P. (1995). *Five little ducks*. New York: North-South Books.

Plourde, L. (1997). *Pigs in the mud in the middle of the rud*. Ill. by J. Schoenherr. New York: Scholastic.

Readers' Workshop in Mr. Marcus Jamal's Second-Grade Class

Mr. Marcus Jamal's second-grade class is learning about friendship. This theme gives the teacher and students a focus for reading, writing, and discussing their ideas during readers' workshop. Mr. Jamal begins the workshop today with OTTER (Our Time to Enjoy Reading). The children and Mr. Jamal independently read from books they have selected until the timer sounds after 20 minutes. Then, for about 10 minutes, they talk about their books. Today Mr. Jamal asks, "Who was reading a book in which friendships are important? Will you tell us a little about those friendships?"

After several children have shared, Mr. Jamal spends about 5 minutes conducting a mini-lesson on a procedure he wants the class to learn—how to discuss a story in a small group independently of the teacher. He wants students to practice sharing their ideas with peers and begin to develop independence in story discussions. He explains how one person brings up a topic (what she thinks about a character's actions or how a certain part confused her) and other people listen and respond to it for a while before someone else brings up another topic. Students will practice this procedure later in the day.

The class has four reading groups, formed on the basis of both interest and reading ability. Each group meets daily with Mr. Jamal for about 20 minutes. Two groups are reading *Katy No-Pocke*t by Emmy Payne (1973), but each group meets separately for discussion to keep the group size at six members or fewer. When one of these groups meets with Mr. Jamal, he begins by having the students share their current response journal entries and inviting comments from the group. As they read and discuss the next section of the book together, he uses the Experience-Text-Relationship approach for guided discussion to help students relate their prior knowledge and experiences to new text ideas.

Mr. Jamal asks the group to share any new or interesting vocabulary they have noted in their response journals as they read. One child has written the phrase *squatting-down*. The group discusses the meaning, using information from the context, including picture cues, as well as visual and structural cues. Mr. Jamal uses this opportunity to talk about root words and endings, helping the group find other words with endings (*crying, cried, rising, squatted, sensible, kindly*) and figure out their roots.

Mr. Jamal determined that students in the other group reading *Katy No-Pocket* could benefit from more guidance with their written response. They use an open-ended response sheet designed by Mr. Jamal to share their story ideas (see Figure 2.2).

Another group is reading *Poppleton and Friends* by Cynthia Rylant (1997). Pairs of children are sitting together to reread a section they read and discussed with Mr. Jamal yesterday. Their rereading helps them build fluency and practice using the word reading strategies they have learned. When they finish, they gather together to talk about a question Mr. Jamal has given them for independent discussion: What do Poppleton, Hudson, and Cherry Sue do to show they are good friends? Children were reminded to use the skills taught in the mini-lesson earlier this day. When they meet with Mr. Jamal later this morning, they will be ready to share their ideas with him.

Another group has finished reading *Hugh Pine* by Janwillem van de Wetering (1992). After their last discussion with Mr. Jamal, each student completed a Response to Literature form to show understanding of the story's problem, characters, main events, and solution, and to give a personal response, interpret the author's message, and apply the message to the student's own life. Right now the group is working on an art project

FIGURE 2.2   SECOND-GRADE STUDENT'S RESPONSE TO LITERATURE

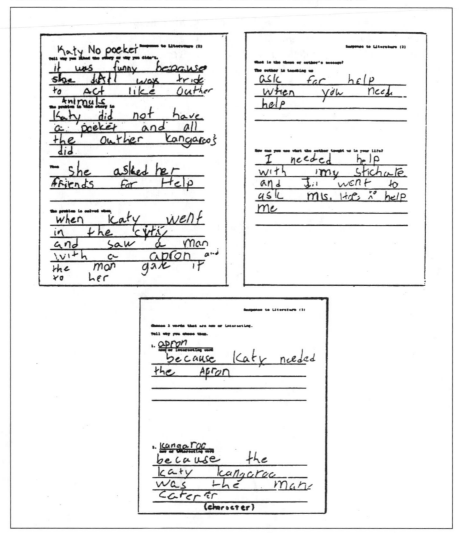

as another way to show what they have learned. Each group can choose the type of project they will do as a culminating activity for their book, and this group has chosen to make puppets and act out their favorite part of the story.

After Mr. Jamal has met with each group, he calls the class together. For the next 10 minutes, he leads a discussion of the common ideas students are discovering among the different books they are reading and helps them add to their class chart on what they have learned about friends. He also asks students to evaluate how their group and independent work time went this morning, and how well they themselves worked.

After recess Mr. Jamal reads aloud from *Runaway Ralph* by Beverly Cleary (1991), a more challenging book than most of his students can read on their own right now, but one with an important theme and interesting vocabulary he wants to share. He reads for about 10 minutes, ending with time for students to comment on the book. He helps them to make connections between this story and the others they have been reading on friendship.

Children's Books Cited

Cleary, B. (1991). *Runaway Ralph*. New York: Scholastic.

Payne, E. (1973). *Katy no-pocket*. Boston: Houghton Mifflin.

Rylant, C. (1997). *Poppleton and friends*. New York: Scholastic.

van de Wetering, J. (1992). *Hugh Pine*. Fairfield, NJ: Morrow Jr. Books.

Readers' Workshop in Ms. Brenda DeRego's Fourth-Grade Class

Ms. Brenda DeRego, a fourth-grade teacher, began the school year by asking her students to think and write about their previous accomplishments in reading and set goals for themselves for the first quarter. After discussion, the students decided to add work samples to their portfolios at least once a month and to look over their goals and review their progress monthly.

For the first 20 minutes of class after morning business, students read independently a book of their choice and record it in their reading logs. Ms. DeRego reads along with her students. Available are text sets and author sets that have been gathered by classroom librarians. This quarter they include text sets on family life (the theme related to their literature study groups) and author sets by Katherine Paterson and Patricia MacLachlan (authors they are reading in literature discussion groups).

On Mondays, Ms. DeRego collects the reading logs, which include students' comments and a parent's signature. Once a month, Ms. DeRego asks the students to complete a book project. Some students create book jackets, some do dioramas, some make mobiles or posters, and others dress as a character and give a presentation to the class.

Ms. DeRego often uses literature she has been reading aloud as a model in her mini-lessons. Today, she spends about 20 minutes reading from *Maniac Magee* by Jerry Spinelli (1990) and discussing how readers develop a sense of theme through character actions and thoughts. She has chosen this topic because the literature study groups have finished or are nearly finished with their novels, and she wants to give them ways to explore themes.

There are four literature study groups reading one of two books on family relationships: *The Great Gilly Hopkins* by Katherine Paterson (1978) or *Journey* by Patricia MacLachlan (1991). Students chose the book they wanted to read after hearing Ms. DeRego's book talks and looking through the books themselves.

The groups meet every two to three days for discussion. On other days, they read and write in their response journals (see Figure 2.3). The groups decide how much they will read before their next meeting together. The groups meet at the same time, with a student serving as facilitator in each group. Earlier in the school year more of the discussions were teacher led. Now Ms. DeRego finds she can move from group to group, listening, making notes, asking questions, and contributing her own ideas to the discussion.

One of the groups reading *Journey* is discussing a "think question" posed by one of the students: Why was it important for Journey to have a sister like Cat? They will also share personal connections they made to the story, new vocabulary words, and interesting words they term "sparkling jewels" from their response journals.

Ms. DeRego is meeting with one of the groups that has finished *The Great Gilly Hopkins*. She is using the Experience-Text-Relationship approach for guided discussion, to have students discuss their feelings about the book's ending, their ideas about the author's message, and their personal evaluations of the book.

After this 40-minute period for literature discussion groups, Ms. DeRego reserves another 10 minutes for pulling things together. Sometimes she asks the students to evaluate how well they have been working individually and in groups. She reminds them to think about their goals and the progress they are making. They write first and then share their evaluations. She uses this time to help them identify and solve problems related to working in groups.

FIGURE 2.3   FOURTH-GRADE STUDENT'S RESPONSE TO LITERATURE

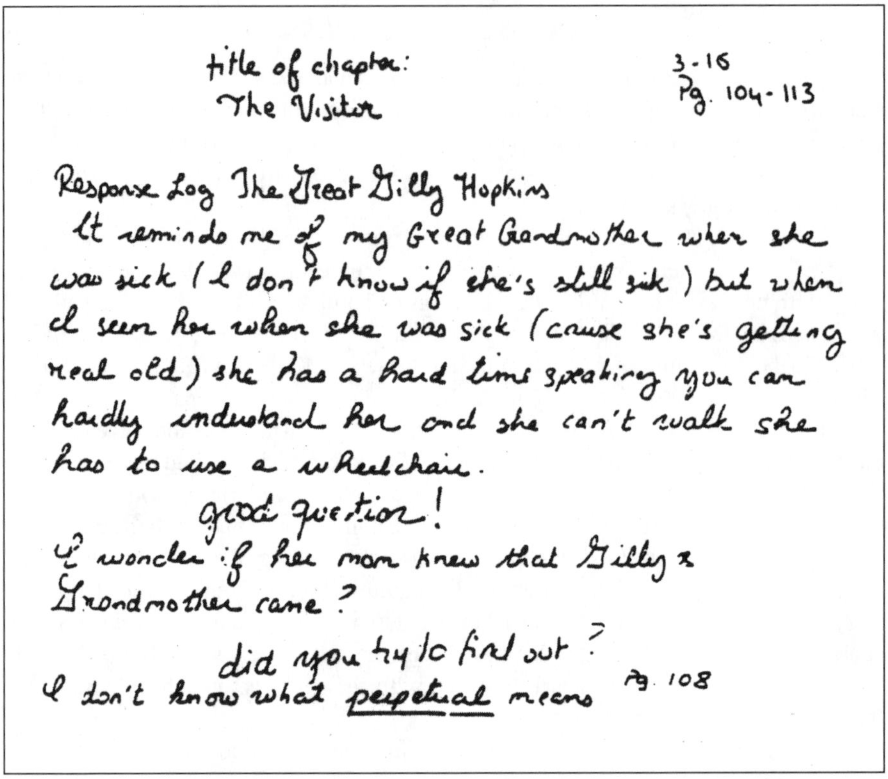

title of chapter:
   The Visitor

3-16
Pg. 104-113

Response Log The Great Gilly Hopkins
   It reminds me of my Great Grandmother when she
was sick (I don't know if she's still sick) but when
I seen her when she was sick (cause she's getting
real old) she has a hard time speaking you can
hardly understand her and she can't walk she
has to use a wheelchair.
                     good question!
   I wonder if her mom knew that Gilly's
Grandmother came?
                     did you try to find out?
   I don't know what __perpetual__ means   Pg. 108

At other times the class talks about the relationships between the books they are
reading in literature groups and others related to the theme they are exploring. Students
have a chance to compare and contrast characters and themes from different books.
Often, as a result of these discussions, students decide to read a book someone else has
been reading.

Children's Books Cited

MacLachlan, P. (1991). *Journey*. New York: Delacorte Press.
Paterson, K. (1978). *The great Gilly Hopkins*. Scranton, PA: HarperCollins.
Spinelli, J. (1990). *Maniac Magee*. Boston: Little, Brown.

The Impact of Louise Rosenblatt: Reader Response Theory

Jasmine and a group of four other third graders sat in a circle discussing a book they had just read, *Encounter* by Jane Yolen (1992). "This book was scary," said Jasmine. "It was really different from that other book Mrs. Bray read us about Christopher Columbus."

"Why didn't anyone listen to the boy?" asked Rob. "That's what bothered me." "A lot of times grown-ups don't believe kids," Nicole commented. "Like I might tell my parents something, but they think I'm just making it up."

As this example suggests, in classrooms with readers' workshops and literature-based instruction, students have the chance to share their ideas and discuss their feelings about and interpretations of text. This approach to instruction differs greatly from traditional approaches in which teachers often ask questions with a single right answer.

The concepts underlying literature-based instruction are found in reader response theory. One of the foremost proponents of reader response theory is Louise Rosenblatt, who is recognized for making the first statements of this theoretical position in the 1930s. In contrast to earlier thinkers, Rosenblatt (1978) suggests that the reader and the text should not be seen as separate entities. Rather, there is a transaction between the reader and the text in which each is shaped by the other. Readers draw upon their background knowledge to construct a new meaning, and this new meaning is the literary work. In other words, literature is not simply a matter of text but a matter of the meaning that readers construct from text and their own background knowledge.

Two Stances

Rosenblatt (1985) states that people read from one of two stances. The first stance is the *aesthetic*. Readers who take this stance are concerned mainly with reading for the sake of reading. She writes:

> In the *aesthetic transaction,* the reader's attention is focused on *what he is living through during the reading-event.* He is attending *both* to what the verbal signs designate *and* to the qualitative overtones of the ideas, images, situations, and characters that he is evoking under guidance of the text. The literary work of art comes into being through the reader's attention to what the text activates in him. (p. 38)

The second stance described by Rosenblatt (1985) is the *efferent*. This term comes from a Latin word meaning "to carry away." Readers who take this stance are primarily concerned with the information to be taken from the text. Rosenblatt states:

> In *efferent* (nonaesthetic) reading, the reader's attention is centered on what should be retained as a residue after the actual reading-event—the information to be acquired, for example, from the label on a medicine bottle; or the operations to be carried out, as in a scientific experiment; the conclusion to be reached, as in a legal brief; or the actions to be performed, as in a recipe. (p. 37)

According to Rosenblatt, the aesthetic and efferent stances are not mutually exclusive. Readers read in a flexible manner, often shifting back and forth between the two stances. For example, the third-grade students may be reading *Encounter* largely from an aesthetic stance but also gain information about 15th century history.

When reading literature, Rosenblatt argues, the predominant stance should be the aesthetic. That is, literature should be read primarily for the enjoyment of the experience of reading. Rosenblatt (1991) expresses the fear that, in the classroom, teachers may tend to approach literature from an efferent, rather than aesthetic stance. She does not endorse this practice, because it gives students the impression that literature should be read for the sake of facts and analysis, rather than for the enjoyment of the experience. She urges teachers not to rush students away from the lived-through experience of reading, but to prolong the aesthetic experience through such activities as drawing, writing, drama, dance, and discussion (see Responding through Drama and Art, chapter 4).

Changing Relationships Between Reader and Text

What do readers do to make sense of literature? Judith Langer (1990) studied the manner in which students build understanding while they read literature, then expand upon or change those understandings through discussion. She uses the word *envisionment* to refer to the understanding of literature a reader holds at any particular moment.

Like Rosenblatt, Langer discusses the different stances a reader may adopt when reading literature. In this case, however, stances refer to the changing relationships between the reader and the text, as the reader builds an envisionment of the text. One of the stances, Being Out and Stepping In, occurs when readers first make contact with the text. They identify its genre, structure, and content and call on background knowledge to begin building an envisionment. For example, when starting *Encounter,* the reader realizes that the story is being told from the boy's perspective.

Another stance discussed by Langer (1990) is Being In and Stepping Out. Here readers take what they have read and, on that basis, reflect on their lives or the human condition. Nicole, for example, expressed the idea that parents sometimes discount what children say, so it wasn't surprising for the boy's warning to go unheeded.

Three-Level Approach

Teachers may find it helpful to keep in mind that students move through different stances while developing their envisionments of the text. James Zarrillo (1991) recommends a three-level approach, beginning with free response. Teachers might begin with an open-ended question, such as "Does anyone want to say anything about the reading?" The discussion then moves toward having students relive the reading experience. Questions might become more specific, perhaps involving imagery and perspective-taking. For example, students might be asked to imagine how they would feel if they were a character in the story. Finally, teachers might have students interpret the reading experience. Students might be asked to make personal connections to the text. Questions that require this kind of thinking include, "Have you ever been in a situation like the one described in the book?" and "Does this book remind you of any other books?"

You may already have your own ideas about how to apply reader response theory to the classroom. The practical implications drawn by two teachers, Terry Jewell and Donna Pratt (1999), include the following:

- Use heterogeneous (mixed ability) grouping.
- Give students choices of the texts they will read and discuss.
- Base discussions on students' responses to the text, not preset teacher questions.
- Take the role of a facilitator rather than question-asker.

You will be reading much more about the application of reader response theory to the classroom in chapters 3, 4, and 5.

In short, reader response theory provides a framework for understanding literature-based instruction and how it differs from traditional instruction. Reader response theory, as advocated by Rosenblatt and others, emphasizes the aesthetic stance and the importance of personal response and interpretation during reading.

References

Jewell, T. A., & Pratt, D. (1999). Literature discussions in the primary grades: Children's thoughtful discourse about books and what teachers can do to make it happen *The Reading Teacher, 52* (8), 842–850.

Langer, J. A. (1990). Understanding literature. *Language Arts, 67* (3), 812–816.

Rosenblatt, L. (1978). *The reader, the text, the poem: The transactional theory of the literary work.* Carbondale, IL: Southern Illinois University Press.

Rosenblatt, L. M. (1985). The transactional theory of the literary work: Implications for research. In C. R. Cooper (Ed.), *Researching response to literature and the teaching of literature: Points of departure* (pp. 33–53). Norwood, NJ: Ablex.

Rosenblatt, L. (1991). Literature—S.O.S! *Language Arts, 68* (6). 444–448.

Yolen, J. (1992). *Encounter.* Ill. by D. Shannon. San Diego: Harcourt.

Zarrillo, J. (1991). Theory becomes practice: Aesthetic teaching with literature. *The New Advocate, 4* (4), 221–234.

Chapter 3

STRUCTURING THE READERS' WORKSHOP

Setting Up Your Classroom

Setting up a readers' workshop takes initial planning and regular monitoring. What looks like a loose collection of activities is really a well-thought out organization of learning experiences that allows both teacher and students to pursue their goals toward reading and learning from print.

Background

Jane Hansen (1987) examined the basic principles around which she organized her classroom for writing instruction and related those principles to reading. She determined that students need

- **time** to choose books, read, think about their reading, and interact with others over what they have read;
- **choice** about the books they read, their purpose for reading a particular book, and the strategies they use to help them comprehend;
- a sense of **responsibility** for their learning and their interactions with the teacher and fellow students;
- a classroom **structure** that allows them opportunities to work with the teacher, each other, and independently; and
- a supportive **community** that fosters diversity and the development of self-confidence and self-esteem.

Procedure

Principles such as those cited by Hansen (1987) call for a classroom that is organized to promote active participation, independence, and interdependence on the part of students (see classroom descriptions in chapter 2 for more specifics). How teachers set up their classrooms communicates these underlying principles to students. As much as possible, planning should be done jointly by the students and the teacher. Students are often a good source of information about routines that make it easier for the class to operate smoothly.

A well-stocked classroom library is the cornerstone of the readers' workshop, since selecting and reading books will occupy much of students' time. For younger students, books will be more accessible when arranged on shelves with the book covers facing out. Kindergarten teacher Mrs. O'Brien grouped some titles by her favorite authors (Cynthia Rylant, Aliki, and Eric Carle) and some by subjects she liked (ocean animals, faraway places, special people), which she placed in labeled bins on tables nearby students' desks. Later, she asked the students to choose their favorite authors and special subjects, and to help her restock and relabel the bins.

For older students, fiction and nonfiction can be grouped separately, alphabetized with spines out. Ms. DeRego's fourth graders made large bookmarks with their names on them that they used to mark the place on the shelf for the book they borrowed. Titles could be reshelved easily when students were finished with their books. Like the younger students, these students still enjoyed making special book displays to feature favorite authors and subjects.

Book titles should be rotated regularly. Some teachers borrow from school or community libraries or exchange with other classrooms. Student-authored books can be shelved with the regular collection or kept in a special display area within the library. Other reading material such as newspapers, magazines, and reference books make up part of the collection. Parents may be willing to donate books and magazines their child no longer needs at home. Teachers can create a comfortable place for students to browse, read on their own, or pair up to enjoy books together by adding a carpet and some large cushions to the library area.

A system for borrowing books to take home should be set up so that students can manage it, perhaps by posting a sign-out sheet and assigning one or two classroom librarians on a rotating basis to check in books on due days. Some teachers of younger children ask them to bring back their books each day, even though the same book can be checked out again for that night. Teachers of older children may require students to bring back books once a week, allowing them to borrow the same book for a second week if they want to renew it.

A large area where the entire class can gather for discussions and sharing, as well as several areas for small groups to meet, is important for creating a supportive community atmosphere. The whole class can meet at an open area, either sitting on the floor or pulling their chairs together in a circle. One teacher arranged students' desks in a squared-off C shape, using the open area in the middle for mini-lessons and having students sit around the perimeter for sharing. Small groups can meet at desks clustered together or at work tables stationed at the back and sides of the room.

Charts, bulletin boards, and displays can contribute greatly to the smooth running of the readers' workshop. For example, Ms. DeRego began a chart during a mini-lesson on how to figure out unknown words, brainstorming with students to produce a list of strategies. The chart was posted for reference and the teacher and other students encouraged anyone who was stuck in their reading to refer to the chart for help. Ms. DeRego used other charts to list possible discussion questions and different types of responses to literature students might want to try.

Bulletin boards can be used to remind students of the daily schedule of activities for readers' workshop, using pictures and simple labels for younger students. Displays might give information about the Author of the Week, including a special collection of the author's books. This could be a student author or a commercially published author. Students should have many opportunities to design displays and bulletin boards to share information of importance to them in their learning. They may want to create a display for their favorite books or authors, set up a book swap table, or post book recommendations for their classmates.

Teachers can use mini-lessons to explain the classroom set-up to students and help them operate within this environment. Students learn their responsibilities for using their time productively, making good choices, and interacting with their teacher and classmates in ways that support their learning and the classroom community. Teachers monitor the operation of the classroom and look for ways to refine any parts that are not running smoothly. They discuss possible changes with students and ask for students'

FIGURE 3.1   MARCUS JAMAL'S CLASSROOM LAYOUT, SECOND GRADE

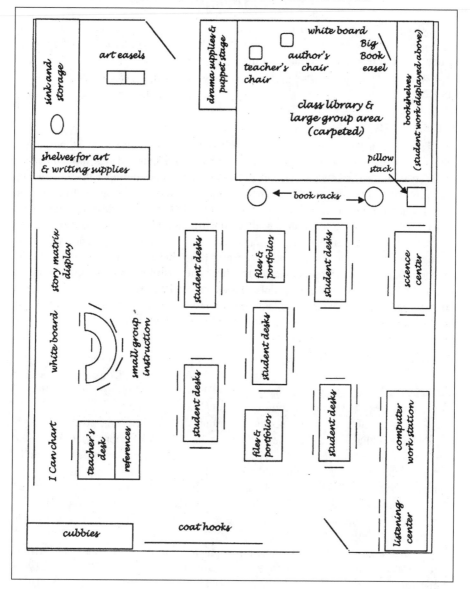

ideas about how to make the classroom function better. Students and teachers working together can create an environment that fosters learning. Figure 3.1 gives a sample layout that teachers may find useful when considering how to set up their classrooms.

References

Hansen, J. (1987). *When writers read*. Portsmouth, NH: Heinemann.

Materials

Selecting books and other materials for the readers' workshop can be one of the most pleasant tasks on a teacher's "to do" list. Here is an opportunity for teachers to collect favorite reading materials and materials for literature responses to share with their students and to impart their enthusiasm and love of reading as they talk about their choices.

Background

The basic materials for a good readers' workshop are high quality literature and other reading matter, not elaborately decorated bulletin boards and classroom displays. Carol Avery (1993) talks about changes she has made in materials selection for her classroom. In her early years of teaching, she chose materials to create an attractive and enticing classroom that "rivaled the fast-paced stimulation of Saturday morning television cartoons" (p. 62). She came to realize, however, that the room was a reflection of her own interests, not those of her students. She noted that although parents and fellow teachers sometimes admired her well-decorated room, no students ever commented on the room's appearance. Now she leaves bulletin boards empty for the children to decorate and concentrates on the essentials: the classroom library, art supplies, props and puppets, games and puzzles, media equipment, and tools for writing.

Procedure

Teachers who value and emphasize reading in their curriculum generally have classroom libraries that house a variety of types or reading materials. Books, of course, are the mainstay of the library, with many types of literature, both fiction and nonfiction, included (also see Selecting Literature, Author Study, and Thematic Units, all in this chapter). Books of different genres can be grouped in labeled bins, so that students inspired by reading an interesting legend or an exciting work of science fiction can find other books of the same genre. Books by the same author or on the same topic can be displayed similarly. Displays (changed regularly) of featured authors, topics, and genres invite readers to try something new. In addition, reference and resource books are useful for both readers' and writers' workshops: various kinds of dictionaries for students with different reading levels, an encyclopedia, a simple thesaurus, an atlas, and other informational books.

Magazines, newspapers, brochures, pamphlets, catalogs, fliers, and other written materials also are important to include in a classroom library. In addition, certain types of maps and posters are designed to be read as well as viewed. It can be a real revelation to students to see the variety of ways print is used by stores, museums, nature centers, theme parks, and other organizations to inform, educate, and entertain people. Including these different formats may even inspire different types of student publications.

Part of the classroom library might include a multimedia center if equipment is available. Books with accompanying audiotapes are popular with some students. A table can be set up with tape players, headsets, and a special display of books and tapes, which are easily kept together in zip-lock plastic bags. And of course a world of information is available via computer, both through the Internet and CD-ROMs.

Other worthwhile materials are props students and teachers can use to tell stories or to re-enact stories they have heard or read. Puppets, flannel boards with accompanying story characters, and other props can be set up in a storytelling corner or a drama center. Special materials for younger readers include big books; easels for holding large sheets of newsprint with poems, songs, chants, and so forth, for choral reading and singing; and pointers. Besides their use by teachers, pointers can be used by students to "read the room." In this procedure, students are given pointers and told they can move around the room to read any of the information on charts or other displays. Young children delight in using the pointer to lead a group of classmates in the reading of a favorite poem or chant.

Materials for written or drawn responses to literature include lined, bound response journals (many teachers use composition books), a variety of pencils and colored pens, erasers, highlighters, various types and sizes of lined and unlined paper, staplers, and other art supplies. Painting in response to stories heard or read is an excellent means of expression, especially for younger students. Easels, paints, and large sheets of newsprint can be set up in a special area for this activity.

Teachers use mini-lessons to let students know early in the school year what materials are available in the classroom and what uses they might make out of them. As the year progresses, teachers may need to remind students how to find materials they need and different uses they can make of the materials at hand. Parents may have supplies they would be happy to donate; a request for donations and a list of possibilities can be included in a classroom newsletter.

References

Avery, C. (1993). *And with a light touch: Learning about reading, writing, and teaching with first graders.* Portsmouth, NH: Heinemann.

Scheduling

Creating a schedule for readers' workshop involves committing time for students to read, reflect, talk, listen, and write. Think about athletes and musicians, who spend countless hours perfecting their skills through practice and performance. Similarly, your students need time to read, think about the ideas presented in books, listen to others' thoughts, and share questions, insights, and discoveries through discussion, writing, and other forms of expression.

Background

Studies such as the one by Anderson, Wilson, & Fielding (1988) show that students who spend more time reading tend to be more successful readers. Yet students are given little time to read in school, and many choose to do little or no reading at home. Nancie Atwell (1998) discusses the importance of making reading the central component of her literature program. Putting reading at the core of the readers' workshop achieves two goals: (a) it allows students the luxury of time to read, and (b) it demonstrates the value the teacher places on the act of reading.

Procedure

Ideally, readers' workshop is held for $1^{1}/_{2}$ to 2 hours per day. During that time, students read (independently, with partners, with stories on computer, with book/audiotape packages), listen and share (teacher read alouds, book talks by the teacher and other students), respond (in writing and drawing, through discussion), and participate in instruction (through mini-lessons, shared reading, and small group lessons). Students also have some time to choose other reading-related activities when they have finished required activities (usually, reading the required pages for their book group and completing written responses). Not all of these events occur every day, and students at different grade levels may need differing amounts of time for activities. Older students reading longer books need more independent reading time, while younger students still learning the reading process generally need more small group instructional time.

For teachers who do not have an uninterrupted block of time in their schedules, parts of the readers' workshop may need to be scheduled at different times of the day. For example, some teachers use one block of time for independent reading, reading aloud, and book talks; they use another block of time for shared reading, small group lessons, literature study groups, and writing in response to literature. Upper-grade teachers who meet with their students for 45- to 50-minute periods may elect to do different activities on alternate days. The examples that follow show how three teachers created schedules for the readers' workshop.

References

Anderson, R. T., Wilson, P. T., & Fielding, L. G. (1988). Growth in reading and how children spend their time outside of school. *Reading Research Quarterly, 23* (3), 285–303.

Atwell, N. (1998). *In the middle: New understandings about writing, reading, and learning (2nd ed.)*. Portsmouth, NH: Boynton/Cook.

FIGURE 3.2   DAILY SCHEDULE—SECOND GRADE

Daily Schedule—2nd Grade
Mr. Marcus Jamal

8:30	Check-In/Morning Business
8:45	Readers' Workshop:

- morning message
- read aloud (Mr. J.)
- reading groups meet w/ Mr. J.
- independent activities*

When your group isn't meeting:

* write in your response journal

* read your group book

* read stories on the computer

* listen and read at listening center

* practice your spelling words

10:15	Snack & recess
10:35	Math
11:30	Lunch
12:00	Readers' Workshop:

- silent or partner reading
- book talks (Mr. J. and others)

12:30	Geography, science, health, art, or music (rotation)
1:30	Break
1:40	Writers' Workshop:

- mini-lesson
- status of the class
- independent writing
- conferences (teacher and peer)
- sharing

2:45	Evaluation, pack up
3:00	School ends

FIGURE 3.3   DAILY SCHEDULE—FOURTH GRADE

**Daily Schedule—4th Grade
Mrs. Brenda DeRego**

8:30	Check-In/Morning Business
8:45	Writers' Workshop:

• teacher read aloud

• mini-lesson

• status of the class

• independent writing

• peer conferences

• teacher conferences

• skill instruction (small groups)

9:45	Math
10:30	Snack & recess
10:45	Readers' Workshop:

• mini-lesson

• silent reading

• literature logs

• Book Clubs meet

11:45	Lunch
12:15	Independent reading
12:35	Science or social studies
1:35	Student book talks
1:45	Art, music, or PE
2:45	Evaluation, pack up
3:00	School ends

FIGURE 3.4   READERS' AND WRITERS' WORKSHOP SCHEDULES—SIXTH GRADE

Readers' Workshop
Period 3 10:15–11:00 a.m.

Mon. and Wed.
Silent reading and response journals—30 min.
Class sharing, book talks—15 min.

Tues. and Thurs.
Mini-lesson & read aloud—15 min.
Literature discussion groups—30 min.

Friday
Choice time—30 min.
Class sharing, weekly reflection—15 min.

Writers' Workshop
Period 4 11:05–11:50 a.m.

Mon. and Wed.
Mini-lesson—10 min.
Writing and conferring—35 min.

Tues. and Thurs.
Writing and conferring—35 min.
Author's Chair—10 min.

Friday
Writing and conferring—30 min.
Class sharing, weekly reflection—15 min.

Grouping

Students routinely have been grouped for reading instruction on the basis of reading ability as measured by standardized test scores, informal reading measures, or their previous year's reading group placement. In readers' workshop classrooms, however, students are grouped for reading instruction according to both needs and interests. Heterogeneous groups accommodate students who, regardless of reading level, are excited about reading a story or novel with their friends or are eager to do research with a group by reading about some aspect of the topic and sharing their findings. Homogeneous groups are useful for instructing students with similar skill needs. Group membership changes with changing interests and needs.

Background

The composition of reading groups and the effects on readers have been studied extensively by researchers (e.g., Allington & Walmsley, 1995; Gamoran, 1992; Slavin, 1989). Within-class ability grouping in one or two subjects, when students were grouped heterogeneously at other times, were found beneficial in some studies. When students were grouped by ability consistently, however, low groups fell further behind each year. Researchers concluded that instructional differences played a part. Students in high groups received fast-paced, challenging instruction. They focused more on silent reading, comprehension, and high-level thinking skills. Those in low groups got slower-paced, less challenging instruction consisting of more skill sheets, practice drills, and low-level discussion questions.

For over eight years, Cunningham, Hall, and Defee (1998) studied students who were grouped heterogeneously to learn to read. In this model, students worked daily in four blocks—guided reading, self-selected reading, writing, and working with words. Teachers were challenged to make the guided reading block work for students of different reading abilities. They chose two books per week for each group, one at grade level and one below. The children read and discussed the same selections several times over the week to improve comprehension and fluency, and those who had difficulty were assigned reading partners. Despite these challenges, the achievement rate for the classes in the study was consistently high over the entire eight years.

Ability grouping has been used successfully in New Zealand classrooms, where literacy rates also are high (Wilkinson & Townsend, 2000). In the early grades, classrooms generally have five or more homogeneous groups, but students do not remain in the same group for the entire term. Instead, teachers move students ahead to higher groups as the students gain in reading abilities. Some students may move to an earlier level, but only when the group the child is in has moved ahead at a faster pace but the earlier level group is moving ahead and meets that child's abilities. Teachers use informal observations and running records to determine when to move students. Half to two-thirds of the class may change groups within a school year.

Wilkinson and Townsend (2000) note several characteristics of the lessons that support lower-ability readers. The New Zealand teachers generally spent more time with their at-risk students. Teachers emphasized reading for meaning, and they used metacognitive questions to promote independent use of comprehension, vocabulary, and word reading strategies. Teachers also selected texts carefully, with attention to both reading levels and interest levels, so that students generally were engaged and on-task when reading.

Procedure

Teachers begin the school year by finding out about their students' reading interests, habits, and attitudes. This may take the form of interviews, surveys, observations as students read and talk about books, and/or observations as teachers read aloud to their students. From this information, some teachers select one book the whole class will read and discuss together. Either following this experience or instead of it, teachers may select several books for literature study around a theme of interest to the students and relevance to the curriculum. Later, students may suggest books they want to read together.

Teachers have found that guided reading groups of no more than six allow each student ample opportunity to be heard. Teachers who are more comfortable having fewer stories to keep track of at any one time may have more than one group read the same book. If students are grouped homogeneously for reading, it is better to have fewer students in the lower groups so that each student gets more attention. The more capable readers can usually manage in a slightly larger group.

For students reading chapter books and novels, the teacher can use book talks to introduce the selections, which are left out a few days for students to browse through and consider. Teachers will want to talk about how challenging each book may be to read. For example, a book with a great deal of specialized vocabulary may be more difficult for students with no background in the area and easier for students with relevant background. Some children are more comfortable with books that have larger type, more illustrations, shorter sentences, fewer words on a page, or shorter chapters. The teacher can alert students to these features in the books students will choose from.

After students have had time to consider the possibilities, they make first and second choices (see Figure 3.5 for a sample form). The teacher then assigns a book after weighing their preferences, reading level, background knowledge, and level of difficulty of the book. Teachers also consider the strong motivation students have for reading a more challenging book that is of personal interest to them. Even after students have begun their books, the teacher gives them a few days to change their selections if the text proves too difficult or not of interest. When the students finish their books, they can evaluate how well they handled the reading. This information is helpful to the teacher as well as the student when choosing books in the future. Over time, students may be able to choose their own books with little or no assistance from the teacher (see Figure 3.6).

Teachers who group students heterogeneously for reading and literature discussions use homogenous groups to address specific areas of need. For example, after observing several students struggle repeatedly with unknown words, Mr. Jamal decided to have these students meet with him for a few sessions to explore strategies for figuring out unknown words. This flexible skills group was not a permanent "remedial" group; the students in it also were members of heterogeneous literature discussion groups. New flexible skills groups can be formed and dissolved as needs arise and are met.

Students just beginning to read usually are placed in homogeneous groups in order to help them interact with text that is challenging but not frustrating. Keeping in mind alternatives for grouping, these students should be placed in different groups for other small group work. For example, students in Mrs. O'Brien's kindergarten class work in heterogeneous small groups on book projects based on favorite stories that have been read aloud.

Mason and Au (1990) recommend that teachers work to improve the status of students perceived as less successful readers, and look for opportunities to evaluate students on multiple dimensions—for example, any special reading talents they may have. Following these suggestions, Mr. Jamal calls on struggling readers as often as he does strong readers during class discussions. He knows that students called on by teachers are perceived as smarter and more knowledgeable by their peers. Since he generally asks open-ended questions, low-achieving readers have equal opportunities to share their insights and contribute thoughtful responses to discussions.

In addition, Mr. Jamal notes and praises other strengths his struggling readers have. One student consistently notices when special vocabulary words in their book have been used in other stories the class has heard or read. Another student knows a lot about taking care of pets and applies his knowledge to a discussion of *Arthur's Pet Business* (Brown, 1990). Teachers who work to balance students' instructional needs with their needs for social acceptance and status find that students become more willing collaborators in their own learning.

FIGURE 3.5   SAMPLE FORM FOR STUDENT BOOK SELECTION

Name _____ Date _____

What book would you like to read?

    Best Friends

    Henry and Mudge

    Freckle Juice

    Arthur's April Fool

Write your 1st and 2nd choices.

1st _____

2nd _____

FIGURE 3.6   A TEACHER'S NOTE TO STUDENTS FOR SUGGESTING BOOKS

Dear 6th Graders,

Since our theme is survival, be on the lookout for good novels for our literature discussion groups that will start next week. Someone suggested <u>Homecoming</u> by Cynthia Voigt, and there's a group that wants to talk about Gary Paulsen's <u>Dogsong</u>. Be ready with ideas when we meet Friday morning.

Mrs. Okamoto

References

Allington, R. L., & Walmsley, S. A., Eds. (1995). *No quick fix: Rethinking literacy programs in America's elementary schools.* Newark, DE: International Reading Association.

Cunningham, P., Hall, D., & Defee, M. (1998). Nonability grouped, multilevel instruction: Eight years later. *The Reading Teacher, 51* (8), 652–664.

Gamoran, A. (1992). Is ability grouping equitable? *Educational Leadership, 50* (2), 11–17.

Mason, J. M., & Au, K. H. (1990). *Reading instruction for today.* New York: HarperCollins.

Slavin, R. E. (1989, September). Synthesis of research on grouping in elementary and secondary schools. *Educational Leadership,* 67–77.

Wilkinson, A. G., & Townsend, M. A. (2000). From Rata to Rimu: Grouping for instruction in best practice New Zealand classrooms. *The Reading Teacher, 53* (6), 460–471.

Children's Book Cited

Brown, M. (1990). *Arthur's Pet Business.* New York: Little Brown.

The Impact of Violet Harris:
Multicultural Children's Literature

While teachers continue to share old favorites such as *Charlotte's Web* (White, 1952) during the readers' workshop, they are also finding new favorites such as *Grandfather's Journey* (Say, 1993) in the growing body of multicultural literature. Noting that the term multicultural literature appears more and more frequently in discussions of children's literature, Violet Harris (1992a) offers the following definition:

Multicultural literature refers to literature that focuses on people of color—African, Asian, Hispanic, and Native American; religious minorities, such as the Amish or Jewish; regional cultures, for example, Appalachian and Cajun; the disabled; and the aged. To some extent, the term encompasses literature that presents women and girls in a multitude of roles that are not gender stereotyped. The element common to each group member is its marginal status and its lack of full participation in "mainstream" institutions. (p. 171)

Harris (1992b), who conducts research on African American children's literature, argues for the place of literature focusing on African, Asian, Hispanic, and Native Americans. In the past, works featuring these groups did not find their way into the curriculum. Harris points out that the exclusion of these works prevents students from gaining a broader perspective, because race and ethnicity can serve as lenses through which experiences and history receive different interpretations.

Culturally Conscious Literature

Sims (1982) developed the term culturally conscious literature to refer to works that depict the culture of a particular group from the perspective of an insider. Through the author's portrayal of language, traditions, settings, and physical appearances, the reader understands that the characters are African, Asian, Hispanic, or Native American. The author presents the culture in a sensitive and authentic manner, showing the characters as complex individuals rather than as stereotypes. For example, in the Newbery Award winner *Roll of Thunder, Hear My Cry*, Mildred Taylor (1976) tells the story of the Logans, an African American family living in the south in the 1930s. Taylor presents Cassie and her siblings as distinct personalities, growing up in a family with strong principles.

Taylor composes realistic works that include acts of violence against African Americans. Harris (1992a) notes that such works serve the crucial function of preserving history, correcting misconceptions, and offering nonmainstream interpretations of events. But she recommends that students' attention also be called to the positive experiences shared by people of color, such as stories showing the close ties of family and community. These works may grow from everyday life rather than from extraordinary or dramatic events. For example, in *Tar Beach* by Faith Ringgold (1991), a young girl dreams of flying through the sky with her baby brother to see significant places the city.

Benefits of Multicultural Literature

Harris notes that students gain the same cognitive benefits from reading multicultural literature as they do from reading and discussing any excellent work. Involvement with multicultural literature can improve students' comprehension and vocabulary and expand their background knowledge. Students can become familiar with works and styles that can serve as models for their own writing.

Multicultural literature offers the additional advantage of raising students' consciousness of their own cultures and the cultures of others. Through multicultural literature, students have the chance to explore both the similarities and differences among groups. Multicultural literature may help students, of both mainstream and nonmainstream backgrounds, to become more tolerant and understanding of others. *Too Many Tamales* by Gary Soto (1993) shows customs that might be unfamiliar to many students. Yet this work can help students recognize that all groups have their own customs. As a follow-up activity, students might be asked to prepare illustrations for their own book of family celebrations.

Harris (1992a) considers the situation in which children have a steady diet only of mainstream literature. This situation can be harmful to mainstream students because it limits their view, fails to develop their knowledge and understanding of other cultural perspectives, and does not prepare them to interact with those of other backgrounds. Reading a multicultural work such as *My First American Friend* (Jin, 1990) may give mainstream students insights about the fears and struggles of immigrant students.

Nonmainstream students need to read multicultural literature to get the message that the contributions and experiences of their cultural groups are valued by the school and by society. Through multicultural literature, teachers can give nonmainstream students the message that they have lives and experiences worth writing about. For example, in *Night on Neighborhood Street*, Eloise Greenfield (1991) presents poems of scenes likely to be familiar to students who live in the inner city.

Practical Considerations

Harris (1992a) recommends that classroom teachers make their own decisions about whether to make multicultural literature part of the classroom literacy program. She believes that multicultural literature is likely to have a positive effect only when teachers sincerely want to share these books with their students. Harris does not think teachers should be pressured to use multicultural literature. If teachers are compelled to use this literature before they feel ready to do so, they may convey a negative attitude about the books and the groups portrayed to their students. "Ideally," Harris writes, "teachers should want to include the literature because it is part of world literature, many of the works are excellent, and children deserve to expand their knowledge of the world's cultures and histories" (p. 193).

Multicultural literature presents new challenges, Harris notes, and teachers have to develop strategies for solving the problems that arise because of the controversial issues in some of the works. For example, *Mississippi Bridge*, another of Mildred Taylor's (1990) works, is historically accurate and tells a powerful story. Yet this book depicts acts of violence against African Americans as well as the use of derogatory terms for African Americans. On the one hand, this book gives teachers the opportunity to explore issues of racism with students. On the other hand, some adults might judge this work inappropriate for use with elementary students.

Harris points out that authors writing from an insider's perspective often portray characters' language just as they might speak in vernacular English. Patricia McKissack (1986), for example, follows this approach in *Flossie and the Fox*. Teachers who share this book with students might need to explain to parents why they have chosen to use a text including a nonmainstream variety of English, instead of sticking to texts written entirely in standard English.

Finally, Harris notes that some authors present historical events from viewpoints that contradict those usually evident in textbooks. For example, some Japanese American authors use the term concentration camp rather than internment camp to refer to the imprisonment of their people during World War II.

Harris does not see a ready resolution to the many potential controversies surrounding the use of multicultural literature. Teachers cannot easily reconcile these conflicting views, although they can come to an understanding of their own positions on the issues. Harris highlights debatable issues not to discourage teachers from using multicultural literature but to remind teachers to use these books in an informed manner. Multicultural literature can provide all students with the pleasures of powerful language, an engaging story, and all joys of reading. Taken a step further, these works offer teachers and students the opportunity to explore issues of critical importance in today's world, in particular, the need for social justice and racial equality.

References

Harris, V. J. (1992a). Multiethnic children's literature. In K. D. Wood & A. Moss (Eds.), *Exploring literature in the classroom: Content and methods* (pp. 169–201). Norwood, MA: Christopher-Gordon.

Harris, V. J. (1992b). Contemporary griots: African-American writers of children's literature. In V. J. Harris (Ed.), *Teaching multicultural literature in grades K–8* (pp. 55–108). Norwood, MA: Christopher-Gordon.

Sims, R. (1982). *Shadow and substance: Afro-American experience in contemporary children's fiction.* Urbana, IL: National Council of Teachers of English.

Children's Books Cited

Greenfield, E. (1991). *Night on Neighborhood Street.* New York: Dial.

Jin, S. (1990). *My first American friend.* Madison, NJ: Raintree Steck-Vaughn.

McKissack, P. (1986). *Flossie and the fox.* New York: Dial.

Ringgold, F. (1991). *Tar beach.* New York: Crown.

Say, A. (1993). *Grandfather's journey.* Boston: Houghton Mifflin.

Soto, G. (1993). *Too many tamales.* New York: Putnam.

Taylor, M. (1990). *Mississippi bridge.* New York: Dial.

Taylor, M. (1976). *Roll of thunder, hear my cry.* New York: Dial.

White, E.B. (1952). *Charlotte's web.* New York: HarperCollins.

Resources

Barrera, R. B., Thompson, V. D., & Dressman, M. (Eds.) (1997). *Kaleidoscope: A multicultural booklist for grades K–8* (2nd ed., covering books published from 1993–95). Urbana, IL: National Council of Teachers of English.

Day, F. A. (1994). *Multicultural voices in contemporary literature: A resource for teachers.* Portsmouth, NH: Heinemann.

Harris, V. J. (Ed.) (1992). *Teaching multicultural literature in grades K–8.* Norwood, MA: Christopher-Gordon.

Lindgren, M. V. (1991). *The multicolored mirror: Cultural substance in literature for children and young adults.* Fort Atkinson, WI: Highsmith.

Selecting Literature

We read literature basically for enjoyment. Yet good literature is important in a child's education for many other reasons. Professor Donna Norton (1999) points to other values of good literature:

- transmitting our literary heritage from one generation to the next
- helping children understand and value not only their own cultural heritage, but the cultures of others
- allowing vicarious experiences that help children better understand the past, speculate on the future, and reflect on the experiences of contemporary characters like or unlike themselves
- connecting children with knowledge and ideas they might not encounter otherwise
- supporting the development of imagination and creativity

Selecting good literature and promoting children's enjoyment of good literature are at the heart of a strong readers' workshop.

Background

What constitutes good literature, literature that is important and worthy of children's time and attention? Much discussion on this issue has involved attempts to define a literary *canon*: an authoritative list of works to be read by all students. In his research, Alan Purves (1993) explores a canon's underlying purposes: to communicate cultural values and promote cultural identity. Of course, there are many canons, based on beliefs as diverse as the groups that devise them. As values change, canons are modified. The "classics" of the 1950s were largely from the Western European tradition; today, we recognize a far greater ethnic diversity and the influence of that diversity on American culture. Native American, African American, Hispanic, and Asian authors and books are now represented in multicultural canons. Yet there is still little consensus as to what belongs in any canon.

Purves (1993) suggests that literature in the curriculum goes beyond the literary canon. In order to select literature "with a full respect for the diverse groups that comprise our society" (p. 105), he proposes teachers choose a broad variety of texts, sometimes grouped by cultures, but other times grouped in other ways. For example, to help students understand cultures other than their own, teachers might select a group of books about a specific culture. To help students understand that certain values are universal, teachers might choose a group of books that show the importance of families and friendships in several cultures. In all cases, to enrich the literary experience, books should be linked to information about the authors themselves—including the cultures in which they live and work.

Procedure

Teachers looking for a wide variety of texts will have no shortage from which to choose. The number of titles currently available may make the task seem daunting at first; a working knowledge of children's literature takes time to build. Browsing in the school library, community library, bookstores, and other teachers' classrooms is a good way to start. Libraries and publishers make available helpful book lists, often on their web sites. There are lists of award winners (Caldecott, Newberry, Boston Globe/Horn

Book, the NCTE Orbis Pictus Award for Outstanding Nonfiction for Children), themed lists (celebrating cultural diversity, understanding environmental issues), lists based on genres (picture books, mystery books, fantasy), and grade level lists. Students, fellow teachers, librarians, parents, and others can be asked to share favorite titles and reasons for their recommendations. Figure 3.7 suggests some resources to use as a starting point. Additional resources are given in the sections on Author Study and Thematic Units (both are in this chapter).

As teachers begin to explore books, they consider their students' interests and needs to determine whether and how a particular title might fit into their curriculum. Some books are chosen to create a classroom library core. Others are selected for reading aloud, mini-lessons, or small group reading lessons. Still others become possibilities for literature discussion groups. Teachers from different grade levels may want to work together to select titles to focus on at each grade in order to avoid duplication across grades. Teachers need to look carefully at reading levels when determining which books will be used for small group reading instruction. A great piece of literature that is beyond the reach of the students in the group is better left for a later grade or a read aloud.

Teachers will want to find titles that help children consider different ways of looking at stories. Miriam Martinez and Nancy Roser (1995) describe three useful categories. One is books that entice readers into the story experience itself, creating a sense of living in the story world and knowing the characters as real people. *A Chair for My Mother* by Vera Williams (1982) and *Charlotte's Web* by E. B. White (1952) are two such examples. A second category is books that lead students to explore story themes, such as *Faithful Elephants* by Yukio Tsuchiya (1988) and *Missing May* by Cynthia Rylant (1992). A third category is books that enable readers to notice author's craft, such as *Fortunately* by Remy Charlip (1964) and *Journey* by Patricia MacLachlan (1991). Other titles that fit these categories are listed in Martinez and Roser's (1995) chapter.

When looking for literature for her fifth-grade classroom, teacher Laura Pardo (1998) considered themes to help her organize her literature selections and related content learning. After identifying a theme, she looked for books that had potential for weighty discussions for Book Clubs (see Literature Discussion Groups in chapter 5) and read alouds. She also chose titles related to this theme for the classroom library and as source material for independent inquiry projects. For a unit on World War II, she chose *Sadako and the Thousand Paper Cranes* (Coerr, 1977) for the Book Club selection and *Faithful Elephants* (Tsuchiya, 1988) as a read aloud. Both books prompted heated discussions by her students about the unfairness of war and its effects on the lives of non-combatants. Based on the quality of discussions of these and other titles, Pardo developed a list of criteria for selecting books. She determined that good literature for discussion

- presented big ideas or themes,
- reflected real issues,
- described the condition of humanity,
- contained mature content, and
- could be considered controversial (p. 223).

Ideally, books should inspire readers in some way—to feel, think, talk, write, draw, act, grow. The best children's books "evoke emotions; they invite thought and reflection; they engender ideas....They explore universal truths with honesty and integrity. Concerned with the whole of human experience, they provide a link with life" (Brett, 1989, p. 18).

FIGURE 3.7   ANNOTATED LIST OF RESOURCES FOR SELECTING LITERATURE

Resources for Selecting Literature

- *Adventuring with Books: A Booklist for Pre-K–Grade 6, 12th Edition*, edited by M. M. Pierce, NCTE, 2000, 605 pp. Carefully chosen selections are categorized by topics, themes, concepts, and types—ways classroom teachers find useful. Many annotations include students' and teachers' personal responses to the stories.

- *Battling Dragons: Issues and Controversy in Children's Literature*, edited by Susan Lehr, Heinemann, 1995, 288 pp. Twenty authors and educators discuss issues of censorship, gender, freedom, violence, racism, family values, children's roles, good and evil, and political correctness in literature.

- *Better Books! Better Readers! How to Choose, Use, and Level Books for Children in the Primary Grades*, Linda Hart-Hewins & Jan Wells, Stenhouse, 1999, 152 pp. Contains a bibliography of good books for beginning (Concept Books, Pattern Books, First Steps), developing (Step a Little Further, Step a Little Faster, Taking Off), and fluent readers (You're Away, Getting Longer, First Novels).

- The New Blue Pages: Resources for Teachers (240 pp.), in *Conversations: Strategies for Teaching, Learning, and Evaluating*, Regie Routman, Heinemann, 1999. Includes professional resources for teachers and recommended literature. Annotated book lists by grade levels (K–8) and additional topics (poetry, author studies, books that invite writing and storytelling, favorites).

- *Reluctant Readers: Connecting Students and Books for Successful Reading Experiences*, Ron Jobe & Mary Dayton-Sakari, Stenhouse, 1999, 160 pp. Books that interest reluctant readers. Includes categories such as books with interactive movement, books with engaging information, language play books, and books about girl power, survival, and horror stories.

- *Research and Professional Resources in Children's Literature: Piecing a Patchwork Quilt*, edited by Kathy Short, International Reading Association, 1995, 288 pp. Sections on research, journals that review children's literature, book lists by topic, and professional books dealing with the use of literature for reading, writing, content area studies, and cultural awareness.

- *Teaching Multicultural Literature in Grades K–8*, edited by Violet Harris, Christopher Gordon, 1992. African American, Asian American, Native American, Mexican American, Puerto Rican, and Caribbean children's literature, as well as issues in common with all multicultural books and authors.

- *Through the Eyes of a Child: An Introduction to Children's Literature*, Donna E. Norton, Prentice-Hall, 1999, 746 pp. A thorough exploration of children's literature, including its history, current issues, extensive book lists, and a searchable CD-ROM with 2,600 titles.

References

Brett, B. M. (1989). Selecting children's books: "The rarest kind of best." In Hickman, J., & Cullinan, B. E., (Eds.), *Children's literature in the classroom: Weaving Charlotte's web* (pp. 13–24). Needham Heights, MA: Christopher Gordon.

Martinez, M. G., & Roser, N. L. (1995). The books make a difference in story talk. In Roser, N. L. & Martinez, M. G., (Eds.), *Book talk and beyond: Children and teachers respond to literature* (pp. 32–41). Newark, DE: International Reading Association.

Norton, D. E. (1999). *Through the eyes of a child: An introduction to children's literature,* Upper Saddle River, NJ: Prentice-Hall.

Pardo, L. S. (1998). Criteria for selecting literature in upper elementary grades. In Raphael, T. E., and Au, K. H. (Eds.), *Literature-based instruction: Reshaping the curriculum.* Norwood, MA: Christopher-Gordon.

Purves, A. C. (1993). The ideology of canons and cultural concerns in the literature curriculum. In Miller, S. M., & McCaskill, B., (Eds.), *Multicultural literature and literacies: Making space for difference* (pp. 105–127). Albany: State University of New York Press.

Children's Books Cited

Charlip, R. (1964). *Fortunately.* New York: Four Winds.

Coerr, E. (1977). *Sadako and the Thousand Paper Cranes.* New York: Putnam.

MacLachlan, P. (1991). *Journey.* New York: Delcourte Press.

Rylant, C. (1992). *Missing May.* New York: Orchard.

Tsuchiya, Y. (1988). *Faithful elephants: A true story of animals, people, and war.* Boston: Houghton Mifflin.

White, E. B. (1952). *Charlotte's web.* New York: Harper & Row.

Williams, V. (1982). *A chair for my mother.* New York: Greenwillow.

Author Study

An author study is an in-depth examination of multiple works by a single author. Teachers use author studies in the readers' workshop to help students explore the craft of writing and discover how authors communicate with their readers.

Background

Author studies can take many forms. Three different types are described in *The Allure of Authors: Author Studies in the Elementary Classroom* (Jenkins, 1999):

- author study as literary biography
- author study as critical response
- author study as aesthetic response

Literary biography looks at literature as "the embodiment of the writer's life and times—his or her relationships with family and friends, the influences and experiences that shaped his or her early life, and the social/historical context in which he or she lived" (p. 27). This type of study examines the author's works to find threads of the author's life, however transformed they may become in the story. Critical response examines the craft of writing. It looks at the story in detail for its style, structure, and complexity, without looking beyond it to what may have influenced the author. Aesthetic response explores the reader's reactions to and connections with the story. It is closely related to Louise Rosenblatt's reader response theory (see chapter 2). In this approach, it is assumed that each reader's interpretation of the story's events, its deeper meaning, and the author's intent will be different, based on the reader's own life experiences.

Jenkins (1999) advocates *author study as multiple response*. She believes that to focus on any one of the perspectives described above at the expense of the others limits our thinking about authors and their literature. She also believes that, although critical response and response to the author as a person and a writer deepens and extends the literary experience, aesthetic engagement must come first.

Procedure

Author studies can be done by the whole class, a small group of students, or an individual. Teachers often use whole class author studies to introduce authors whose works seem to have the ability to communicate strongly to readers. Author studies also may evolve from a student's (or group of students') love for a book, leading to the exploration of other works by that author.

When selecting an author for study, the teacher looks for someone whose work she enjoys and admires. That positive attitude will be reflected in her discussions with the students, and she will have genuine points of interest to share. Some authors write about strong characters readers identify with or may emulate. Some write plots that grab the reader and keep him engrossed in wanting to know what happens next. Others engage readers with powerful themes or a unique style. While authors of fiction are frequently selected for study, many authors of nonfiction are good choices also. Some examples of both are listed in Figure 3.8, and resources for finding information about authors and author studies are listed in Figure 3.9. (See also Figure 3.7 in Selecting Literature and Figure 3.12 in Thematic Units.)

The teacher gathers as many different titles as possible, including multiple copies of some titles so students can read and discuss in small groups or do paired reading. A letter to parents informing them of the planned study may result in students bringing in their own copies of the author's books to share. The teacher also locates background information about the author. Publishers may have web sites with photographs, interviews, and facts about their authors. Some authors have their own web sites. Videotapes and books showing authors at work and home are another good source for helping students see the author as a real person. For example, students reading Lois Lowry's (1998) books should enjoy *Looking Back: A Book of Memories*, which is full of family photos, short reflections, and quotes from her many writings. Additional resources about authors are listed at the end of this section.

FIGURE 3.8   SUGGESTED AUTHORS FOR AUTHOR STUDIES

Fiction Authors	**Nonfiction Authors**
For lower grades (K–3):	
Marc Brown	Aliki
Jan Brett	Joanna Cole
Eric Carle	Tomie de Paola
Beverly Cleary	Jean Fritz
Tomie de Paola	Gail Gibbons
Mem Fox	Dick King Smith
Eloise Greenfield	Patricia Lauber
Dick King Smith	Bianca Lavies
Leo Lionni	Milicent Selsam
Patricia Polacco	Diane Stanley
Cynthia Rylant	
Allen Say	
William Steig	
John Steptoe	
For upper grades (4–6):	
Avi	Carolyn Arnold
Betsy Byars	Brent Ashabranner
Rhold Dahl	Isaac Asimov
Sid Fleischman	Leonard Everett Fisher
Jean Craighead George	Russell Freedman
Lois Lowry	Jean Fritz
Scott O'Dell	James Haskins
Katherine Patterson	Kathryn Lasky
Mildred Taylor	David Macaulay
Yoshiko Uchida	Milton Meltzer
Lawrence Yep	Seymour Simon

Teachers often share the author's biographical information in mini-lessons, highlighting interesting facts about how the author works or something in the author's background that has contributed to his or her style of writing or choice of content. Mini-lessons can include brief book talks about some of the titles available in the classroom, using them as illustrative examples of the author's style. After that, the teacher may want to give students several sessions to select books and read independently.

As with thematic literature units, the teacher may want to read aloud one book as an anchor piece, a book all students will have in common for discussion. For younger students, the teacher may read aloud several of the selections. Some teachers tape record as they read so that students can play the tapes later and follow along in the book. The book chosen for the read aloud may be a more challenging book that the students could not read on their own, an autobiography or biography of the author, or simply a favorite book by that author.

From these experiences, the students and the teacher begin to discuss what they notice about this author, the author's writing, or their own personal connections. The discussions might start with the whole class and move into small groups as students do more reading and find others who want to talk about the same books they do. With older or more able students who are reading longer books, the teacher may set up a plan in advance, working with the class to decide which titles will be read in common.

When doing critical response, the teacher can help students focus on issues such as how the author sets up story conflict, shows characters' growth and change, takes a point of view, develops themes, uses language to convey mood, and other aspects of author's craft. For example, the first graders in Mrs. Shima's class reading Marc Brown's books learned how he included his children's own names in his illustrations and other "fingerprints" in his work. A group of students in Mr. Jamal's second-grade class reading Jan Brett's books noticed how much factual information came through in her illustrations, especially in the borders. When some of Ms. DeRego's students did an author study of Katherine Patterson, they noted and admired the strong characters she created and explored how these characters dealt with major events in their lives.

Follow-up activities give students opportunities to put together their findings in interesting and informative ways. Students have made posters, charts, bulletin board displays, and book jackets. They have given speeches, choral readings, and dramatic performances. They have shared their learning with other classes and visitors to the classroom; they have taken home portable items to show parents and other family members. These and other activities provide evidence that students are making connections with authors and that authors are helping them acquire and improve their literacy.

References

Jenkins, C. B. (1999). *The allure of authors: Author studies in the elementary classroom.* Portsmouth, NH: Heinemann.

Lowry, L. (1998). *Looking back: A book of memories.* Boston: Houghton Mifflin.

FIGURE 3.9   ANNOTATED LIST OF RESOURCES FOR AUTHOR STUDY

Resources for Author Study

* *The Allure of Authors: Author Studies in the Elementary Classroom*, Carol B. Jenkins, Heinemann, 1999, 280 pp. A thorough examination of the topic of author studies. Describes different focuses an author study can take (literary biography, critical response, reader response), and gives detailed examples of studies using authors Carolyn Coman, Mem Fox, Avi, Joanna Cole, Patricia Polacco, Mildred Taylor, Kathryn Lasky, and Cynthia Rylant.

* *The Author Studies Handbook: Helping Students Build Powerful Connections to Literature,* L. Kotch & L. Zackman, Scholastic, 1995. How-to strategies for using real authors as models for writing and making connections among authors, books, and readers.

* *Books That Invite Talk, Wonder, and Play,* A. A. McClure & J. V. Kristo, (Eds.), National Council of Teachers of English, 1996. Children's authors share their thoughts on how they develop plot, create authentic characters, invent realistic dialogue, and other aspects of writing.

* *Get to Know.* Harcourt Brace videotape series on authors and illustrators. Designed to help students see the person behind the story.

* *Lifetime Guarantees*, Shelley Harwayne, Heinemann, 2000, 384 pp. plus appendices. Includes Across the Grades Guide to Author Study and Results of Children's Literature Survey (favorite authors listed by grade levels).

* *Meet the Author.* A series of books about authors published by Richard C. Owens.

* The New Blue Pages: Resources for Teachers (240 pp.), in *Conversations: Strategies for Teaching, Learning, and Evaluating,* Regie Routman, Heinemann, 1999. Annotated book lists by grade levels (K–8) and additional topics (poetry, author studies, books that invite writing and storytelling, favorites).

* *Through the Eyes of a Child: An Introduction to Children's Literature,* Donna E. Norton, Prentice-Hall, 1999, 746 pp. A thorough exploration of children's literature, including its history, current issues, extensive book lists, and a searchable CD-ROM with 2,600 titles.

Genres

All teachers seem to know those students who read only one type of book—science fiction, perhaps, or books about sports, or all the books featuring the character Encyclopedia Brown. While teachers want to support these reading passions, they also hope to widen students' horizons. When planning for the readers' workshop, teachers need to consider how to excite students about books of different genres.

Background

A genre is a type of literature in which the books of that type share common characteristics, says children's literature professor Rebecca Lukens (1998). Having said that, however, she cautions that there are often as many differences as there are similarities among works in a given genre. Yet she finds genre classifications useful for several reasons. One, they make us aware of the scope of children's literature beyond familiar stories and nursery rhymes. Two, in different genres, literary elements such as plot and characterization function differently. Three, using genre classifications helps teachers and children explore the rich variety of literature.

The broadest classifications of literature are fiction and nonfiction. Within fiction, the three main categories are traditional literature, realism, and fantasy. Figure 3.10 shows a diagram of different genre types.

Traditional literature encompasses many types of stories passed down from the oral tradition, before writing recorded our stories. Variations on the same tales may come from many cultures, attesting to the universality of human needs and desires. Folk tales, fables, myths, legends, and epics are common types of traditional literature. Since these stories are handed down from one generation to the next by word of mouth, they have no identifiable author. The authors' names we see on traditional tales today are simply the writers of a particular version of the original tale.

Realism, as the label implies, deals with stories that could happen. Realistic children's stories may have contemporary or historical settings, and they often deal with social issues or problems common to children and adolescents. Historical fiction is a type of realism that has become increasingly popular in classrooms. Teachers find it gives students a vivid sense of life in a particular period in history while immersing them in conflict, suspense, and believable characterizations.

Fantasy employs settings (imaginary worlds), characters (such as animals or plants that speak), and situations (the use of magic to generate events, for example) that are not known to exist. Good fantasies, nevertheless, make their worlds believable. In science fiction (one type of fantasy), scientific laws as we understand them are the foundation for futuristic inventions and scenarios. In fantastic stories involving animals that speak, the animals often retain characteristics that fit their species.

Nonfiction generally is divided into two main categories: biographies and informational books. Biographies (and autobiographies) give factual accounts of the lives of individuals. Informational books tell facts and related concepts about numerous topics in science, social studies, history, and so forth. Nonfiction books are written in both narrative and expository format.

Procedure

Teachers can introduce students to different genres through mini-lessons, reading aloud, discussions, and book talks. During these activities, teachers will want to talk with students about literary elements (such as character, plot, theme, setting, point of view, style, and tone) and how they are treated in various genres. For example, setting is obviously a more important element in historical fiction or science fiction than it is in most contemporary realistic fiction. However, in some realistic fiction, it is the setting that develops the main character (e.g., *Hatchet* by Gary Paulsen, 1999). Stock characters in traditional tales—the wicked stepmother, the cruel giant—are very different than the multidimensional portraits of characters in most realism and fantasy. Yet some characters in realism and fantasy are flat characters who do not change throughout the story (e.g., Annemarie's younger sister in *Number the Stars* by Lois Lowry, 1987). Students can explore similarities and differences in genres as they read and talk about books.

A third grade teacher developed a unit on traditional literature by beginning with myths. She read aloud several creation myths from different cultures and talked with students about what they noticed. She also set up a special book display of myths on other natural phenomena (earthquakes, lightning) for students to browse and borrow from. Students were encouraged to give book talks during whole class sharing about the titles they had read. From these experiences, the students were able to develop a list of characteristics of myths and begin to understand the genre of traditional literature.

The unit continued with folktale variants. Students were asked to read and compare two or more versions of Cinderella, the Gingerbread Boy, or Rumpelstiltskin. They discussed their findings in small groups with others who had read about the same character. The groups charted their conclusions by using a genre matrix (see Figure 3.11) to note the characteristics all versions of a story had in common as well as differences in plots, settings, and characters. The group that read about Cinderella chose to dramatize their favorite version, which was the Chinese tale *Yeh-Shen* (Louie, 1982). The teacher also encouraged students who wanted to write myths and folk tales of their own during writers' workshop time. The students used information about the characteristics of these types of tales to help them develop their own stories.

Reference

Lukens, R. J. (1998). *A critical handbook of children's literature, 6th ed.* New York: Addison Wesley Longman.

Children's Book Cited

Louie, A. (1982). *Yeh-Shen: A Cinderella story from China.* New York: Philomel.
Lowry, L. (1989). *Number the stars.* Boston: Houghton Mifflin.
Paulsen, G. (1999). *Hatchet.* New York: Simon & Schuster.

FIGURE 3.10 A DIAGRAM OF LITERATURE GENRES

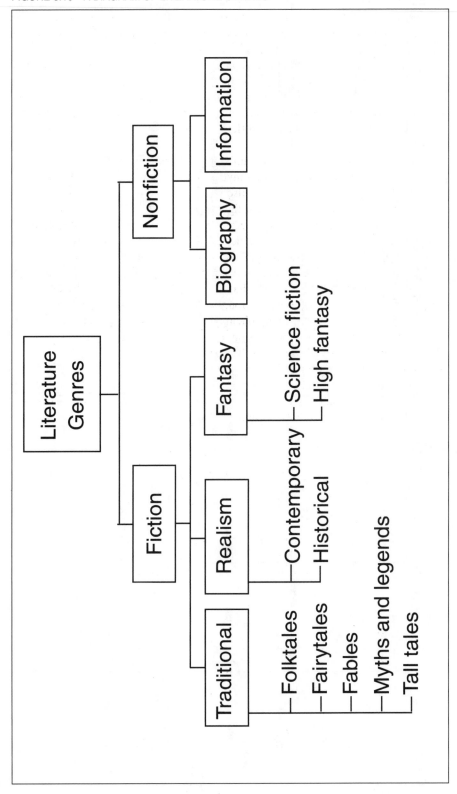

FIGURE 3.11 GENRE MATRIX

Story	Characters	Setting	Problem	Events	Solution	Theme
Cinderella by Paul Galdone (McGraw-Hill, 1978)	Cinderella Stepmother 2 Stepsisters Godmother King's son	A place long ago that has castles.	Cinderella's stepsisters are mean and she can't go to the ball.	Godmother gives her pretty clothes. She meets Prince. Loses glass slipper at ball. Prince finds her. They get married.	Cinderella is married and moves to a castle. She is still nice to her stepsisters.	If you're nice to other people, something good will happen to you.
Yeh-Shen by Ai-Ling Louie (Philomel, 1982)	Yeh-Shen Stepmother 1 Stepsister Magic fish King	Southern China long ago. In a cave and a palace.	Yeh-Shen lives with a cruel stepmother. She can't go to the festival.	Stepmother kills magic fish. Bones give Yeh-Shen pretty clothes. Loses golden slipper at festival.	King falls in love with Yeh-Shen. They get married & live in palace. Stepmother and stepsister stay in their cave.	Being good pays off and being bad doesn't.
The Rough Faced Girl by Rafe Martin (Putnam, 1992)	Rough Faced Girl (has scars from fire) 2 Sisters Father Invisible Being & his sister	Indian village by Lake Ontario.	The sisters are mean to Rough Faced Girl. All the girls want to marry the Invisible Being, but you have to see him first.	The 2 sisters dress up nicely. They lie and say they see him but they don't. Rough Faced Girl dresses in strange clothes but she really sees him.	Rough Faced Girl washes in the lake and loses her scars. She and the Invisible Being get married.	Even if you don't look nice on the outside, you can be beautiful inside.

Thematic Units

Thematic units can be used to plan instruction in the readers' workshop. With this structure, book selection and study are organized around themes that enable teachers and students to connect reading, writing, listening, and speaking with science, social studies, art, music, mathematics, and other subjects. The purpose of using thematic units is to help students explore complex concepts using a variety of reading materials and learning activities.

Background

Teachers and researchers are in agreement about the values of using thematic units for instruction (Valencia & Lipson, 1998). Both groups cite the following benefits for students:

1. in-depth learning with a focus on important ideas and concepts,
2. better connections among the language arts (reading, writing, listening, and speaking), across subject areas (for example, language arts and social studies, science, math, etc.), and between school studies and the larger world outside school,
3. greater student interest and engagement in instructional activities, and
4. more efficient use of the limited time available for instruction.

However, Valencia and Lipson (1998) also offer some cautions. One, thematic units must be based on worthwhile and powerful ideas, not simply on interesting activities that are topically related. Two, thematic units should not shortchange language art instruction for the sake of the content being studied. So teachers need to be sure they are teaching students reading and writing skills and strategies, not just how to complete unit activities that apply these skills and strategies. Three, thematic units should not shortchange the content area for the sake of literature. For example, when using historical fiction to meet social studies and language arts goals, teachers need to be sure students also are learning history from factual sources to acquire a well-rounded understanding of the issues. Four, although thematic teaching can save time in the classroom, well-planned units take time to create outside of the classroom. Teachers should plan on a multi-year process to develop, teach, and refine their units.

Procedure

The best thematic units are based on *enduring questions*, which Valencia and Lipson (1998) describe as questions that "have relevance for people of a diverse society in many aspects of their lives, both in and out of school" (p. 101). These also have been called *guiding questions*, "a fundamental query that directs the search for understanding" (Traver, 1998, p. 70). Guiding or enduring questions go beyond topics (e.g., ancient Egypt, recycling, friendship) to ask about deeper issues (e.g., Why did the ancient Egyptian civilization rise and fall? What is waste, and what should we do about it? What is friendship?). Even if you already have ideas about the answers, posing questions allows the students to explore issues and come to their own conclusions (e.g., Being a friend means having respect for each other. People have a responsibility to care for the environment that sustains us all.).

One way to develop a strong thematic unit is to begin by looking at the topics and texts you have been teaching. From there, identify guiding questions that can motivate students to explore deep issues and do high level thinking as they read and learn. Some schools have specified topics and literature selections for each grade level, giving teachers a starting point in planning. Another way to develop your unit is to start with a guiding question and then look for activities and resources to explore different aspects of that question. Figure 3.12 lists some resources to help with thematic planning. Additional resources are given in Selecting Literature and Author Study in this chapter.

Mrs. O'Brien's kindergartners study ocean animals each year. She developed a guiding question for this unit: How do people help or harm ocean animals and the ocean environment? For his second-grade students, Mr. Jamal's unit on friendship included as one of his guiding questions: How do the characters in our stories become friends? Ms. DeRego's unit on the works of Jean Craighead George included the following guiding question for her fourth graders: How does this author's knowledge of the natural world shape her writing?

The teacher may elect to read some of the selections aloud, especially for younger students or less-experienced readers. Mr. Jamal decided to begin his friendship unit by reading aloud Aesop's "The Lion and the Mouse" followed by *Amos and Boris* by William Steig (1971). He led discussions about these stories by asking his students about the characters. How were they alike? How were they different? How did the characters feel about each other? How did they show their feelings? What could the author's message be? Students discussed how the characters in each story helped each other when each one needed help, and how that showed friendship. Later, students read other friendship books independently, choosing from a collection Mr. Jamal assembled that included some of Russell Hoban's stories about Francis, Arnold Lobel's stories about Frog and Toad, and Cynthia Rylant's Poppleton stories.

For older students or more able readers, the teacher may give book talks about the selections in the unit and then ask students to choose one or two books to read independently (see Figure 3.13 for one teacher's ideas). Questions to guide the readings and discussions may be handed out or posted. The teacher may want to read aloud one book as a focus for initial discussions. As students read their selections, further discussions center around their books, with comparisons and contrasts to the book read aloud.

Discussions may be conducted with small groups, the whole class, or even partners. Recording key points on charts, in response journals, or by other means will help students as they work toward the objectives for the unit. New learning should be related to prior knowledge. The teacher may want to have students express and share new insights and information through the visual or dramatic arts as well as by writing.

Teachers may involve their students in developing discussion questions, suggesting follow-up activities, and even selecting books for the unit. Units may be based on expressed interests of students. Students should be asked to evaluate the books, the discussions, and other unit activities as well as their growing understandings of the unit's theme and guiding questions.

References

Traver, R. (1998). What is a good guiding question? *Educational Leadership, 55* (6), 70–73.

Valencia, S. W., & Lipson, M. Y. (1998). Thematic instruction: A quest for challenging ideas and meaningful learning. In T. E. Raphael & K. H. Au (Eds.), *Literature-based instruction: Reshaping the curriculum* (pp. 95–122). Norwood, MA: Christopher-Gordon.

Children's Books Cited

Steig, W. (1971). *Amos and Boris.* Scranton, PA: Farrar, Straus, and Giroux.

FIGURE 3.12   ANNOTATED LIST OF RESOURCES FOR THEMATIC UNITS

Resources for Thematic Units

Books

• *Adventuring With Books: A Booklist for Pre-K–Grade 6, 12th Edition,* edited by M. M. Pierce, National Council of Teachers of English, 2000, 605 pp. Recent titles are categorized by topics, themes, concepts, and types.

• *The Complete Guide to Thematic Units: Creating the Integrated Curriculum, 2nd Edition.* A. M. Meinbach, A. Fredericks, and L. Rothlein. Norwood, MA: Christopher Gordon, 2000. Ideas for developing and assessing thematic units. Includes nine primary and ten intermediate grade units emphasizing key concepts in science, social studies, language arts, mathematics, and the arts, all with a strong literature component.

• *Kaleidoscope: A Multicultural Booklist for Grades K–8.* R. B. Barrera, V. D. Thompson, & M. Dressman, Eds. Urbana, IL: National Council of Teachers of English, 1997. Information on 600 fiction and nonfiction titles that reflect different cultures, grouped by theme or genre to emphasize cultural similarities and differences.

Periodicals

• *Book Links.* American Library Association. Contains essays on books with similar themes, bibliographies, book reviews, and other articles on children's literature.

• *The Horn Book Magazine.* Horn Book, Inc. Reviews children's books, organized by topic and appropriate grade level. *The Horn Book Guide,* published twice a year, reviews and rates children's books, and includes interviews of authors and illustrators.

• *The New Advocate.* Christopher-Gordon. Includes articles by and about children's authors and illustrators, articles by teachers about teaching with literature, and book review columns.

• *Language Arts.* National Council of Teachers of English. "Talking About Books" (bimonthly column) and "Notable Children's Books in the Language Arts" (annual column) review recent children's books.

• *The Reading Teacher.* International Reading Association. "Children's Books" column reviews books by topics. Recent columns have dealt with topics such as: characters, enduring themes, international literature, imagination, and traditions. Each October issue includes "Children's Choices" for the year, and the November issue, "Teachers' Choices." Both are also available as separate reprints.

FIGURE 3.13 A SIXTH GRADE TEACHER'S NOTE TO THE SCHOOL LIBRARIAN

Maddie,

I'm starting a unit on survival. My guiding question for the unit is: "What does it mean to survive?" Will you please reserve copies of the following books for me:

Island of the Blue Dolphins, Scott O'Dell
Julie of the Wolves, Jean Craighead George
Call It Courage, Armstrong Sperry
Hatchet, Gary Paulsen
Monkey Island, Paula Fox
The Wild Children, Felice Holman
Number the Stars, Lois Lowry
River Rats, Caroline Stevermer
The Giver, Lois Lowry

These are the titles my students and I know about. Any other suggestions? I'll drop by the library soon.
Thanks!

Charlene

Connections to Home and Community:
Communicating with Parents

Reading experiences are enhanced when students see themselves as members of a community of readers that includes their families and other important people in their lives. Teachers can increase communication with parents to improve parental understanding of what occurs in the readers' workshop and how families can be a part of the reading community.

Background

Au, Mason, and Scheu (1995) examined classrooms where teachers built connections with families and communities. They noted two areas where teachers worked to strengthen parent involvement: communication with parents and enlisting parent participation in children's literacy activities. Communication with parents included many types of written communication (letters, notes, newsletters), conferences, and open houses. Enlisting parent participation included activities parents could do outside of school, such as reading aloud their children and taking them to the public library, and activities within school, such as volunteering to be readers, listeners as children read to them, and presenters of information or special activities. Other family members were welcomed also, since some parents were not able to participate in the classroom.

Procedure

Before the school year starts, the teacher will want to begin building connections between the school and the home. Some teachers mail or e-mail letters to incoming students and their parents, others telephone to talk, and still others pay personal visits to as many homes as possible. This early communication is used to let students and families know that the teacher is interested in them and their lives beyond the classroom. The teacher tries to learn more about his students—special interests and talents, special challenges they face in their lives, the family structure. The teacher also may describe his plans for the upcoming school year, discuss his beliefs about teaching and learning, invite parents and other family members to support classroom efforts in whatever ways they can, and ask for their ideas on strengthening the connections. Some teachers ask parents to complete a questionnaire telling about their child's reading habits and attitudes, interests, and any other information parents feel the teacher should know in order to help their child learn best. Figures 3.14 and 3.15 give a sample of a teacher's letter to parents and of one parent's response.

Once school starts, regular communication can be accomplished efficiently through monthly newsletters. Students can participate in helping to determine what goes into each newsletter, and older students can be responsible for much of the content and layout. Computers, if available, make this an easier task. Newsletters are a good place for teachers to communicate the themes, authors, genres, and so forth being studied that month and to ask parents for support. For example, when the class studies Native American tribes in their area, parents could be asked if they have books on this topic, titles to recommend, or any artifacts they could share. Families could be asked if any members have special knowledge they would be willing to share with the students.

Another vehicle for communication is a journal that circulates between the student, teacher, and parent. Some teachers write weekly to each child's parent, some write to half the families one week and half the next, and some write to each student on a similar schedule. In these classes, students write weekly to their parents also, telling them of school happenings and personal news. Parents are encouraged to respond to their child and to the teacher in the same journal, creating a record of positive events and special memories, a place to share concerns anyone (parent, teacher, or student) has, and a place for dialogue in everyone's busy schedules.

Some teachers send home additional information on topics they think will be of interest to parents. Topics such as parents and children using the library together, building a low-cost library of books at home, and reading with your child are addressed in one-page essays in *Parent Power: Energizing Home-School Communication* (Power, 1999). These essays are available for duplication and distribution, and the book includes a CD-ROM for this purpose.

In addition to keeping up with what the class is learning, parents need to know how their own child is progressing. Involving parents more fully in the assessment and evaluation process is discussed in Connections to the Home and Community: Three-Way Conferences (see chapter 11).

Parents can be wonderful resources for information. In a typical class, students' parents hold jobs in a variety of fields and have different interests and areas of expertise. Inviting parents to talk about their work or their interests, especially as these activities relate to an area of study going on in the classroom, can add an important new dimension. More importantly, parent participation helps students see how people in the community are a part of their learning environment.

Connections to the school community can be promoted through activities such as the Great American Read Aloud Day, when adults nationwide are asked to visit school classrooms to read to children. A first-grade teacher invited Mr. Trujillo, the school's physical education teacher, to read to her students and share how reading was important in his own life. First he displayed the worn repair manual for his 1989 Honda, explaining to the children how it had recently helped him replace his car's carburetor. Next he shared a memoir by Tim Allen given to him as a Christmas gift. He suggested why a family member had chosen the book for him, described how he discovered connections between his life and Allen's while reading it, and read aloud a humorous excerpt showing Allen's relationship to his own family car. Last, Mr. Trujillo introduced *The Gym Teacher From the Black Lagoon* (Thaler, 1994), and he and the children joyfully compared the fictional with their real gym teacher as he read the story.

References

Au, K. H., Mason, J. M., & Scheu, J. A. (1995). *Literacy instruction for today.* New York: HarperCollins.

Power, B. (1999). *Parent power: Energizing home-school communication.* Portsmouth, NH: Heinemann.

Children's Books Cited

Thaler, M. (1994). *The gym teacher from the black lagoon.* Jefferson City, MO: Scholastic.

FIGURE 3.14 BEGINNING-OF-YEAR LETTER FROM TEACHER TO PARENTS

September 5

Dear Parents,

I have enjoyed getting acquainted with your child during these past two days. We have begun to settle into the school routine and come together as a classroom community.

In order to help me work more productively with your child, I would appreciate your responses to the following questions. Please take some time to respond and send this sheet back on Monday if possible.

Sincerely,

— —

Student's name _____ Parent's name_____

1. What would you like me to know about your child?

2. How does your child spend time on his/her own at home?

3. What are your goals/expectations for your child this year?

FIGURE 3.15 ONE PARENT'S RESPONSE TO THE TEACHER'S BEGINNING-OF-YEAR LETTER

August 23, 1996

Dear Parents,

   I have enjoyed getting acquainted with your child during these past two days. We have begun to settle into the school routine and come together as a classroom community.

   In order to help me work more productively with your child, I would appreciate your responses to the following questions. Please take some time to respond and send this sheet back on Monday if possible.

                              Sincerely,

                              Judy Scheu

                              Judy Scheu

Student's name _Billy Penaroza_ Parent's name _Susan & Bill Penaroza_

1. **What would you like me to know about your child?**

   Billy is very athletic (started surfing at 5yrs.), and I know he's going to excel in sports. This type of enthusiasm spills over to all aspects of his life. He's very motivated about school.

2. **How does your child spend time on his/her own at home?**

   We've moved into a new home, so of course he's mostly interested in going out and playing with the new friends in the neighborhood—friends are very important to him. He loves nature and exploring, things that make you think

3. **What are your goals/expectations for your child this year?**

   Billy's very happy inside, and though I don't wish to be a demanding parent, I find it very easy to just expect of Billy continued happiness, and success in reading, growth, and learning about the world.

Troubleshooting: What About Commercial Reading Programs?

In our opinion, the best way to improve students' reading achievement is to develop a reading curriculum at the school level, tailored to the strengths, needs, and interests of the students, community, and teachers.This reading curriculum reflects the school's philosophy of teaching, learning, and literacy, and is based on its vision of the excellent reader. It specifies grade level benchmarks (see article in chapter 11), provides recommendations for instruction, describes instructional materials, and includes assessment procedures. We want to outline the reasons why this approach, rather than merely choosing a commercial reading program, is the preferred path to long-lasting change.

On the surface, it may seem like a commercial reading program, developed by experts and for sale to a school, may be the best solution to the problem of how to teach reading. Several reasons are commonly seen for reaching this conclusion. These include

- Test scores need to be raised.
- Federal, state, or district funds have been set aside for the purchase of certain programs.
- The school's administration does not trust teachers to do a good job in developing a curriculum.
- Teachers feel they lack the expertise needed to develop a reading curriculum.
- Too much work is involved in developing a reading curriculum at the school level.

These reasons will be familiar particularly to teachers who work in schools in low-income areas.

We are not against the use of commercial reading programs. If a commercial program can be found that matches a school's philosophy, vision, and grade-level benchmarks, adopting that program could certainly save time. It is not necessary to reinvent the wheel. However, too often educators at a school do not go through the process of discussing philosophy, vision, students' needs as readers, and grade-level benchmarks in order to establish criteria for determining the kind of reading program that will best promote students' learning. In the absence of this process, no commercial program, no matter how well designed, can be the answer, because staff members have not gone through the deeper thinking that contributes to a clear sense of direction and purpose.

If your school is considering adopting a commercial program, you will want to encourage a process of careful thinking about this process. Here are some of the questions that should be considered as your school engages in a discussion of the criteria the program should meet. These criteria should relate to your school's philosophy, vision, and grade-level benchmarks.

First, does the program support students' development of higher-level thinking about text? In higher-level thinking about text, we include making personal connections, constructing a theme or main idea, and critical evaluation. Many commercial programs focus on the teaching of skills in isolation, particularly phonics. These programs take a "back to basics" approach. We caution against an overemphasis in this direction. For one thing, goals at the national level emphasize higher-level thinking with text, including the idea that students should use their minds well while dealing with challenging subject matter (National Education Goals Panel, 1995). For another thing, we do not want children to get the impression that reading is nothing more than accurate word calling. This misunderstanding frequently occurs with struggling readers, who are more likely than more capable readers to receive a steady diet of skill-and-drill, with little instruction to promote comprehension (Allington, 1983).

Research points toward some common understandings of what it takes to be a successful reader (International Reading Association, 1999; Snow & Griffin, 1998). Students need the motivation to read, strategies for constructing meaning from print, sufficient background information and vocabulary to understand text, fluency, decoding skills, and knowledge of sound-print relationships. We emphasize higher-level thinking about text because of its importance in the national picture, because it is not easy to teach, and because it is an area often neglected in the instruction of struggling readers. Therefore, looking at how well a commercial program addresses higher-level thinking about text is a good test of the program's strength.

Second, does the program provide for a balance of motivation and systematic skill instruction? Many commercial programs put much greater emphasis on skill instruction than on motivation, contributing to an imbalance in instruction. Students will be motivated to read if they hear read alouds from wonderful picture storybooks and novels, and if they have access to a well-stocked classroom library. A well balanced commercial program will certainly include these elements. Enthusiasm for reading is contagious. If teachers do not feel excited about teaching reading, students will not feel excited about learning to read. Be sure that you feel enthusiastic about the activities specified by the commercial program, and that you can see yourself motivating students to read by using these activities.

Third, does the program have a record of success with students from backgrounds similar to those of your students? Success can be defined in various ways, and the results themselves depend on the definition of reading success used. Some studies declare success if children learn to read words in isolation; others, if children answer questions on multiple-choice tests correctly. We believe success should be defined in terms of promoting ownership of literacy and higher-level thinking about text, and in terms of lasting effects on reading achievement through the upper grades. For many programs, there is no evidence either of promoting ownership or of higher-level thinking about text, and the only results presented are for narrow measures of decoding and lower-level comprehension. Also, it is wise to note that no commercial program, with results published in a refereed journal, appears to have been successful in raising the achievement of struggling readers, so that they are at or near grade-level by the fifth grade (Pogrow, 1998).

Fourth, does the program allow teachers to make adjustments they find necessary to meet the needs of individual students? The fact is, there is no one method that can meet every child's needs, as noted in the International Reading Association's (1999) position statement on the use of multiple methods in beginning reading. This position is based on the finding that every reading approach ever studied has been successful with some students but unsuccessful with others. This means that, regardless of the approach used, including commercial programs, the teacher always has the responsibility for making adjustments in order to help individual children. A commercial program should allow teachers the flexibility to use a repertoire of strategies, as needed to meet children's needs.

Teachers must use their knowledge of students' needs along with their knowledge of sound reading practices to make informed decisions about what to teach and how to teach. They must know when, for example, to move from shared reading to guided reading or when to teach specific word reading strategies. They must incorporate a variety of activities and practices to reach all students in their classroom. These decisions have to be made at the student level, not at the school or district level. Teachers should not be deprived of the opportunity to make wise decisions based on their students' needs, and students should not be deprived of the chance to benefit from instruction that is geared to their needs.

Finally, does the program provide ongoing opportunities for teachers' professional development? Here we would emphasize the distinction between teachers being "trained" in a program and ongoing professional development. Training involves learning to implement a particular program and does not emphasize the larger picture of theory, research, and instruction in the field of reading and language arts as a whole. Training tends to stress the hows rather than the whys drawn from theory and research. Or if the whys are presented, they may focus just on one narrow perspective. Teachers who are trained in a program learn a great deal about what the program developers expect, but they are not necessarily guided to understand how they can grow as reflective practitioners. Professional development differs from training in that it has the goal of helping teachers to grow as reflective practitioners (Schon, 1983), by expanding their knowledge of theory and research, as well as of specific instructional practices. Professional development is a process informed by teachers' own strengths, needs, and interests, not just by the structure of a commercial program. Professional development helps teachers to feel empowered, to expand upon or revise existing curricula, and to think in new ways about the teaching of reading. While training may limit teachers' options in the classroom, professional development expands teachers' options in ways that will help them adjust instruction to meet the needs of all learners.

In short, commercial reading programs can be beneficial in improving students' achievement if they are selected as part of a thoughtful process of ongoing curriculum development and improvement at the school level. Commercial programs are not likely to improve students' achievement over the long run if they are chosen as a quick fix or seen as a default solution for raising test scores. A school that sees a commercial reading program as a shortcut or as a substitute for an ongoing process of curriculum development and improvement is likely to find itself going around in circles, looking for a new program every few years. In matters of improving reading instruction so that students' achievement rises, there are no shortcuts (Allington & Walmsley, 1995).

References

Allington, R. L. (1983). The reading instruction provided readers of differing abilities. *Elementary School Journal, 83* (5), 548–559.

Allington, R. L., & Walmsley, S. A. (Eds.). (1995). *No quick fix: Rethinking literacy programs in America's elementary schools*. New York, NY and Newark, DE: Teachers College Press and International Reading Association.

International Reading Association. (1999). Using multiple methods of beginning reading instruction: A position statement of the International Reading Association . Newark, DE: International Reading Association.

National Education Goals Panel. (1995). *The national education goals report: Building a nation of learners 1995*. Washington, DC: U. S. Government Printing Office.

Pogrow, S. (1998). What is an exemplary program, and why should anyone care? A reaction to Slavin and Klein. *Educational Researcher, 27* (7), 22–29.

Schon, D. A. (1983). *The reflective practitioner: How professionals think in action*. New York: Basic Books.

Snow, C., & Griffin, M. (1998). *Preventing reading difficulties in young children*. Washington, DC: National Academy Press.

Chapter 4

TEACHER-DIRECTED ACTIVITIES IN THE READERS' WORKSHOP

The Impact of Shelley Harwayne: Teachers As Readers

In her book *Lasting Impressions*, Shelley Harwayne (1992) discusses the place of literature in her life, personally and as a teacher. "I'm fussy about books," she writes, "because I put great trust in literature" (p. 10). Harwayne, an avid reader of books for children and adults, has a vast knowledge of literature that she can call upon during the readers' workshop. As a result, she is able to help her students connect to literature. If she knows a student's interest (for example, in baseball), she can often recommend an appropriate book. If a student is struggling with an issue in writing (for example, how to structure a piece about her experiences as an immigrant), Harwayne often can suggest a book that might serve as a model.

Reading Club for Teachers

As Harwayne points out, the starting point for literature-based instruction is good books. Often, teachers hesitate to begin this type of instruction because they are not familiar with a wide range of wonderful children's books and with how to guide open-ended discussions of literature. One approach to these challenges is to form a Teachers As Readers group, a kind of reading club in which teachers read and discuss children's books.

In 1988 Harwayne started a Teachers As Readers program in New York City. She found that these book discussion groups helped teachers to see how much fun it could be to read and discuss books. Many felt like college students again as they rediscovered the joys of reading. Book clubs for staff members continue to play an important role in Harwayne's (1999) work at the Manhattan New School.

Many Teachers As Readers groups are in existence today. Cardarelli (1992) describes a program for middle school and junior high teachers. Some groups involve administrators, school board members, and parents. In the program run by the Virginia State Reading Association, participants agree to read and discuss at least four children's books during the school year. Some groups meet monthly, some more often. Participants keep journals in which they write their responses to the books.

Teachers As Readers groups give teachers knowledge of children's literature and personal experience with literature discussions and written responses to literature. In these groups, teachers are involved in the same activities that their students pursue in the readers' workshop. One of the key insights teachers gain is that children and adults alike may have very different responses to the same work of literature (Lehman & Scharer, 1996). Understanding and learning from this diversity of response is an important step forward for many teachers.

Teacher's Role

The idea of Teachers As Readers developed because the role of the teacher in literature-based instruction is different from that of the traditional teacher. In traditional forms of teaching, teachers often lecture students about what it is they want them to do and understand. In literature-based instruction, teachers generally do less telling and more demonstrating. When these teachers want their students to read, discuss, and write in response to literature, they know that they must be reading, discussing, and writing in these same ways themselves.

Experienced teachers of literature-based instruction know the dramatic effects that serving as a model of lifelong reading can have on students. A fourth grade teacher came to school one day with a shopping bag full of the reading materials she had taken from her night stand. One by one, she took the items from the bag and explained to the students why she was reading each one. This demonstration showed students just how important reading was in their teacher's life and could be in their own (Carroll, Wilson, & Au, 1996).

References

Cardarelli, A. F. (1992). Teachers under cover: Promoting the personal reading of teachers. *The Reading Teacher, 45* (9), 664–668.

Carroll, J. H., Wilson, R. A., & Au, K. H. (1996). Explicit instruction in the context of the readers' and writers' workshops. In E. McIntyre & M. Pressley (Eds.), *Balanced instruction: Skills and strategies in whole language* (pp. 39–63). Norwood, MA: Christopher-Gordon.

Harwayne, S. (1992). *Lasting impressions: Weaving literature into the writers' workshop.* Portsmouth, NH: Heinemann.

Harwayne, S. (1999). *Going public.* Portsmouth, NH: Heinemann.

Lehman, B. A., & Scharer, P. L. (1996). Reading alone, talking together: The role of discussion in developing literary awareness. *The Reading Teacher, 50* (1), 26–35.

Continuum of Reading Strategies

Instruction in the readers' workshop centers on a continuum of instructional strategies (Au, 1998). These strategies allow teachers to meet the needs of students at different levels of reading proficiency. A continuum showing the six strategies is presented in Figure 4.1. Each of these strategies is discussed in detail later. Here you will read an overview so you can get a sense of the big picture and see how the strategies fit together and build upon one another.

Two strategies—teacher read alouds and sustained silent reading—are used across the grades and are appropriate for all students. In fact, these strategies continue to be appropriate at the high school and even college levels. Read alouds allow teachers to model enthusiasm for reading and to win students over to good books. Sustained silent reading, or the reading of books students have chosen for themselves, is also a key instructional strategy across all grades. This is the time for students and teachers to engage in the "real reading" of books they enjoy and to share these books with others.

The next four strategies in the continuum are used with students who show differing levels of proficiency as readers. Shared reading, in which the teacher introduces big books that children eventually learn to read themselves, is the starting point for young readers whose literacy is still emergent (Holdaway, 1979). Shared reading allows children to participate as readers while learning concepts about prints and the very beginning skills of word identification. Shared reading is generally used in kindergarten and first grade classes but may also be used with older students who require extensive scaffolding when dealing with text.

Guided reading begins with the reading of little books of only a few pages, with brief and relatively predictable text (Fountas & Pinnell, 1996). Books become longer, with less predictable text, as children progress. After the teacher has introduced the book, the children attempt to read it independently. The teacher monitors the children's reading and provides scaffolding and mini-lessons to develop children's word identification and comprehension abilities. Guided reading is usually introduced in kindergarten or first grade and continues until children have gained proficiency in identifying words.

At this point students are ready for instruction in the next strategy, guided discussion. As in guided reading, the teacher introduces the text and students read independently, perhaps just a paragraph or page at a time in the beginning. The texts used for guided discussion are less predictable in language and tell a story or convey information. After students have read a short section of text, the teacher leads them in discussion. The focus has shifted from word identification to comprehension, although new words may still form the basis for mini-lessons. The teacher attempts to stretch the students' minds and lead them to interpretations, insights, and connections they might not otherwise gain. Later, when students are able to comprehend longer sections of text, they may read chapters of a novel on their own before meeting with the teacher for guided discussion.

The final strategy is literature discussion groups, also known as Book Clubs (Raphael & McMahon, 1994). Students read novels, often a chapter at a time, and meet for discussion in a small group of peers. The teacher monitors the groups and may serve as a facilitator of the discussions, building on and extending ideas students have introduced. Literature discussion groups provide time for students to manage their own discussions. However, teachers must spend considerable time helping students develop the social skills needed to interact in a comfortable manner with other students and to express agreement or disagreement in a respectful way.

Guided discussion and literature discussion groups continue to be useful strategies, even at the secondary level. Guided discussion is used when the teacher wants to promote students' comprehension ability and the text is a rather challenging one. Literature discussion groups are used when students are expected to be able to comprehend much of the text on their own and the goal is to foster independent reading and thinking. These strategies are not mutually exclusive, and both strategies may be used with the same group of students. For example, guided discussion may be used with the first few chapters of a novel. Students may then read and discuss the remaining chapters in literature discussion groups.

Teachers conducting Readers' Workshops find it valuable to understand all of these strategies, because of the range of readers who may be present in the classroom. Strategies generally used with younger children may be useful in the teaching of struggling readers, just as strategies generally used with older students may be beneficial for capable younger readers.

References

Au, K. H. (1998). Constructivist approaches, phonics, and the literacy learning of students of diverse backgrounds. In T. Shanahan & F. Rodriquez-Brown (Eds.), *Forty-seventh yearbook of the National Reading Conference* (pp. 1–21). Chicago: National Reading Conference.

Fountas, I. C., & Pinnell, G. S. (1996). *Guided reading: Good first teaching for all children.* Portsmouth, NH: Heinemann.

Holdaway, D. (1979). *The foundations of literacy.* Sydney, Australia: Ashton Scholastic.

Raphael, T. E., & McMahon, S. I. (1994). Book Club: An alternative framework for reading instruction. *The Reading Teacher, 48* (2), 102–116.

FIGURE 4.1 CONTINUUM OF READING STRATEGIES

Reading Aloud

Reading aloud is a powerful activity. Anyone who was read to as a young child probably remembers the thrilling new worlds that unfolded as they listened to story books and factual books. When teachers read aloud, students hear firsthand the excitement and fascination books can hold and they learn that reading is pleasurable. When students come to associate worksheets and skill practice with reading, they just don't get that message. Teaching children *how* to read is wasted if children never learn to *want* to read.

Background

According to research findings, reading aloud to children is "the single most important activity for building the knowledge required for eventual success in reading" (Anderson, Hiebert, Scott, & Wilkinson, 1985, p. 23). In a worldwide study of reading practices and results (Elley, 1992), two major factors associated with high achievement in reading were: (a) the frequency of teachers reading aloud to their students, and (b) the frequency of sustained silent reading in classrooms.

When adults read aloud to children, they give children access to language and ideas they might not otherwise acquire through their own reading. Improving children's listening comprehension supports better reading comprehension over time. This social support for learning (see The Impact of Lev Vygotsky in chapter 1) parallels the process parents use to teach their child to talk and to increase the child's ability to use more sophisticated language as he or she grows.

Jim Trelease (1995) has done extensive research on the value of reading aloud and spoken to thousands of audiences, including students in classrooms. He cites the enthusiasm kindergartners show when he asks them how many want to learn to read (usually 100%!), and notes with grave concern the statistics showing that only about 46% of fourth graders, 27% of eighth graders, and 24% of twelfth graders read for pleasure. He believes that with the overwhelming influence of television (the average child views 1,300 hours of television and video in a year), an interest in reading must be promoted strongly in schools and in homes.

Procedure

Reading aloud should be a regular activity in classrooms, daily if possible. Reading aloud generally includes time for the students to discuss what they have heard, tell what they think about it, and ask questions after the teacher finishes the selection. Sometimes the teacher may pause during the reading to allow for comments and questions, although this is kept brief so as not to disrupt the flow of the story.

Depending on the grade level of the class, teachers may devote more or less time to reading aloud. Younger students and less able readers benefit greatly from listening to stories and informational books. Teachers of these students often read several books aloud each day, including the rereading of favorite books along with introducing new ones. Particularly with less able readers, hearing books read aloud helps them keep up with the information and ideas their peers are getting from reading independently.

Older students and more capable readers benefit just as much from being read to, but their teachers may have less time to devote to this activity due to the increased demands of teaching specific content areas. If so, these teachers may use reading aloud as an enticement to expose their students to the wide range of good literature available, perhaps reading selected chapters of a longer book and providing several copies for students to borrow and finish independently, or reading short stories, poetry, or folktales.

Teachers may want to begin the year with exciting, humorous, or other highly engaging books that seem to fit the needs and interests of their students. A first-grade teacher, whose lively students had some unplanned adventures on their first field trip, read aloud *The Day Jimmy's Boa Ate the Wash* (Noble, 1980), a comical story of Jimmy's pet boa constrictor coming along on a class field trip. A second-grade teacher began the year with *The Stray* by Dick King-Smith (1998), a humorous story of a 75-year-old woman who runs away from a retirement home, finds a wonderful family to live with, foils a car thief, and wins the lottery. A third-grade teacher decided to read aloud *Harry Potter and the Sorcerer's Stone* by J.K. Rowling (1998) after hearing how many of her students were excited about this series. A fourth-grade teacher whose class was made up of students from two different campuses started the year by reading aloud *Be a Perfect Person in Just Three Days* (Manes, 1984), a humorous look at a young boy's attempts to fit in and be accepted.

As the year progresses, teachers report being able to read more thought-provoking works because students have become attuned to listening carefully and critically to stories, and to thinking about themes, characterization, complexities of plot, style, and other story elements. The same fourth-grade teacher read aloud *Bridge to Terabithia* (Paterson, 1987) part way through the school year; her students enjoyed this sophisticated book about friendship and death.

Reading aloud is a skill that improves with practice. Teachers may want to rehearse with the selection they have chosen, particularly if the text is long or complex. Changing voice tones and facial expressions to represent different characters, varying speed to match story action, pausing at dramatic moments, reading smoothly through intricate sentence structures, and taking time to show illustrations will enhance the story for the listener. Whether or not you get a chance to rehearse, it is always a good idea to read the selection all the way through ahead of time. That way, you will be prepared for any surprising events or character revelations.

Reading aloud fits well with other parts of the readers' workshop. Thematic units, author studies, and genre studies can all be introduced with the teacher reading aloud one of the books in the collection chosen for study. In all these cases, the book read aloud serves as the anchor piece, a common denominator students can refer to and use as a basis for comparison with other works (by the same author, on the same theme, or in the same genre).

Reading aloud has another benefit. A student may want to join a particular literature discussion group because she wants to read the book selected by the group, even though it is beyond her reading capabilities. For a student who has good listening comprehension, the teacher may be able to arrange for a "reader"—an adult volunteer, for example. Thus, a less able reader can participate in more sophisticated literature discussions and increase her experience with literature that challenges her thinking.

An excellent resource for choosing good literature to read aloud is Trelease's *The Read-Aloud Handbook* (1995). Other publications by Trelease (1992, 1993) include a book of read aloud stories for primary grade students (*Hey! Listen to This*) and a book of stories, poems, and newspaper pieces for preteens and teens (*Read All About It!*). Carol Avery's *And With a Light Touch* (1993) contains lists of suggested books for reading aloud that were compiled with the help of her first graders. *In the Middle* (Atwell, 1998) contains lists of novels, picture books, short stories, poems, and informational books Nancie Atwell has read aloud to her seventh and eighth graders, as well as tips for reading aloud and linking the read aloud with writing. Perhaps the best source of recommendations comes from fellow teachers and from the students themselves. Ask your students to tell you their favorite read alouds, and keep the list for your next year's class.

References and Resources

Anderson, R. C., Hiebert, E. H., Scott, J. A., & Wilkinson, A. G. (1985). *Becoming a nation of readers: The report of the Commission on Reading.* Champaign-Urbana, IL: Center for the Study of Reading.

Atwell, N. (1998). *In the middle: New understandings about writing, reading, and learning,* 2nd ed. Portsmouth, NH: Heinemann.

Avery, C. (1993). Chapter 16: Suggestions for reading aloud to children. In *And with a light touch.* Portsmouth, NH: Heinemann.

Elley, W. R. (1992). *How in the world do students read?* Newark, DE: International Reading Association.

Trelease, J. (1992). *Hey! Listen to this: Stories to read aloud.* New York: Penguin Books.

Trelease, J. (1993). *Read all about it!: Great read-aloud stories, poems, and newspaper pieces for preteens and teens.* New York: Penguin Books.

Trelease, J. (1995). *The read-aloud handbook,* 4th ed. New York: Penguin Books.

Children's Books Cited

King-Smith. D. (1998). *The Stray.* New York: Alfred A. Knopf.

Manes, S. (1984). *Be a perfect person in just three days.* New York: Bantam.

Noble, T. H. (1980). *The day Jimmy's boa ate the wash.* New York: Dial.

Paterson, K. (1987). *Bridge to Terabithia.* New York: Harper.

Rowling, J. K. (1998). *Harry Potter and the sorcerer's stone.* New York: Scholastic.

Mini-Lessons

Mini-lessons are brief (5–10 minute) or longer (20 minute) lessons given in the readers' or writers' workshop to teach a specific skill or strategy, to give information, or to develop ideas collaboratively among teacher and students. Mini-lessons are a form of teaching, demonstration, and sharing that allows the teacher to focus on an area of student need (rather than on the next skill listed in a workbook), give students the information they require, and let them apply what they have been taught as they read and write. Mini-lessons can be taught by the teacher, a student, a group of students, or they can be a collaborative effort by the whole class.

Background

Nancie Atwell (1998) adapted Lucy Calkins' mini-lesson from the writers' workshop for use in her readers' workshop. Atwell divides mini-lessons into three broad categories. One focuses on procedures for the workshop, such as how to choose books that interest you or what to write about in response journals. Another type of mini-lessons deals with author's craft, for example, learning how authors reveal things about their characters. The third category is skill lessons, such as what to do when encountering unfamiliar words while reading. Figure 4.2 gives more examples of the three types of mini-lessons. Atwell's mini-lessons often include reading aloud, especially when she teaches different aspects of author's craft or introduces students to new authors or genres.

Atwell uses mini-lessons as a forum for sharing what she knows. She also uses them to give her students a forum for sharing what they know. A third type of sharing comes from the mini-lessons the teacher and students do together to work out what they know collectively. Mini-lessons used in this way help to build the reading community that supports everyone in the classroom.

Procedure

Determining what topics to teach during mini-lessons requires a balance between planning and flexibility. Many teachers start by examining the reading/language arts standards from their school district, grade level, and commercially published teacher's guides. These sources give a teacher new to readers' workshop, or new to the grade level, a good general background. If there are benchmarks for the district or school, these are obviously a good source for mini-lesson topics. Other teachers who have taught at the grade level for several years can provide additional ideas, and teachers at the next grade level can describe what a student entering their grade should know.

The most important aspect of mini-lessons, however, is that they are responsive to students' needs. This means the teacher will not have a set list of topics to teach in a given order. Instead, he will need to observe students during small group discussions, examine written responses to literature, and talk with students about their reading to determine which topics are appropriate at a given time. A written questionnaire asking students about their reading and writing habits, attitudes, strategies, and interests is a useful beginning-of-year tool for identifying needed mini-lesson topics (see Setting Up Your Classroom, chapter 7, for a sample questionnaire).

Certain topics lend themselves to getting the readers' workshop started. Teaching students the basic expectations for operating during readers' workshop time is an important first mini-lesson. Since the mini-lesson is by definition short (even longer mini-lessons are only about 20 minutes), subsequent mini-lessons will be needed to cover other topics students need to know to work productively in the readers' workshop. For example, students need ideas for how to respond to literature. Some mini-lessons may be devoted to written responses, and others to oral, artistic, and dramatic responses. If students' behaviors when asked to choose books for independent reading (or their responses to a questionnaire) indicate they do not know strategies for book selection, this topic should be addressed in an early mini-lesson. If students do not have favorite authors, introducing them to good authors should be another group of mini-lessons. Two or three authors whose works have some connection could be introduced, compared, and contrasted during a single mini-lesson. Other mini-lessons can be devoted to specific authors whose books the teacher feels every student in the class should know and read.

For older students who receive grades, the grading system for the readers' workshop should be a topic explained fairly early in the school year. For all students, discussing the evaluation system is important. Even very young students need to know the teacher's long-range expectations. How students' own goals fit into the evaluation system is also a good mini-lesson topic.

Deciding on other mini-lesson topics as the year progresses requires an ongoing assessment of students' immediate and long-term needs. For example, fourth-grade teacher Chris Tanioka noticed that many of her students responded to literature in a static way, looking at their reading from the same angle each time they wrote. She began her next mini-lesson (described in Carroll, Wilson, & Au, 1996) by putting up an overhead of an article she had read in a research journal. She explained how researchers had looked at the written responses of fifth and sixth graders and noticed four different types of responses—writing down what you visualized as you read, putting yourself in the character's shoes, responding in another form such as poetry, and making connections to your own life. As she described each one, she read an example of a student's response from the article. Then she said, "See if you can use one or two of these ideas when you write in your response logs this morning." Later, during whole class sharing, one boy read part of his response to a chapter from *On My Honor* (Bauer, 1986): "I could feel my stomach muscles rise in fright. How could Tony drown so quick? Why didn't he yell or something?" This student was able to apply the mini-lesson by putting himself in the place of one of the characters.

Mini-lessons can be effective with small groups or individuals. For example, as the teacher leads a literature discussion, he may note that one or more students are having difficulty with some of the story vocabulary. He might decide to take a few minutes to review the use of cross checking for decoding and finding the meaning of unfamiliar words. Or he may feel that the discussion is not being greatly hampered and decide to conduct a mini-lesson with the individual or group at a different time to address this need. Skill lessons are more efficiently handled this way, with students forming flexible skill groups as needed and not being assigned to a remedial group on a permanent basis.

Many teachers keep a list of the mini-lessons they have taught as a resource for future years. Even with a personalized list though, teachers will find themselves making changes in response to the differing needs of each successive class. This balance of planning and flexibility is what makes mini-lessons a powerful teaching tool.

References

Atwell, N. (1998). *In the middle: New understandings about writing, reading, and learning, 2nd edition.* Portsmouth, NH: Boynton/Cook, Heinemann.

Carroll, J. H., Wilson, R. A., & Au, K. H. (1996). Explicit instruction in the context of the readers' and writers' workshop. In E. McIntyre & M. Pressley (Eds.), *Balanced instruction: Strategies and skills in whole language* (pp. 39-63). Norwood, MA: Christopher-Gordon.

Children's Book Cited

Bauer, M. D. (1986). *On my honor.* New York: Dell.

FIGURE 4.2   IDEAS FOR READING MINI-LESSONS

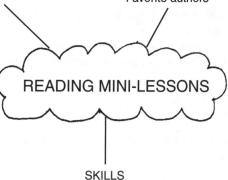

PROCEDURES

Expectations for readers' workshop
Sources for finding good books
Choosing a book that fits you
Responding to literature
   (through writing, drama, art)
Discussing literature
Keeping a book log
Keeping a reading folder
Using the class library
Individual goals and self-evaluation
Keeping a portfolio
Grading and report cards
Conferences

CRAFT

How authors reveal characters
Types of conflict in stories
Titles, leads, and endings
Parts of a book
   (e.g., title page, prologue,
   epilogue)
Elements of fiction
Theme/author's message
Genres
Authors and their styles
The use of language
Poetry (forms, rhythm, sounds)
Favorite authors

READING MINI-LESSONS

SKILLS

Concepts about print
Main idea/supporting details
Cause/effect relationships
Sequence of events
Understanding story elements
Reading for different purposes
Activating prior knowledge

Decoding by analogy
Using meaning cues
Dividing words into syllables
Prefixes, root words, & suffixes
Study skills
Test taking skills
Fluency and proficiency

Phonemic Awareness

Phonemes are the smallest sounds of speech that can convey differences in meaning. For example, the *P* and *B* sounds are phonemes in English. We know this because we hear *pat* and *bat* or *pin* and *bin* as different words with different meanings. Yopp (1995) defines phonemic awareness in the following way:

> Phonemic awareness, as the term suggests, is the awareness of phonemes, or sounds, in the speech stream. It is the awareness that speech consists of a series of sounds. (p. 20)

The child demonstrates phonemic awareness when she can perform tasks such as the following:

- Given a word such as *Jill*, the child can think of a rhyming word such as *Bill*.
- Given a word such as *mat*, the child can divide the word into its constituent sounds: /m/, /a/, /t/.
- Given a word such as *found*, the child can substitute another beginning sound, such as /r/, to make the word *round*.

In other words, a child who has phonemic awareness is conscious of the different sounds in words and can manipulate those sounds.

Phonemic awareness is purely auditory and should not be confused with aspects of learning to read involving print, including letters, letter-sound relationships, and phonics (Clay, 1998). However, while it has nothing to do with print, phonemic awareness is important in learning to read because it establishes the foundation for a later understanding of letter-sound relationships. Yopp (1995) reminds us that phonemic awareness is not an end in itself but a step along the way.

What can teachers do to develop children's phonemic awareness? Clay (1998) suggests that teachers help children to focus on the sounds in words through playful activities involving:

- rhymes, poems, and songs
- stories read aloud
- rereading that emphasizes rhyme, alliteration, or segmentation of words
- games such as "I'm thinking of a word that begins with the same sound as..."
- manipulative activities, such as working with magnetic letters, that call attention to sounds as one way of referring to letters
- shared writing of messages in which the teacher asks children the sounds they hear at the beginning, middle, and end of words

At times during these and other reading and writing activities, teachers may want to say words slowly, stretching them out so that children can hear the sounds within them. For further ideas, refer to Ericson and Juliebo (1998) and Yopp & Yopp (2000), who detail numerous activities for developing phonemic awareness.

Remember that some kindergarten children may already be reading. Phonemic awareness activities will not be necessary for these children, who are at the point where they can benefit from more advanced activities involving letters and sounds.

References

Clay, M. (1998). *By different paths to common outcomes.* York, ME: Stenhouse.

Ericson, L., & Juliebo, M. F. (1998). *The phonological awareness handbook for kindergarten and primary teachers.* Newark, DE: International Reading Association.

Yopp, H. K. (1995). A test for assessing phonemic awareness in young children. *The Reading Teacher, 49* (1), 20–29.

Yopp, H. K., & Yopp, R. H. (2000). Supporting phonemic awareness development in the classroom. *The Reading Teacher, 54* (2), 130–143.

Shared Reading

Shared reading is aptly named—it is the act of sharing a reading experience between a reader and an audience who is invited to participate by reading along. In the readers' workshop, shared reading is a delightful way to build on children's experiences of being read to at home or to introduce children who have not had such experiences to the world of books and reading. (To review how shared reading fits with other strategies, refer to the section on the Continuum of Reading Strategies earlier in this chapter.) Recent research suggests that shared reading, including a home component involving audiotapes, can be highly beneficial to children who are learning English as a second language (Koskinen et al., 1999).

Background

Don Holdaway's (1979) descriptions of the shared-book experience in kindergarten classrooms in New Zealand formed the foundation of our understanding of shared reading. Holdaway and his fellow teachers began by making their own big books— enlarged versions of favorite tales such as "The Gingerbread Man" and "The Three Billy Goats Gruff" and presenting them as a read aloud and read along experience. Their teaching methods followed a model of developmental language learning. This model is characterized by

- immersion in an environment where language is being used purposefully;
- reinforcement of most language approximations, even those that are far from the correct or expected response, as long as they seem to be moving toward the desired response;
- allowing the learner a lot of control over the task of learning language, and
- expecting and accepting individual differences in the acquisition of proficiency.

Applying this model in the classroom, Holdaway (1979) discovered three stages of the literary experience that take place over the course of a few weeks. The first, *discovery*, is an introductory stage where teachers attempt to give all the children an enjoyable story experience they want to repeat on subsequent days, encourage participation, provide a spoken model for the language of books, and support word solving strategies. The second stage, *exploration*, focuses on rereading to familiarize children with stories, deepen understanding and response, give opportunities for language practice, and teach relevant reading skills. Finally, in the stage of *independent experience and expression*, children are able to recreate the experience for themselves in reading or reading-like ways and extend the experience through creative exploration and expression.

Procedure

A relaxed atmosphere where children enjoy favorite stories and feel encouraged to chime in, even if they make mistakes, is critical to the success of this method. The teacher will want to find a comfortable place for shared reading—perhaps the carpeted area where class meetings are held, with children sitting in a cluster and the reading materials placed on an easel or stand so everyone can see. Commercially published big books are standard items these days; teachers will find many favorite titles in both big book and little book form. Books that use rhyme, repetition, and predictable text—for example, *Brown Bear, Brown Bear, What Do You See?* (Martin, 1983) and *Noisy Nora* (Wells, 1973)—are good choices. Big books used during shared reading can be left in an accessible spot for groups of students to reread together, while the little book versions of the same story can be used during small group instruction or placed in the classroom library for individual rereading.

The teacher typically begins shared reading with a familiar song, chant, or poem, usually written in large letters on chart paper but sometimes displayed on a screen with the use of an overhead projector. He points to each word as he reads it, beginning with the title and looking forward to cries of, "Oh! I know this!" as he continues. Smiles, nods, and encouraging comments as some children spontaneously try to read along will invite others to try also. Favorite stories in big book format are next, with the teacher rereading those requested by the children if possible. During rereading, the teacher encourages children to read along as much as they can. With these familiar texts, he can highlight a reading strategy or skill he wants the children to practice.

In the early lessons, he will focus more on concepts about print, such as showing children how we read from top to bottom and left to right, how we identify the front and back of books, and how we recognize individual words by the spacing between them. In later lessons, he will focus more on features of print, such as teaching children to notice the beginning consonants of selected words and use known words (for example, a child's name) to figure out the sounds of those consonants (see the discussion of Masking at the end of this article).

A new story is introduced after the familiar texts are shared. Here, the teacher will focus children on enjoying the story and developing story comprehension. The children may be asked to make predictions from the title and cover before the story is read. The teacher may ask a few questions during the story to solicit further predictions. When he is finished, he will give the children the opportunity to tell what they liked and noticed about the story. Then he may ask the children to retell the story, with volunteers making contributions to a group reconstruction of the story.

At some time during the day, there should be time for the children to reread their favorite stories as they sit in the classroom library or sing and chant together in front of the charts of the songs and poems they learned. Art, craft, and drama activities can be connected to the stories to enrich the children's experiences and allow for creative expression. The teacher may organize the making of masks or puppets for dramatic reenactments of a story, encourage painting or drawing of a favorite part of a story, or help children put together a group mural. Connections to writing include text reproductions (using the same text with the children's own illustrations) and text innovations (creating new text following the same pattern as a familiar text). Using these techniques, the class can create their own big books—which are often the most popular texts—during independent reading time. A first grade class did a text innovation of the poem "A Hunting We Will Go," creating new lines such as, "We'll catch a toad and put him in the road, and then we'll let him go."

Shared reading typically is used with beginning readers, but the procedure can be equally effective for older students, especially second language learners or reluctant and struggling readers. Koskinen et al. (1999) found that second language learners enjoyed taking favorite shared reading books home, especially when these books were accompanied by audiotapes of the text. Children could read the books at home by following along with the audiotapes, even if no one at home was able to assist them. Interestingly, the children who were least proficient in English seemed to appreciate the practice with the tapes more than other children.

Songs, chants, raps, and poems are particularly effective for learning language, and predictable stories help readers learn word families and other patterns without drill exercises. Shared reading can also provide opportunities for choral reading, an enjoy-able experience for older as well as younger students. An individual or small group of children can take turns reading lines, verses, or stanzas, alternating with another indi-vidual or small group. Paul Fleischman's (1985, 1988) poetry volumes for two voices, *I Am Phoenix* and *Joyful Noise* are good resources for the shared reading of poetry.

Masking

Masking is a way of calling children's attention to the words within a text and to the letters that make up those words. When used during the shared reading of big books, it can be an effective approach for developing children's knowledge of phonics and other decoding skills. Like other word identification activities, masking should be used after the children have had the chance to enjoy the big book on a number of occasions and have become thoroughly familiar with the text.

Holdaway (1979) discusses three different forms of masking. The first involves a simple cardboard mask or frame. In this case the mask is used to isolate the target word so that it is easy for children to focus on it. The mask may also be used to isolate a phrase or sentence, rather than just a single word.

The second kind of masking discussed by Holdaway (1979) involves the use of a sliding mask. Figure 4.3 provides a pattern for a sliding mask, which can be enlarged to fit the size of text in the big books the teacher is using. This type of mask allows the teacher to reveal the letters of the word one at a time. The purpose of the activity is to encourage children's active attention to print.

Often, because children have read the big book so many times, their knowledge of the order of words in the text lets them predict what word should come next. For ex-ample, in *Meanies* (Cowley, 1990), children may know the entire sentence:

Meanies drive old tin can cars.

Suppose that the target word is *cars*. The teacher puts the mask over the word and asks the children what word they think it is. The children will know that the word is *cars*. The teacher asks, "If this word is *cars*, what letter do you expect to see first?" As the children name the letters they expect to see, the teacher slides the center strip of the mask back, revealing the letter and allowing the children to confirm or correct their predictions.

Holdaway's (1979) third approach to masking uses an overhead projector. On a transparency, the teacher writes the portion of the text she wants the students to inspect. She attaches the transparency to a cardboard frame. The frame has strips of cardboard that can be pulled back to reveal each line of the text gradually (see Figure 4.4). The teacher follows the same type of questioning as with the sliding mask, asking the chil-dren what they think the word will be and then having them predict the letters they expect to see. In short, masking is a valuable strategy for having children learn and apply word identification skills (in particular, visual cues or phonics) as part of shared reading.

References

Holdaway, D. (1979). *The foundations of literacy.* Sydney: Ashton Scholastic (dis-tributed in the United States by Heinemann).

Koskinen, P. S., Blum, I. H., Bisson, S. A., Phillips, S. M., Creamer, T. S., & Baker, T. K. (1999). Shared reading, books, and audiotapes: Supporting diverse students in school and at home. *The Reading Teacher, 52* (5), 430–444.

Children's Books Cited

Cowley, J. (1990). *Meanies.* Bothell, WA: Wright Group.

Fleischman, P. (1985). *I am phoenix: Poems for two voices.* New York: Harper & Row.

Fleischman, P. (1988). *Joyful noise: Poems for two voices.* New York: Harper & Row.

Martin, B. (1983). *Brown bear, brown bear, what do you see?* New York: Henry Holt.

Wells, R. (1973). *Noisy Nora.* New York: Dial.

FIGURE 4.3   MAKING A MASK

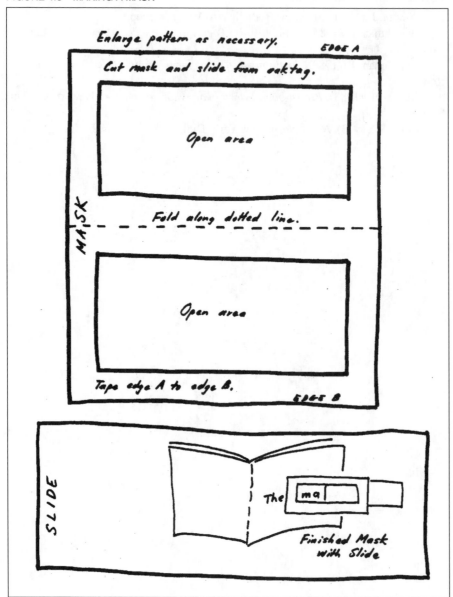

FIGURE 4.4   MASKING WITH AN OVERHEAD TRANSPARENCY

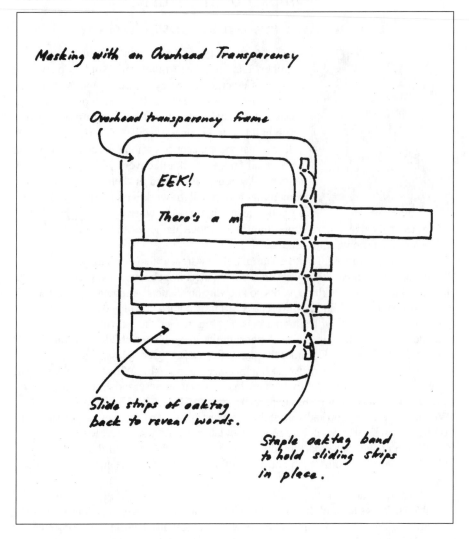

The Impact of Marie Clay:
Literacy Awareness and Cross Checking

 Marie Clay, a New Zealand educator and researcher, has conducted pioneering studies on young children's emergent literacy development. She is well known for founding Reading Recovery, a program of intensive individual instruction that helps struggling first grade children to become effective readers. Clay (1998) believes that the concept of awareness can help teachers understand how to work effectively with young literacy learners. Awareness is defined as "being able to attend to something, act upon it, or work with it" (p. 42). She suggests that learning can occur when

- teachers give children opportunities to notice literacy events,
- children show an awareness of literacy, or
- adults interact with children around the awareness they are showing.

Awareness in emergent literacy covers a broad range, from knowing how a book is organized, to knowing how writing works, to knowing how letters go together to form words.

Understanding children's awareness certainly comes into play during the readers' workshop, as teachers of beginning or struggling readers help their students learn to decode words. The trick is to create opportunities to build upon children's awareness of strategies for decoding. Consider this scene from a first-grade class.

Karen is reading aloud from a book as her teacher, Mrs. Williams, looks on. The picture shows the face of a boy with three freckles over his nose, and the text reads, *I have three freckles*. When Karen tries to read the sentence, she says, "I have three spots." Mrs. Williams has Karen stop and look at the last word again. "*Spots* makes sense," says Mrs. Williams. "But if that word were *spots*, what letters would you expect to see?"

Karen knows that *spots* would start with an *s* and that this word began with an *f*. Mrs. Williams continues, "Can you think of another word for the spots on someone's face that starts with *f*?"

"I know," Karen answers. "Freckles!"

"Right," says Mrs. Williams. To highlight the awareness that Karen has shown, she comments, "You chose a word that made sense and that also began with the correct first letter. When you do both those things, that shows good thinking!"

Information Cues: Meaning, Structural, and Visual

Clay (1991, 1993a) points out that children need to learn to use cues from different systems in order to read words accurately. (In the United States, related ideas about children's reading were developed by Goodman, see chapter 1.) The cue systems highlighted by Clay are

- meaning or sense,
- structure or grammar, and
- visual cues.

Meaning or sense cues have to do with the meaning of the passage or the text as a whole. In this case, Karen was reading a story about a boy named Carlos (Womersley, 1996), and she knew that every sentence had something to do with Carlos. In books for young children, pictures may be an additional source of meaning cues. Karen's guess of *spots* showed that she was using meaning cues provided by the picture.

Structure or grammar cues are those that involve the order of words in the sentence. For example, in English we know that if a sentence begins, *I have three...*, the next word is likely to be a noun. Karen showed that she was using structure cues by substituting the word *spots*. The sentence she produced, *I have three spots*, while inaccurate, is grammatically correct. Texts written for young children often follow predictable language patterns. In the story about Carlos, every sentence began with the words *I have* followed by a number word. The predictable language in a text encourages children to use structure and grammar cues when they read.

Visual cues are those that involve the appearance of the word and the letters the word contains. At first, Karen did not look at the unknown word closely and guessed that it was *spots*. After Mrs. Williams had her study the word, Karen noticed that it began with an *f*, not an *s*. Mrs. Williams' prompting encouraged Karen to use a cue system that she had previously ignored.

Proficient readers learn to use all three cue systems simultaneously to help themselves identify unknown words. Young, developing readers, such as Karen, have not yet learned to use information from all three cue systems at the same time. In this case, we saw how Karen used meaning and structure cues but neglected visual cues.

Cross-Checking

It is important to use all three information or cue systems, and not just to rely on one or two. When all three cue systems are used, the reader can engage in what Clay calls *cross-checking* and *self-correction*. Cross-checking is the practice of checking one's reading of a word against all three cue systems. Karen's reading of *spots* for *freckles* was consistent when checked against the meaning and structural cue systems, but was shown to be incorrect when checked against the visual cue system. Mrs. Williams encouraged Karen to cross-check her guess by adding information from the visual cue system. Eventually, as she learns to use visual cues consistently, Karen will be able to self-correct. She will notice on her own if her reading of a word does not fit with information from one of the cue systems, and she will spontaneously correct her own error. When this happens, Karen's reading might go something like this: "I have three spots . . . no, I mean, freckles."

Clay does not recommend that teachers simply tell children the correct word, because this approach does not develop children's awareness and help them to become independent readers. Instead, she suggests that teachers ask questions to lead children to figure out the word for themselves. The questions teachers ask depend on the cue system the child is neglecting. Suppose a child read the sentence differently from Karen, saying instead, "I have three friends." This reading, which leads to a grammatically correct sentence, shows that the child is using structural cues. It also shows that the child is using visual cues, because *friends* has the same beginning letters as *freckles*. However, this reading suggests that the child is not using meaning cues, because the sentence, *I have four friends*, appeared on the previous page, and the picture on this page shows Carlos by himself.

In this case the teacher might say, "*Friends* fits with the first letters of that word, but *friends* doesn't make sense because we just had a sentence about friends, and on this page we see only Carlos' face. Look closely at this page and see if you can think of another word that begins with *fr-* but makes sense."

Pointing Out Present Behavior

Clay (1993a) suggests that teachers begin by pointing out children's present reading behavior. This heightens their awareness of the kind of thinking they are doing.

Then they can call children's attention to the cue system that was ignored.

- If meaning cues were ignored, the teacher says, "You said . . . Does that make sense?"
- If structure or grammar cues were ignored, the teachers says, "You said . . . Does that sound right?" or "Can we say it that way?"
- If visual cues were ignored, the teacher says, "You said . . . If that word were . . . , what letters would you expect to see?" or "Does that look right?"
- If children are at the point where they are beginning to use all cue systems, the teacher simply says, "What's wrong?"

Teachers in the Reading Recovery program, as well as regular classroom teachers, find it useful to take a *running record* of children's oral reading. Clay (1993b) uses the term running record to refer to observations the teacher makes while observing the child's oral reading. Goodman (1969) uses the term *miscue analysis* to refer to a similar procedure. The purpose of taking a running record is to see which cue systems the child is consistently using on her own and which cue systems she may be ignoring. The teacher puts a check mark for every word read correctly. When a word is misread, the teacher writes the word in the text with the child's response above it. For example, Karen's reading would have been recorded in this way:

spots

freckles

If Karen had corrected her own mistake, the teacher would have written an *SC* for self-correction. Usually, children read a sample of from 100 to 200 words. After the running record has been taken, in addition to looking for patterns of errors, the teacher calculates the rate of accuracy of the child's reading. An accuracy rate below 90% indicates that the text is probably too difficult for the child. Clay notes that when a child is making errors on one word out of ten, it becomes difficult for her to judge whether her attempt at a word is a good one; and her coordinated use of cue systems begins to break down. To help the child progress as a reader, the teacher should have her read easier text. For detailed information about running records, refer to Clay (1993b).

Clay's ideas about awareness and information or cue systems provides a useful, practical framework for thinking about issues of word identification. Thinking in terms of the three cue systems helps teachers to keep their teaching focused on understanding children's present level of awareness and moving them forward from their present reading behavior. In contrast, focusing on a lengthy list of skills may cause instruction to be diverted to issues that do not relate to children's present level of awareness and immediate needs as readers.

References

Clay, M. M. (1991). *Becoming literate: The construction of inner control.* Portsmouth, NH: Heinemann.

Clay, M. M. (1993a). *Reading recovery: A guidebook for teachers in training.* Portsmouth, NH: Heinemann.

Clay, M. M. (1993b). *An observation survey of early literacy achievement.* Portsmouth, NH: Heinemann.

Goodman, K. (1969). Analysis of oral reading miscues: Applied psycholinguistics. *Reading Research Quarterly, 5,* 9–30.

Womersley J. (1996). *Carlos.* Boston: Houghton Mifflin Early Success.

Guided Reading

Guided reading follows shared reading in the continuum of teaching strategies in the readers' workshop (see article earlier in this chapter). Children are ready for guided reading when they have gained a preliminary understanding of how print works. They can point to words as they read, they know some letter-sound relationships, and they know a few common words (such as *the* and *is*) by sight. At this time the teacher's job is to lead children to greater knowledge of word identification and toward independence in decoding. Simultaneously, she wants to make sure that the children keep sight of the larger goal of reading, which is to construct meaning from text.

During guided reading, the teacher selects a little book that the children will be able to read largely on their own. The text of books used early on in guided reading might be very simple. For example, the first page might have the words "Black cat" below the picture of a black cat, while the second page might have the words "Yellow cat" below a picture of a yellow cat. At this level children's reading is supported both by the strong picture-text connection and the simple patterning of the words. The text of books used later in guided reading are longer and less predictable. For example, here are the last lines of a little book about a mockingbird (Lawrence, 1996):

He sings when day is done.

He sings his song for everyone.

In other words, during guided reading, children move through a leveled set of little books. A list of books at different levels of difficulty is provided by Fountas and Pinnell (1996).

How can teachers help children improve their word identification skills so that they will be able to read increasingly challenging text? Fountas and Pinnell (1996) provide a view of guided reading based on Clay's (1991) research. While shared reading is usually conducted with the whole class, guided reading takes place with a small group of children who have similar needs in learning to read.

Guided reading has a "before reading" phase, during which the teacher introduces the little book to the small group. When children are new to guided reading, or the little book is expected to be somewhat difficult for them, the teacher begins with a picture walk. During the picture walk, the teacher holds up her own copy of the book and calls the children's attention to the title. She goes through the book, referring to the pictures to help the children predict what the text will be about. For example, in the little book entitled *My Garden* (Keane, 1996), Ms. Hall calls the children's attention to the different tools the child uses when working in the garden. Because the children do not know the terms *watering can* or *trowel*, she introduces that vocabulary. If this were shared reading, Ms. Hall would read the text aloud to the children. However, because this is guided reading, Ms. Hall uses the picture walk to prepare the children to read the text for themselves.

The next part of guided reading is the "during reading" phase. Ms. Hall passes out the children's individual copies of the little book and has them start reading. Most beginning readers need to hear their own voices, so Ms. Hall reminds them to read quietly to themselves. She listens carefully as the children point to the words as they read, tracking the print, and attempt to figure out the words on their own. She provides help if children get stuck, but she is careful not to step in too soon. She makes a mental note that words with *-ing* endings have posed a problem for most of the children.

The last part of guided reading involves the "after reading" phase. When the children have finished reading the last page, Ms. Hall engages them in a retelling of the little book and asks them how they liked the story. She makes sure the children have understood the text so that the larger purpose of reading, to gain meaning, is not lost. Then she conducts a mini-lesson based on her observations of words that proved challenging to the children. She holds up her copy of the book, and she and the children read aloud the following sentence together:

> In my garden I have
>
> a favorite seat for reading,
>
> a big tree for climbing,
>
> and a swing for swinging. (pp. 12-13)

Ms. Hall prints the sentence on the chalkboard and has volunteers circle the words that contain the letter pattern *-ing*. She and the children discuss how *-ing* can be added to words such as read, climb, and swing. The children notice that *-ing* occurs twice in the word swinging.

The next day, Ms. Hall has the children reread *The Garden*. She conducts a mini-lesson to review *-ing* and has the children reread the text to see if they can find other words with *-ing*. The children discover digging, seedlings, and hiding, and Ms. Hall leads them in a discussion of the similarities and differences among these three words. Two children are chosen to copy all the *-ing* words on a chart to which new *-ing* words will be added as the children notice them.

As this example shows, the main event during guided reading is the children's own independent reading of the text. As the children read, the teacher carefully monitors their performance. The teacher uses what Fountas and Pinnell call "small detours" in giving children the assistance they need to finish reading the text. Fountas and Pinnell (1996) advise teachers to be very brief during individual interventions, so that children can immediately return to their efforts at meaning construction. In guided reading the teacher often focuses on moving children toward independence in word identification, so the children's own reading is often followed by a mini-lesson on skills. However, attention to comprehension or the meaning of the text is always maintained.

References

Clay, M. M. (1991). *Becoming literate. The construction of inner control.* Portsmouth, NH: Neinemann.

Fountas, I. C., & Pinnell, G. S. (1996). *Guided reading: Good first teaching for all children.* Portsmouth, NH: Heinemann.

Keane, S. (1996). *My garden.* Boston: Houghton Mifflin.

Lawrence, A. (1996). *The mockingbird.* Boston: Houghton Mifflin.

Decoding By Analogy

Clay's work on cue systems (see earlier article in this chapter) suggests that students must attend to three different kinds of cues: meaning, structural, and visual. During the readers' workshop, teachers in grades K–2 usually need to focus a considerable amount of instruction on the visual cue system. This involves teaching children to use the systematic relationships between letters and sounds in English. The process of identifying words by using visual cues (or what Goodman, 1969, terms graphophonic cues) is called decoding. Phonics, or letter-sound relationships, is one aspect of the visual or graphophonic cue system (see Troubleshooting: What About Phonics? in this chapter).

Efficient Approach

Pat Cunningham (1975–1976; see also Cunningham, 1991) introduced the idea of teaching decoding by analogy, or by comparing the unknown word to familiar words. This approach is based on research showing that proficient readers do not decode words by sounding them out letter by letter. Instead, they use the more efficient approach of looking for similarities between parts of the unknown word and known words. Suppose that the unknown word is *paronym*. The proficient reader might notice that the first part of the word begins like *party*, while the last part looks like the end of *synonym*. Using this knowledge, she can arrive at a reasonable pronunciation of the word.

Of course, beginning readers are not faced with words quite so difficult. The words they read are often only one syllable long. They start the process of decoding by separating the beginning consonant or consonants from the rest of the word, for example, *b-at*. The first consonant (in this case *b*) is called the onset. The remainder of the word (in this case *at*) is called the rime. In the word *throw*, the onset is *thr*, while the rime is *ow*. A word such as *and*, that begins with a vowel, has a rime but no onset.

A child who has learned to decode by analogy uses the following approach when confronted by an unknown word. Suppose the unknown word is *blame*. First, the child separates the onset from the rime, noticing that the word begins with *bl* and ends with *ame*. She knows that *blue* begins with *bl*. She also knows that *came* ends with *ame*. By putting the beginning and ending sounds together, she can pronounce the word.

The concept of decoding can often be made clear to children by showing them how to decode letter by letter. However, once children have grasped the idea of consistency in letter-sound relationships, it is wise to move them forward toward decoding by analogy. Letter-by-letter decoding works quite well with consonants but breaks down when it comes to vowels. Traditionally, children were taught that each vowel had two sounds, a "short" sound and a "long" sound. Children learned, for example, that there were two sounds for *a*, the short *a* sound as in *cat* and the long *a* sound as in *cane*. This teaching was not very useful to children because a vowel can be associated with up to 20 sounds. What helps a proficient reader to pronounce vowels accurately are the consonants that follow the vowel. These consonants give the vowel a stable, predictable sound. That is why proficient readers consider the rime in the word, not just the individual vowel.

Compare-Contrast

In decoding by analogy, the reader is comparing the unknown word to words already known. For this reason, decoding by analogy is also called the "compare-contrast" approach (Gaskins, Gaskins, & Gaskins, 1991; Center for the Study of Reading, 1991). For decoding by analogy to work efficiently, the reader must have a store of words in her mind to which the unknown word can be compared. A list of the 37 common spelling patterns or rimes most useful to children in the primary grades is given in Figure 4.5 (Wiley & Durrell, 1970, cited in Adams, 1990). Teaching students these patterns gives them a good foundation for using the compare-contrast approach.

FIGURE 4.5   COMMON RIMES

—ack	—ail	—ain	—ake	—ale	—ame	—an
—ank	—ap	—ash	—at	—ate	—aw	—ay
—eat	—ell	—est				
—ice	—ick	—ide	—ight	—ill	—in	—ine
—ing	—ink	—ip	—ir			
—ock	—oke	—op	—ore	—or		
—uck	—ug	—ump	—unk			

However, many of the most frequently occurring English words, such as *the* and *was*, do not follow these spelling patterns. These frequently occurring words, called *glue words* because they hold sentences together, should also be taught to children. A list of glue words is presented in Figure 4.6 (Adams, 1990).

Decoding by analogy is a useful strategy not just for words of one syllable but for multisyllabic words as well. Sometimes one multisyllabic word may be compared directly to another (for example, *mountain* and *fountain*). At other times, it may be necessary to break the multisyllabic word into parts, in order to compare the parts to familiar words. For example, *detain* could be divided into two parts: *de-tain. De-* could be compared to the familiar word *be* and *-tain* to the familiar word *rain*.

In the balanced literacy program, decoding by analogy is directly taught to children as part of the Readers' Workshop. Children's ability to decode by analogy is also strengthened through spelling instruction that occurs during the Writers' Workshop (see Spelling Strategies, chapter 8). For decoding by analogy to work efficiently, the child must know the spellings of many words to which the unknown word can then be compared.

Word Wall

How does instruction on decoding by analogy fit within the readers' workshop? As part of the readers' workshop, the teacher and students spend time each week adding to a word wall. Most of the words added to the wall incorporate the common rimes listed in Figure 4.5. Glue words may also be added to the wall. The word wall is a physical representation of the process the teacher wants to have taking place in students' minds. Students are encouraged to learn and memorize the spellings of words added to the wall. Once words have gone up on the word wall, students are expected to spell them correctly. As the spellings of more and more words are stored in students' minds, they have more and more words to which an unknown word may be compared. As a result of having a larger store of words in their minds, students can improve in decoding by analogy. The lessons that lead to words being added to the word wall grow out of children's reading of literature (for details, refer to Wagstaff, 1994, 1997-1998).

FIGURE 4.6   GLUE WORDS

274   Chapter 11

Table 11.4
The 150 must frequent words in printed school English according to the American Heritage *Word Frequency Book.* "Soundable" words are italicized.

the	*but*	into	long	also
of	what	*has*	little	around
and	all	more	very	another
a	were	*her*	after	came
to	when	two	words	come
in	we	like	called	*work*
is	there	*him*	*just*	three
you	*can*	see	where	*word*
that	*an*	time	most	*must*
it	your	could	know	because
he	which	no	*get*	does
for	their	make	through	part
was	said	than	back	even
on	*if*	*first*	much	place
are	do	been	before	*well*
as	*will*	*its*	go	such
with	each	who	good	here
his	about	now	new	take
they	how	people	write	why
at	*up*	my	our	things
be	out	made	used	*help*
this	them	over	me	put
from	then	*did*	*man*	years
I	she	down	too	different
have	many	only	any	away
or	some	way	day	again
by	so	find	same	*off*
one	these	use	right	*went*
had	would	may	look	old
not	other	water	think	number

References

Adams, M. J. (1990). *Beginning to read: Thinking and learning about print.* Cambridge, MA: MIT Press.

Center for the Study of Reading (1991). Teaching word identification. In Teaching reading: Strategies from successful classrooms, six-part videotape series. Champaign-Urbana, IL: University of Illinois (available through the International Reading Association).

Cunningham, P. (1975–1976). Investigating a synthesized theory of mediated word recognition. *Reading Research Quarterly, 11,* 127–143.

Cunningham, P. (1991). *Phonics they use: Words for reading and writing.* New York: HarperCollins.

Gaskins, R. W., Gaskins, J. C., & Gaskins, I. W. (1991). A decoding program for poor readers—and the rest of the class, too! *Language Arts, 68* (3), 213–225.

Goodman, K. (1969). Analysis of oral reading miscues: Applied psycholinguistics. *Reading Research Quarterly, 5,* 9–30.

Wagstaff, J. (1994). *Phonics that work! New strategies for the reading/writing chassroom.* New York: Scholastic.

Wagstaff, J. (1997-1998). Building practical knowledge of letter-sound correspondences: A beginner's word wall and beyond. *The Reading Teacher, 51* (4), 298–304.

Fluency

Making sure that students have sound strategies for word identification, such as decoding by analogy, is an essential part of instruction in the readers' workshop. Yet teaching students to identify words accurately is only part of the job. The reader who plods through the text in a slow, choppy manner, laboriously reading one word at a time, is not going to be an effective reader. Such a reader will be focusing so much attention at the word level that she will have no attention left for comprehension of the text as a whole. The other part of the job, then, is to help students read with fluency. Fluency involves reading quickly as well as accurately (Samuels, 1979). In addition, a fluent reader breaks the text into meaningful phrases, pauses at the proper points, and reads with expression (Martinez, Roser, & Strecker, 1998–1999).

Martinez, Roser, and Strecker (1998–1999) recommend that teachers use Readers Theater to promote students' reading fluency. Readers Theater is a highly motivating interpretive activity in which students read aloud from scripts like those that might be used in a play. However, unlike a play, Readers Theater does not require sets or costumes. Simply by reading expressively, the performers help the audience to visualize the scenes and actions.

Readers Theater can be effective in promoting fluency when teachers attend to four points. First, teachers should select or develop scripts at just the right level of difficulty. If the texts are too challenging, and students have to stumble through many unknown words, they will not be able to read the text quickly and with proper expression. Also, the best scripts are based on stories with a straightforward plot, but in which the character has to work out a dilemma. The script makes the characters inner thoughts and feelings clear. Scripts based on Mark Brown's Arthur books (1991, 1992) worked well with second graders.

Second, teachers should model what it means to read a text with expression. This does not mean that the teacher is reading the text in an exaggerated manner. Rather, the teacher shows students how a reader uses her voice to communicate the sense of the text to listeners. Third, teachers provide students with ample opportunity to read the same text over and over again. This method, known as repeated reading (Samuels, 1979), has been shown to improve the fluency of struggling readers. Finally, teachers give students feedback about their reading and provide instruction on fluency, as needed. Here are examples of feedback a teacher gave her students:

- "Remember that D. W. just rode her bike for the first time. How do you think she might sound?"

- "Could you read that again and pause for the comma? Let's see if it makes more sense."

- "I noticed how you 'punched' the word *never* in that sentence. That really helps the listener get the meaning." (Martinez et al., 1998–1999, p. 330)

Lessons might address the kind of intonation readers use when a sentence ends with a question mark or an exclamation point, or how to use one's voice to communicate a character's emotions.

Martinez et al. (1998–1999) found that Readers Theater improved the fluency of second graders. The approach should prove effective, as well as enjoyable, for students of all ages. Students in other classrooms provide an appreciative audience for the performances.

References

Martinez, M., Roser, N. L., & Strecker, S. (1998-1999). "I never thought I could be a star": A readers theatre ticket to fluency. *The Reading Teacher, 52* (4), 326–334.

Samuels, S. J. (1979). The method of repeated readings. *The Reading Teacher, 32,* 403–408.

Children's Books Cited

Brown, M. (1991). *Arthur meets the president.* Boston: Little, Brown.

Brown, M. (1992). *Arthur babysits.* Boston: Little, Brown.

Experience-Text-Relationship Lessons

Small group, teacher-guided reading lessons, for the purpose of developing students' reading comprehension, play a central role in the readers' workshop especially at first grade and above. The Experience-Text-Relationship or ETR approach (Au, 1979) provides a framework for planning and conducting guided discussions in small group reading lessons. This approach is based on the strategy of beginning with students' background knowledge and linking new text ideas to this knowledge. (To review how ETR fits with other strategies, refer to the Continuum of Reading Strategies earlier in this chapter.)

In traditional reading groups, students engage in round-robin reading, taking turns reading aloud from the text. The appropriate model for small group reading lessons in the readers' workshop is not round-robin reading but guided discussion. In guided discussion, the teacher leads students to construct a theme (Au, 1992). Students engage in silent reading, and the focus of the lessons is on appreciating and understanding the literature, not on oral reading performances.

The ETR approach involves three phases of discussion. In the first or experience phase of discussion, the teacher has students discuss background experiences related to the theme she intends to develop for the story. In the text phase of discussion, she uses questioning to guide students through the text, section by section, clarifying points unclear to students. Finally, in the relationship phase, she guides students to draw relationships between the text and their own background experiences. A single ETR lesson usually lasts from 20 to 30 minutes. The series of lessons based on a particular work of literature may take from three days to several weeks. The description of ETR lessons presented below focuses on picture storybooks. Following this description, methods of adapting the ETR approach to novels are discussed.

Planning

Figure 4.7 is a sheet for planning ETR lessons. The teacher first selects a high-quality piece of literature appropriate to the thematic unit and to students' interests. The literature should be at the instructional level of most students in the reading group, since students are expected to read the text independently. Because this piece of literature will be the focus of reading and discussion for three or more lessons, it should be a text with ideas worthy of this amount of attention.

The teacher then decides upon a possible theme to be pursued in discussions. Many works of literature offer several possible themes. For example, in *Halmoni and the Picnic* by Sook Nyul Choi (1993), one possible theme is that grandparents strengthen families by keeping traditions alive. Another possible theme is that students should take pride in their cultural heritage. The teacher chooses a theme in order to plan the course of the discussion. In this case, the teacher selects the theme of grandparents keeping traditions alive.

After deciding upon a theme, the teacher looks for a "hook," or a way of drawing the students into the story. She thinks of what she knows about the students' backgrounds and interests. Then she jots down the question she will use to start the discussion, for example, "What special traditions have you learned from your grandparents?"

The teacher completes the planning process by dividing the text into sections or chunks for silent reading. With a picture storybook the chunks may be small, just a couple of pages. Students will do the reading during the lesson, while the teacher observes.

Experience Phase of Discussion

During the first lesson, the teacher guides students in a discussion of their background experiences related to the literature and the theme. The teacher begins with the question she developed. Follow-up questions are based on the answers students generate. Once the students have shared their experiences, the teacher introduces the book and connects it to the discussion. For example, the teacher might say,

> The book we're going to be reading is about a girl named Yunmi and her grandmother. Please be thinking about how Yunmi's experiences with her grandmother are similar to or different from your experiences with your grandparents.

The teacher should also call students' attention to the ETR strategy itself, so that students become aware of the kinds of thinking they need to do to comprehend text (Dowhower, 1999). The teacher might say:

> This story will help you to learn a strategy to understand what you read. It is called Experience-Text-Relationship, or ETR for short. It gets us thinking about what has happened in our lives and how that fits with the character's experiences. (Adapted from Dowhower, 1999, p. 676)

Text Phase

The teacher tells the students the pages they will read for the first chunk of the story. She also sets a purpose for reading. For example, to begin *Halmoni and the Picnic*, the teacher might say, "Read to find out about the characters and setting in the story. Also see if you get any hints about what the problem in the story is going to be." The teacher monitors the students as they read and responds to questions they may have about difficult words. When the students have finished reading, the teacher resumes the discussion by picking up on the purposes set for the reading. In the example, the teacher would first have the students discuss the characters and the setting. She will make sure the students have identified the main characters, Yunmi and Halmoni, her grandmother. Then she will see if students are beginning to sense the tension in the story—Yunmi understands and values American customs while Halmoni finds them very strange.

Writing

At the end of each lesson, the teacher gives the students a written assignment. The assignment may be a review of the discussion, or it may be connected with the reading the students are supposed to do on their own. In this example, at the end of the first lesson, the teacher may ask the students to write about what they think is going to happen in the story. At the start of the second lesson, the teacher has the students share their writing. As students become more independent, the teacher can let them choose how they wish to respond in writing to the literature. At this point, the teacher will let students pick from a menu of possible writing ideas (see Written Responses to Literature, this chapter).

Relationship Phase

When the students have finished reading and discussing the last chunk of the text, the teacher begins the relationship phase of discussion. She first has the students summarize the story, to review the key events and issues. Then she has the students reflect on the theme of the story, in this case, how Halmoni is keeping Korean traditions alive although she and her family are living in America. Finally, the teacher has the students draw relationships between the ideas in the story and their own lives. For example, the teacher might ask how the customs students have learned from their grandparents are similar to or different from those that Yunmi is learning from Halmoni. The purpose of the relationship phase is to help students think deeply about the literature and make personal connections to it.

FIGURE 4.7   ETR PLANNING SHEET

ETR Planning Sheet

Author _____

Title _____

Possible Themes (Put an asterisk by the theme selected.)

"Hook" to Draw Students into the Story

Question to Open E Phase of Discussion

Chunks of Silent Reading

Adapting the ETR Approach to Novels

By the time they are in the third or fourth grade, most students are able to read novels with several chapters. These students can read silently without monitoring from the teacher. The teacher may wish to use the ETR approach with small groups of students if she believes the novel will be particularly challenging for them. Otherwise, the teacher may prefer to let students lead their own literature discussion groups (see article in chapter 5).

The ETR approach may be adapted for use with a novel by taking the following steps. The teacher conducts a small group lesson to introduce the novel with an Experience discussion. She sets purposes for the reading of the first chapter and has students write in response to literature, perhaps choosing from a number of options, as shown in Figures 4.10 and 5.2. The students read the first chapter silently, back at their seats, and complete their written responses. The next day, the teacher has students share their writing and follows up with a discussion of the first chapter. After this lesson, students read and respond in writing to the second chapter. In the following day's lesson, they share their writing and have a discussion of the second chapter. The pattern continues until students have finished the novel. During these discussions of the literature, the teacher pursues a line of questioning to highlight the theme. Finally, the teacher conducts a Relationship discussion, as described above.

In summary, the ETR approach allows teachers to provide students with guidance during the reading of literature. Through questioning, teachers can raise the level of students' thinking about literature and improve their comprehension. The ETR approach gives teachers a framework for making literature meaningful, by drawing relationships to students' background knowledge and experiences.

References

Au, K. H. (1979). Using the experience-text-relationship method with minority children. *Reading Teacher, 32* (6), 677–679.

Au, K. H. (1992). Constructing the theme of a story. *Language Arts, 69* (2), 106–111.

Dowhower, S. L. (1999). Supporting a strategic stance in the classroom: A comprehension framework for helping teachers help students to be strategic. *The Reading Teacher, 52* (7), 672–688.

Children's Books Cited

Choi, S. N. (1993). *Halmoni and the Picnic.* Ill. by K. M. Dugan. Boston: Houghton Mifflin.

Vocabulary Development

As students move through the grades, they read texts with an ever-growing number of new words. Research suggests that teachers cannot directly teach the meanings of all the words students will encounter—there are far too many words (Nagy & Anderson, 1984). A more effective approach to vocabulary development in the readers' workshop is to foster students' interest in words, connect the new words to what students already know, and teach students strategies for figuring out the meanings of new words on their own.

Blachowicz and Lee (1991) recommend that the teacher select the vocabulary to be taught from the literature and content materials students are going to be reading. In this way vocabulary instruction can take place as an on-going part of the readers' workshop and does not have to occur through a separate program. An ideal time to present vocabulary mini-lessons is in connection with ETR discussions (see article in this chapter).

Attention to vocabulary development begins at kindergarten and continues through all the grades that follow. During the readers' workshop in kindergarten and first grade, lessons on vocabulary usually grow from the teacher's reading aloud of picture storybooks. (Usually, the books that children can read on their own in kindergarten and first grade contain few vocabulary words that are not already part of the children's oral language.)

Sparkling Jewels

The "sparkling jewels" approach to be followed in kindergarten, first grade, and above is illustrated in this example, based on *Tar Beach* by Faith Ringgold (1991). The teacher reads the book aloud to the children and has them discuss the story. The teacher then returns to several pages to point out examples of the author's use of interesting language. For example, she rereads the page in *Tar Beach* in which the girl's baby brother is "lying real still on the mattress, just like I told him to, his eyes like huge floodlights tracking me through the sky." The teacher has children discuss the images that this sentence brings to mind. She writes the new word, *floodlights,* on the board and has the children think about it. If the children do not do so spontaneously, she helps them recall instances when they might have seen a floodlight (such as at a mall or theater). She also guides the children to look closely at the word itself, so that they can see that *floodlights* is a compound word.

The teacher tells the class that these examples of interesting language can be called "sparkling jewels," and she starts a chart with examples from *Tar Beach*. On the following days, when she reads books aloud, the teacher asks the children if they noticed any sparkling jewels. If the children have not noticed any sparkling jewels on their own, the teacher points out an example or two. Examples selected by the children and teacher continue to be added to the sparkling jewels chart. As this example shows, the teacher's beginning goal for vocabulary development is to help students become aware of new and interesting words and phrases. This goal is accomplished by developing lessons based on vocabulary and language drawn from literature.

Concept Wheels

Students will learn and remember new vocabulary when teachers make connections between the new word and words and concepts students already know. Rupley, Logan, and Nichols (1998–1999) highlight the use of visual displays to help students make these connections. With concept wheels, students draw a circle and divide it into

FIGURE 4.8   CONCEPT WHEEL AND SEMANTIC WEB

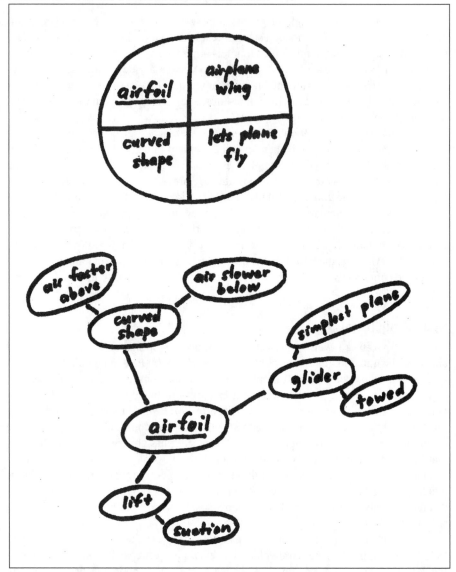

quarters, as show in Figure 4.8. They write the word being learned (for example, air-foil) in one quadrant. In the other quadrants they write words or phrases that will help them remember the new word (for example, airfoil, airplane wing, curved shape, lets plane fly). As illustrated in the bottom half of Figure 4.8, student may also develop semantic webs, either working alone or in small groups. In the center of a sheet of paper, students write the new vocabulary term, then draw an oval around it. As they think of a word associated with the new term, they write the word at the end of a line radiating out from the new term.

Look In, Look Around

At the third grade and above, teachers continue to promote interest in new words. In addition, they teach students strategies for deriving the meanings of new words as they read. One approach to teaching students to get a sense of what a word means is called "look in, look around" ((Herman & Weaver, 1988). The example is based on *Mufaro's Beautiful Daughters* by John Steptoe (1987). First, the teacher has the students read the literature, following an appropriate method. Students are given slips of paper and asked to make a note of any new or interesting words or phrases encountered while reading the story. In *Mufaro's Beautiful Daughters*, students might note the word *transfixed* in the sentence, "She stood *transfixed* at her first sight of the city."

The teacher tells the students that she will be teaching them how to figure out what a word might mean by doing two things: looking around the word and then looking in it. The strategy can be represented visually for students, as shown in the chart in Figure 4.9. The teacher explains that looking around the word means thinking about what is happening in that part of the story. It also means looking at the sentence in which the word is found. In having students look around the passage, the teacher elicits from students that Nyasha and her father had left their village to see the king. In having students look around the sentence, the teacher guides them to notice that the word has something to do with how Nyasha felt when she first saw the city.

After she has shown the students how to look around the word, the teacher explains how to look in the word. This process involves analyzing the word itself: seeing if it is a compound word, checking for familiar words or word parts, and looking for the base word and affixes. In the case of *transfixed*, the students might spot the base word *fix* and the *ed* ending. Some might recognize the common syllable *trans*, which appears in words such as *transportation*. The teacher guides the students to make inferences about what *transfixed* might mean, reminding them that the word tells something about how Nyasha felt when she first saw the city. Students might infer that someone who is fixed in one place does not move, and that in this case Nyasha might be surprised, amazed, or stunned by her first glimpse of the city.

The teacher concludes the lesson by telling the students that they can use the "look in, look around" approach whenever they want to know something about the meaning of a new word. Follow-up lessons on the look in, look around approach might be conducted at least once a week until the teacher is confident that students have an under-

FIGURE 4.9   LOOK IN, LOOK AROUND CHART

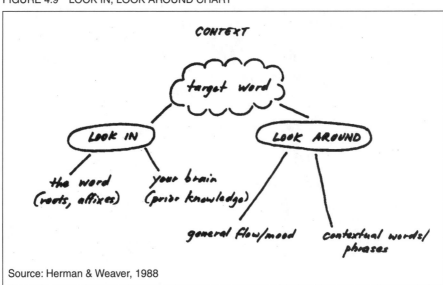

Source: Herman & Weaver, 1988

standing of the approach and are able to apply it when reading.

The "look in, look around" approach is consistent with the idea that people do not have dictionary-style definitions of words in their minds. Instead, they have a general sense of what a word means. A person's knowledge of a word's meaning is built up gradually, through encountering the word in a number of different contexts, perhaps through hearing someone speak or watching television, but usually while reading (Nagy, Herman, & Anderson, 1985). Of course, teachers will still want to teach students how to use a dictionary, but with the understanding that people learn the meanings of most words through wide reading over time, not through memorizing dictionary definitions.

Kuhn and Stahl (1998) reviewed studies of different approaches to teaching students to derive word meanings from context. They concluded that no one approach was superior to all the others, but that the important factor seemed to be how much practice students received. While we recommend look in, look around, you may find another approach that works just as well in your classroom. Whatever approach you use, be sure to have your students practice it on many occasions, preferably several times a week. Be sure to use look in, look around and other vocabulary approaches when students are reading content area textbooks or articles with a heavy load of new concepts and vocabulary.

References

Blachowicz, C. L. Z., & Lee, J. J. (1991). Vocabulary development in the whole literacy classroom. *The Reading Teacher, 45* (3), 188–195.

Herman, P. A., & Weaver, C. R. (1988). *Contextual strategies for learning word meanings.* Paper presented at the National Reading Conference, Tucson, AZ.

Kuhn, M., & Stahl, S. (1998). Teaching children to learn word meanings from context: A synthesis and some questions. *Journal of Literacy Research, 30* (1), 119–138.

Nagy, W. E., & Anderson, R. C. (1984). How many words are there in printed school English? *Reading Research Quarterly, 19*, 304–330.

Nagy, W. E., Herman, P., & Anderson, R. C. (1985). Learning words from context. *Reading Research Quarterly, 20*, 233–253.

Rupley, W. H., Logan, J. W., & Nichols, W. D. (1998–1999). Vocabulary instruction in a balanced reading program. *The Reading Teacher, 52* (4), 336–346.

Children's Books Cited

Ringgold, F. (1991). *Tar beach.* New York: Crown.

Steptoe, J. (1987). *Mufaro's beautiful daughters.* New York: Lothrop, Lee & Shepard.

The Impact of Maryann Eeds and Deborah Wells: Grand Conversations

Eeds and Wells (1989) introduced the term grand conversations to refer to discussions of literature during the readers' workshop. In these discussions, teachers and students participate in a genuine dialogue to construct the meaning of a text. Grand conversations develop students' comprehension of a text but are less structured and teacher-directed than ETR lessons (see article in the chapter). Here is an example of a grand conversation based on *After the Goat Man* by Betsy Byars (1974):

Tim: I want to talk now.

Teacher: Okay.

Tim: I thought the Goat Man would be more sensitive near the end because, well, he helped Figgy out.

Carrie: It was different. That grandfather just walked with Harold to where Figgy was, and he was real quiet and he just, he really cared. I think he really cared.

Teacher: That part of the story was real, real touching for me, too, because Betsy Byars [told us] he was real grouchy and hated children, and then you're seeing a different side of him.

Joy: I thought the grandfather was getting close to Figgy and I thought, well, it was kind of sad. What happened to his grandfather?

Teacher: If you look at page 112…

Tim: Another thing. His rabbit's foot. I thought his rabbit's foot like had a name. I thought it would be like a main character.

Teacher: The rabbit's foot?

Tim: Yeah. (Wells, 1995, p. 134)

This example illustrates the features of a book discussion that qualifies as a grand conversation. Notice that Tim, not the teacher, initiates the topic of discussion. Similarly, Joy, not the teacher, raises a question. No single person dominates the discussion. The teacher is an active participant, sharing her own feelings about the story, but she does not attempt to impose her views on the group. Speakers build on one another's comments, and the conversation moves forward as new ideas and issues are raised. Grand conversations are consistent with a constructivist philosophy (see The Impact of Lev Vygotsky, chapter 1), in which students actively use language to create their own understandings of literature.

Differences from IRE Pattern

A grand conversation may be contrasted with traditional, teacher-dominated discussions that serve as a form of interrogation. In these discussions interaction follows the initiation-reply-evaluation or IRE pattern (Mehan, 1979). The teacher initiates the discussion by asking a question, and students raise their hands if they wish to answer. The teacher then chooses a student to reply. Finally, the teacher evaluates the student's answer. In the IRE pattern the teacher maintains tight control over the topic of discussion and over who speaks on the topic. Students have little or no opportunity to initiate topics or to respond to one another's ideas. They learn that these discussions are a time when the teacher tests their comprehension of the text and that their job is to give the "right" answers, those expected by the teacher.

What steps can teachers take to promote grand conversations about literature in their classrooms? Wells (1995) provides several suggestions. First, teachers need to keep in mind that students' only previous experiences with literature discussions may have been in teacher-directed interrogations. Students may have to learn a whole new way of discussing and responding to literature, a process that will take time. An atmosphere of trust must develop before students feel free to take risks in expressing their ideas and feelings about literature.

A second suggestion made by Wells (1995) is that teachers may wish to reflect upon their own role in discussion groups. Many teachers are accustomed to thinking of themselves as the leader who conducts discussions to check students' comprehension. For grand conversations to take place, teachers must see themselves instead as fellow readers and collaborators. Together, students and teachers share their thinking about the text, explore connections to their lives, and reflect upon central themes.

Comments That Promote Discussion

Wells (1995) identifies three kinds of comments teachers can use to support students' responses during grand conversations: encouragement, synthesis, and inquiry. Encouragement comments further discussion by showing interest in students' ideas. Through these comments the teacher assures students that what they are saying matters to the group. Examples of encouragement comments are:

- Excellent point!

- Please say more about that.

When the teacher uses encouragement comments, she usually is not adding new ideas but simply facilitating the flow of conversation. In fact, encouragement can also be provided by nodding or by giving a simple "um-hm" to express agreement.

Synthesis comments also keep the conversation going. Synthesis comments allow the teacher to get the conversation started, to acknowledge the contributions individual students have made to the discussion, and to promote the exploration of thoughts and feelings. Examples of synthesis comments are:

- We ended yesterday by discussing the idea that . . . Do you still agree with that idea, or do you have a different idea today?

- Oh, so that part of the story made you feel . . . (relieved, anxious, etc.).

- What I think you're saying is that . . . (teacher paraphrases students' ideas). Is that what you mean?

Finally, through inquiry comments the teacher can show students the processes a mature reader uses to construct meaning from text. Teachers demonstrate the processes by thinking aloud. For example, they may share how they make predictions, read on, and confirm or alter their predictions. Or they may talk with students about a part of the text that raised questions in their minds. Wells (1995) gives the following example of a teacher's inquiry comments. The students were reading *Tuck Everlasting* by Natalie Babbitt (1975).

Teacher: Debora mentioned the stranger . . . and I wondered . . . did you notice that the author didn't tell you everything about the man? I wondered what would be the reason why she wouldn't tell you? (Wells, 1995, p. 138)

In this example, the teacher lets the students know of her own questions about the text and invites them to respond. The teacher's inquiry comments promote the students' engagement with the text and invite their collaboration in the group's efforts to interpret the literature.

In conclusion, grand conversations about literature require that teachers rethink their roles in discussions. The teacher's role changes from that of interrogator to fellow reader. However, teachers still fulfill their responsibility for developing students' ability to understand and respond thoughtfully to literature. By using encouragement, synthesis, and inquiry comments, teachers promote a conversational environment in which students gain the confidence to take risks and to share original thoughts. Grand conversations lead students to think about literature more deeply and with greater independence.

References

Eeds, M., & Wells, D. (1989). Grand conversations: An exploration of meaning construction in literature study groups. *Research in the Teaching of English, 23*, 4–29.

Mehan, H. (1979). *Learning lessons.* Cambridge, MA: Harvard University Press.

Wells, D. (1995). Leading grand conversations. In N. L. Roser & M. G. Martinez (Eds.), *Book talk and beyond: Children and teachers respond to literature* (pp. 132–139). Newark, DE: International Reading Association.

Children's Books Cited

Babbitt, N. (1975). *Tuck Everlasting.* New York: Farrar, Straus, & Giroux.

Byars, B. (1974). *After the Goat Man.* New York: Viking.

Story Structure and Story Matrix

Understanding how authors construct stories is an important strategy for increasing reading comprehension, because it lets readers look inside a piece of writing to see the underlying structure. This is particularly helpful to young readers as they build background knowledge about what to expect when they hear and read similar stories in the future. In its simplest form, story structure examines the basic elements of a story: characters, setting, plot, and theme. The story matrix is an organizational tool that students and teachers use to keep a record of these literary elements, and to record similarities and differences across stories.

Background

All works of literature are related to one another in that they all express the human need for unity and identity, elementary teacher and university professor Glenna Davis Sloan (1991) tells us. Characters search for their place in the world, and through them we experience the wonderful and terrible things that can happen to people in their quest for belonging. From this perspective, children can view the joys and pains of childhood and adolescence through the eyes and experiences of the characters in their books.

Sloan (1991) believes that, first and foremost, literature is art and should be read for aesthetic purposes before any other considerations (see also The Impact of Louise Rosenblatt and aesthetic and efferent reading in chapter 2). As with any art, literature cannot be "taught," but its appreciation can be learned. Children can and should be taught to critique what they read, Sloan reasons. To do so will enable them to see literature not as a collection of unrelated works, but as "the continuous journal of the human imagination" (p. 46). In her examination of how children respond to literature, Carol Jenkins (1999) affirms that children are capable of making critical responses to literature. They can and do examine symbolism, plot, character development, theme, and point of view in their oral and written responses to literature. She believes that nurturing these types of responses "deepens and extends the literary experience" (p. 55).

Procedure

Children need a broad range of experience with literature to grow in their ability to study, analyze, and critique it. Accordingly, the teacher needs to be sure that reading aloud, book talks, shared reading, paired reading, and independent reading are frequent activities in her readers' workshop. Children who have favorite authors, who read stories, plays, and poetry, and who know fantasy, realism, and traditional literature—these children have a body of literature to draw from during discussions. This is especially important for children who are slow or struggling readers. Too often these children are given less time for reading or listening to stories and assigned more decoding skills work. Rather than helping them catch up with their classmates, this practice only contributes to widening the gap.

As students read and hear good literature, they should be encouraged to respond to the aesthetics of the work. The teacher might ask questions such as: Did you like the story? Why (or why not)? How did you feel about the characters? Did their actions make sense to you? Was the story believable to you? What did you think about the way the author used language? Did anything in the story remind you of something that happened in your life? Each child's response should be respected and valued; the children should understand that there are no right or wrong answers here. As students reflect on their feelings, both in writing and during discussions, the teacher can show them how to go back to the text to locate examples of passages that affected them and influenced their views.

In further discussion and writing about a story or a poem, the teacher encourages higher-level thinking skills—imagining, hypothesizing, predicting, evaluating, synthesizing—through questioning and by modeling her own thinking (see also Grand Conversations in this chapter and Literature Discussion Groups in chapter 5). The following questions were suggested by Sloan (1991, pp. 119–124) to help students consider the form and structure of stories. The alternative questions in brackets (from Au, Mason, & Scheu, 1995, pp. 89–90) are suggested for younger students.

- What incident, problem, conflict, or situation gets the story going?

  [What is the problem in this story? How does the problem get solved?]

- What are the main events of the story? Is it possible to change their order? Leave any out? Why or why not?

  [What happened first? Then what happened?]

- Do any of the characters change in the story? If so, how are they different at the end? What changed them? Does the change seem believable?

- Did you have strong feelings throughout the story? What did the author do to make you feel strongly?

- What is the idea behind the story that gives point to the whole?

  [What do you think the author wanted you to learn from the story? What is the author's message?]

- Is this story, though different in content, like any other story you have read or watched in its form and structure?

  [Does this story remind you of any other story? Why? How is it the same? How is it different?]

Teachers can show students how stories are similarly constructed using a story matrix. In this matrix, elements common to all stories are listed across the top line, and information from each story can be entered underneath. This is particularly effective for genre studies, author studies, and thematic units, where students can examine similarities in characters, settings, story problems, events, solutions, and themes (see Figure 4.10 for an example). When students complete a matrix, the teacher can use it in discussions that lead students to generalizations about particular authors, genres, or themes in stories.

As students learn to examine the form and structure of stories they read, they discover ideas for their own writing. Analyzing how and why characters change, and what makes the changes believable, can greatly improve children's own stories, that otherwise may have one-dimensional characters who do things with little apparent motive. Looking at how plots are driven both by external events and by characters' internal reactions and motivation can help students create more believable and imaginative plots when they write. Examining authors' use of language can provide students with excellent examples for their own poetry and prose.

References

Au, K. H., Mason, J. M, & Scheu, J. A. (1995). *Literacy instruction for today.* New York: HarperCollins College Publishers.

FIGURE 4.10   STORY MATRIX USED FOR FRIENDSHIP STORIES

Story	Main Characters	Setting	Problem	Solution	Friendship Message
We Are Best Friends Aliki (Greenwillow, 1982)	Robert, Peter, and Will are the main characters.	The setting is the neighborhood.	The problem is Peter moved away and Robert thought he would not be happy.	The problem was solved when Robert and Peter wrote messages to each other and when they both found a new friend.	The friendship message is if someone is alone, make new friends.
Best Friends Steven Kellogg (Dial, 1986)	Louise and Kathy are the main characters.	It takes place in the imagination and in their neighborhood.	The problem is that Louise went to camp and Kathy thought Louise was having more fun than her. So she was jealous of Louise.	Louise came back and they were still best friends	Good friends don't get mad at each other. They cooperate by sharing.
Ira Sleeps Over Bernard Waber (Houghton Mifflin, 1972)	The main characters are Ira and Reggie.	The setting is Ira's house and Reggie's house.	Ira's sister thinks that Reggie will laugh if Ira brings his teddy bear to Reggie's house.	Reggie had a teddy bear like Ira.	The friendship message is they will understand if they are good friends.
Fun In the Sun S. Michaels (Troll, 1986)	The characters are Billy Beaver, Mandy Mouse, Fred Fox, and Ron Raccoon.	It takes place in the forest.	Nobody wanted to play with Billy Beaver because it was so hot.	Billy Beaver built a dam so that Mandy Mouse, Fred Fox, and Ron Raccoon could swim.	Friends are good to have around. They have good ideas.

Jenkins, C. B. (1999). *The allure of authors: Author studies in the elementary classroom.* Portsmouth, NH: Heinemann.

Sloan, G. D. (1991). *The child as critic: Teaching literature in elementary and middle schools* (3rd ed.). New York: Teachers College Press.

Written Responses to Literature

During the readers' workshop, students write in response to the literature they are reading (Routman, 1991; Parsons, 1990). The main purpose of having students engage in written response is to give them the chance to express their individual thoughts and feelings. Often, these responses are personal reactions to the literature, and the content of each student's written response is unique (see Rosenblatt, chapter 2). Many teachers have students do their writing in tablets referred to as literature response logs.

A Menu for Second Graders

Mrs. Young, a second-grade teacher, introduced her class to a menu of responses. For the first six weeks of school, she conducted mini-lessons to familiarize her students with different ways of responding to literature. She introduced one new way of responding each week. She gave the children ideas of the words they could use to begin their written responses, although they did not have to use these exact words. On the day she introduced a type of written response, the teacher asked all the children to try it. In this way, she made sure that everyone in the class became familiar with each type of response. Sometimes, she had children experiment with the new type of response for two or three days in a row.

After this introduction, the children could choose from any of the options on the menu. The menu was written on a large sheet of chart paper and posted at the front of the room. As the year progressed, many of the children departed from the sentence starters and used their own wording. They also began to combine two or even three types of responses in their literature response log entries.

The menu of responses Mrs. Young introduced, along with the suggested sentence starters, are listed below:

> Favorite part—My favorite part of the story is when . . .
>
> Feelings—This story made me feel . . . because . . .
>
> Diary entry written by a character—Dear Diary . . .
>
> Letter from one character to another—Dear [name of story character] . . .
>
> Personal connection—This story reminds me of the time when . . .
>
> Author's message—I think the author wrote this book to show that . . .

As the year went on, the teacher and children added new items to the menu. These items included the following:

> Characters—My favorite character is . . . The reason I like [name of character] is because . . .
>
> Similarities and Differences—I am like [name of character] because . . . I am different from [name of character] because . . .
>
> New Ending—Another way this story could have ended is . . .

Children in these first- and second-grade rooms were encouraged to talk with peers about their responses to literature before writing. They learned to share their written responses with classmates in literature discussion groups. At first, the children simply read their responses one after the other. With the teachers' help, the children learned to make comments and to ask one another questions. Mrs. Young also guided the children in noting similarities and differences in the responses written by members of the group.

Mrs. Young found that written responses to literature provided an effective means of assessing students' ability to understand, interpret, and see the significance of the texts they were reading. She did not have to administer special tests of reading comprehension for assessment purposes, because daily writing in response to literature provided her with ample evidence of students' progress.

Written Responses in Upper Grades

As a key component of the readers' workshop, written responses to literature fit within the teacher's plans for the development of the workshop over the year. Pat Nakanishi, a language arts resource teacher who taught fifth grade, incorporated the approach to written responses to literature shown in Figure 4.11 in her readers' workshop. Mrs. Nakanishi called the literature response logs in her classroom "Thinking Journals," because she wanted her students to think deeply about the literature. She taught her students to write responses with four parts: a summary, a personal response, think questions, and vocabulary and language (for information about Look In, Look Around, listed in the fourth column, see the article in this chapter). Mrs. Nakanishi presented mini-lessons on each of the four parts, and students practiced and received feedback on their efforts. (For another approach to written responses in upper-grade classrooms, refer to Literature Discussion Groups, chapter 5.)

For much of the year, Mrs. Nakanishi's students were divided into three groups, each reading a different novel, during the readers' workshop. She moved her students into groups following a three stage process. In the first stage, at the start of the year, Mrs. Nakanishi had the whole class read the same novel. She read the first chapter aloud, and she taught students to write a summary and personal response to this chapter. She explained that the summary dealt with "what's in the book," while a personal response addressed "what's in your heart."

The students shared their written responses in small groups. Mrs. Nakanishi emphasized the importance of responding in a positive manner to each person's efforts. Each group identified the one response it thought best, and these responses were shared with the whole class. The teacher led the class in a discussion of the strengths shown in these responses.

Mrs. Nakanishi taught the students to write personal responses and think questions as the basis for future literature group discussions. When she introduced the students to think questions, she emphasized that these questions should be about something the students really wanted to know. The answer to these questions should not have been given in the chapters the students had read so far.

In the second stage, Mrs. Nakanishi taught the students to engage in paired or partner reading (see Paired Reading, chapter 5). Although the students read in pairs and could discuss their responses, they were responsible for writing individually in their thinking journals. When the students began to share their written responses in literature discussion groups, Mrs. Nakanishi taught them to evaluate their performance in these groups. Each student was asked to

- participate
- listen
- be positive

In the third stage, Mrs. Nakanishi had the students read chapters of the novel independently and continue to prepare their own written responses. This stage brought the students closer to her goal of developing independent, lifelong readers.

This third stage led students to experiment with many types of written responses.

FIGURE 4.11   FORMAT FOR LITERATURE RESPONSE LOG ENTRIES

Summary	Personal Response ♡	Think Questions ?	Vocabulary—Page # and New Word
– Main Idea	– Like or don't like	– Why?	– Look In
– Beginning Middle End	– Agree or don't agree	– How?	– Look Around
– Characters Setting Problem Solution	– Favorite part or favorite character	– What would happen if?	– Look It Up
– Important events or information	– Prediction	– I wonder	Language
Author's Message and how I can use it in my life	– Connection to life		– Awesome adjectives
	– Walk in my shoes (If I were [character's name], I would . . .)		– Vivid verbs
			– "Show not tell"
			– Similes
			– Other "powerful language"

Source: Pat Nakanishi, 1996; revised 1999 (Reprinted with permission of Pat Nakanishi)

Here is Mrs. Nakanishi's description of what happened in her classroom during this stage:

> As the year progressed, students were introduced to variations on the written response format. For example, they had the option of doing a double-entry journal, which allows the reader to write an interesting event (type of summary), side by side with her thoughts and feelings about the event. (An example of a double entry, used by the teacher to model the approach for students, is shown in Figure 4.12.)
>
> Also, to add variety and creative thinking, sometimes the literature groups had the option of doing "visual retells" instead of written summaries (e.g., story map, matrix, character map, flow chart, timeline, etc.). When doing visual retells, students usually still wrote the personal responses and think questions because they worked so well to activate higher-level thinking and meaningful small-group discussions.

FIGURE 4.12   TEACHER MODELING OF DOULE-ENTRY JOURNAL

My Side of the Mountain   *Chapter 1—Snowstorm*

Ⓢ

Sam is living in a 6 ft. tree on a mountain because he ran away from home. He has survived for 8 months by fishing, hunting, and gathering.

When a blizzard came, he was terrified even though he had a fire to keep warm and lots of food.

When the storm is over, it is beautiful and peaceful. Sam thinks about his crowded apartment in NYC and is glad to be on his great-grandfather's land instead.

 Ⓟℝ

It reminds me of how the Native Americans survived off the land.

I would have been scared too—scared of dying—not of starving.

I grew up in NYC, too, and love the "country" more. When we go camping, nature is extreme like that—sometimes rough and violent, sometimes peaceful and beautiful.

 Ⓣ𝓠: *What adventures will Sam have and how will he survive?*

 Ⓥ: *pg. 7—tethers*
pg. 8—cascades

Mrs. Nakanishi also used the web of ideas for written responses shown in Figure 5.2. As with Mrs. Young in second grade, Mrs. Nakanishi found students' written responses to literature an excellent means of assessing their reading comprehension.

These examples show how students in both the primary and upper grades can be taught to write in response to literature. Written responses play an important part in the readers' workshop. They serve the purposes of allowing students to respond individually to the literature, preparing students to participate in literature discussion groups, and providing teachers with evidence to assess students' ability to understand and appreciate literature.

References

Parsons, L. (1990). *Response journals.* Portsmouth, NH: Heinemann.

Routman, R. (1991). *Invitations: Changing as teachers and learners K–12.* Portsmouth, NH: Heinemann.

Responding Through Drama and Art

Students may respond to literature in a variety of ways during the readers' workshop. These include discussions in Experience-Text-Relationship lessons (see article in this chapter), teacher-led grand conversations (see The Impact of Wells and Eeds, this chapter), or in literature discussion groups (see article in chapter 5), and writing in preparation for these discussions (see Written Responses to Literature, this chapter). Drama and art provide students with other valuable ways of responding to literature and developing comprehension ability.

Creative Drama

Creative drama involves having students act out parts of the literature using gestures, movements, facial expressions, sounds, changes in voice, and so on. Mary Jett-Simpson (1989) argues that creative drama can readily be used both to develop and assess students' comprehension of literature. Creative drama can occur before, during, and after the reading of literature. Drama has the benefits of involving all the language arts—reading, writing, speaking, and listening—while encouraging students to express their feelings as well as to gain deeper insights into the text (McMaster, 1998).

Before reading, creative drama can be used to activate background knowledge. *Lon Po Po*, translated and illustrated by Ed Young (1989), is a version of the Red Riding Hood story from China. Before students read this story, the teacher can have them act out the scene in which Red Riding Hood is questioning the wolf. The teacher can ask the students to think about how the story they will be reading, *Lon Po Po*, is similar to or different from the story of Red Riding Hood.

During reading, teachers can guide students to engage in what Jett-Simpson (1998) terms predictive creative drama. In planning, the teacher selects a key episode to be dramatized. As students read through the story, the teacher guides them to make predictions. After students have read each section of the text, the teacher has them decide whether their predictions were correct or need to be revised. Before students read the key episode, the teacher has them dramatize what they think will happen. In *Lon Po Po*, the teacher can have the students stop reading at the point where Shang, the oldest child, has asked the wolf to tie the rope to the basket. The teacher asks the students to work in small groups to develop a dramatization of what will happen next. After different groups of students have presented their dramatizations, the teacher leads the students in a discussion of similarities and differences in their presentations and has them look for evidence in the text that supports each of the predicted outcomes. Jett-Simpson suggests concluding the lesson at this point, leaving the students in suspense. The next day, students read to find out what happened, and they compare the author's decision about the course of the story with their own predictions.

When students have completed the story, creative drama offers an excellent means both of deepening comprehension and of assessing what the students have learned. The teacher leads students to identify episodes in the story. Students make storyboards, series of sketches showing the episode they will be acting out, and they practice their acting. When the complete dramatization is performed, it can be videotaped.

Readers Theater

In this approach students create a script from the literature. The script may cover the whole story or perhaps just a scene or two. When performing, the students read the script with expression.

The teacher begins by having students discuss the part of the story that they would like to highlight, and together they review that section of the text. The teacher familiarizes students with the format for creating the script, showing them how the characters' names will be followed by a colon and the words to be spoken by each character. *Lon Po Po* is a relatively easy story for students to convert into a Reader's Theater script, because the text contains a lot of dialogue. The teacher reminds the students that they may wish to change the author's wording, and that they may need to add dialogue of their own.

When the group rehearses its reading of the script, the teacher has the opportunity to promote expressive oral reading. For example, the teacher can have the student playing the part of the wolf lower his voice and speak with a growl. As discussed in an earlier article in this chapter, Readers Theater is an excellent means of building fluency. Students can have several rehearsals to practice and improve their performances, before making their presentation.

Art Activities

Instead of asking students for a written response, teachers may ask them to make a sketch reflecting their impressions and understanding of the literature. In *Sketch to Stretch* (Hoyt, 1992), students are given a short time to make a quick sketch to capture their feelings and ideas. The teacher makes a sketch of her own. The students share their sketches, explaining why they they chose to present that image. Students gain by seeing the way others choose to visually display their ideas.

Having students draw comic strips can help them understand the sequence of events and cause-effect relationships in a novel. The teacher and students prepare for this activity by bringing in examples of comic strips. The teacher guides students in noticing and discussing the conventions used in comic strips, such as speech balloons and headings. Students can decide upon the episodes they would like to capture in comic strips, and the strips can be published as a comic book retelling of the novel.

Dioramas allow students to visualize scenes in three dimensions. Students create scenes within a shoe box or other small box. The inside of the box is first painted to add background effects. Students use a variety of materials, such as clay, cloth, toothpicks, cotton balls, and so on to complete the scene. Dioramas may be left open, so the scenes appear as if on a small theater stage. Or the box may be covered and two holes cut, one for light to enter and one to allow the viewer to peer at the scene.

Technology can be used to capture art for sharing with a wider audience. For example, pages of the comic book can be scanned and saved on a CD-ROM for viewing on computers in school or at home. The dioramas can be photographed with a digital camera, and the photos can be uploaded to a classroom web site. Photos of literature-related art projects can be added to students' portfolios.

Of course, drama and art activities may be time-consuming. Au, Mason, and Scheu (1995) note that these activities probably should not be used with every book children read. Furthermore, the time spent on drama, art, and other expressive activities should never be greater than the time originally spent reading and writing about the literature.

As these examples suggest, drama and art activities can serve the dual purpose of having students reflect upon and express their understandings of literature, and of getting other students interested in these works. Drama and art activities add interest and excitement to the Readers' Workshop. They are not mere extras but valid and enriching approaches for deepening students' appreciation for and understanding of literature.

References

Au, K. H., Mason, J. M., & Scheu, J. A. (1995). *Literacy instruction for today.* New York: HarperCollins College Publishers.

Hoyt, L. (1992). Many ways of knowing: Using drama, oral interactions, and the visual arts to enhance reading comprehension, *The Reading Teacher, 45* (8), 580–584.

Jett-Simpson, M. (1989). Creative drama and story comprehension. In J. W. Stewig & S. L. Sebesta (Eds.), *Using literature in the elementary classroom* (pp. 91–109). Urbana, IL: National Council of Teachers of English.

McMaster, J. C. (1998). "Doing" literature: Using drama to build literacy. *The Reading Teacher, 51* (7), 574–584.

Children's Book Cited

Young, E. (1989). *Lon Po Po: A Red-Riding Hood story from China.* New York: Philomel.

K-W-L

K-W-L is both a method of teaching and an organizational tool that can be used to help students read and process informational text. Teachers from primary grades to high school and college have used this method to help learners consider their prior knowledge of a topic, explore new information through reading, and make connections between the new and the known.

Background

Donna Ogle (1986) developed K-W-L to help students be active readers of informational text. In her model, the first step (K) is to have students identify what they already *know* about a topic. As they do, Ogle suggests that teachers ask questions such as "Where did you find that out?" and "How can you prove that is true?" These questions prompt students to think about their own sources of information and whether their uncertainties can be verified through reading. Students also are asked to think about the kinds of information they are likely to find in the text. They try to think of categories to prepare themselves for the reading.

The second step (W) asks students to identify what they *want* to learn. They may want to verify what they think they know, and they may have other questions leading from what they already know. The students' questions help them set their own purposes for reading. When students complete their reading, they record what they *learned*, which is the final step (L) in the model. Ogle developed a three-column chart that students use as they follow the K-W-L steps. A variation of this chart is given in Figure 4.14.

Procedure

Teachers can model the K-W-L procedure when they begin reading a single informational book or start a research project that requires reading several types of informational text (books, brochures, web pages, etc.). Teacher Brenda DeRego began a study of marine animals with her fourth graders by developing her own K-W-L chart in front of the class. The students, as a group, already had a long list of animals they might choose to study. Ms. DeRego told them, "As we listed all these animals, I've been thinking about which one I want to know more about. I thought maybe I would choose a shark, because we think they are all dangerous, but maybe some aren't. But then I thought about the humpback whales. I saw some once, and I was so excited! I don't really know much about them, but I want to know more." Ms. DeRego used an overhead transparency to record what she knew in the K column of her form. "They are huge. They make special noises to communicate. The noises sound like songs. They migrate from Alaska to Hawai'i every year to give birth. Then they go back to Alaska to find food for themselves and their young." Then she completed the W column, listing the questions she had so far.

The students chose an animal from the list and began writing down what they knew and wanted to know. Then Ms. DeRego had them find a partner and share their information and questions. After that, the whole class met and Ms. DeRego asked, "Who had a conference that helped them?" David said, "Chantel wrote, 'How fast does a seal swim?' That made me think, 'How fast can a penguin swim? So I put it on my list." Over the next several days, students read trade books, fact sheets, informational posters, brochures, and other materials Ms. DeRego and they found. As they read, they made notes in the L column of their K-W-L forms. Later, they would decide on a form for their reports and begin writing their drafts.

As teachers have worked with this method over time, they have made their own modifications (Hill, Ruptic, & Norwick, 1998). One is the K-W-L-W model. The final W represents what students still *wonder* about even after they have completed their reading and research. The questions students write for this section can help set a direction for further research, either by individuals, groups, or the whole class. Another variation is K-W-H-L. The H stands for *how* students will find the information they need. This is useful when students use the K-W-L method for research that requires them to access multiple sources of information. In these variations, the basic K-W-L form can be revised to include extra columns.

FIGURE 4.14. K-W-L FORM

Topic or question:		Name:
K I already know . . .	**W** I want to know . . .	**L** I learned that . . .

References

Hill, B. C., Ruptic, C., & Norwick, L. (1998). *Classroom based assessment.* Norwood, MA: Christopher-Gordon.

Ogle, D. M. (1986). K-W-L: A teaching model that develops active reading of expository text. *The Reading Teacher, 39* (6), 564–570.

Troubleshooting: What About Phonics?

For nearly 50 years, the topic of phonics has been at the heart of controversies in the language arts field. Among literacy educators, the term phonics refers to the systematic relationships between letters and sounds in the English language. Clearly, knowledge of these systematic relationships is required if children are to become good decoders, as concluded in Adams' (1990) review of research on beginning reading. This finding implies that phonics instruction can be highly beneficial to many children. However, if phonics instruction is to be effective, it is important to understand its proper place in children's overall development of word identification ability.

Development of Word Identification

Stahl (1997) summarizes research indicating that children go through three phases in learning to identify words. These phases are

- awareness
- accuracy
- automaticity

Children enter the awareness stage getting meaning from pictures rather than print, and they are happy to retell stories in their own words by looking at pictures. In the awareness stage they need to learn about the functions of print (for example, that print can be used to label objects). They must gain an understanding of concepts about print (for example, words are read from left to right), as well as the forms of print (for example, the difference between letters and numbers). They must develop phonemic awareness, or an understanding of how sounds go together to form words (see article in this chapter).

Children in the accuracy stage are attending to print and tracking it carefully. Unlike children in the awareness stage, they may refuse to retell a story from a book, protesting, "I don't know the words." Children in the accuracy stage can benefit from phonics instruction much more readily than children in the awareness stage, and this is the time that phonics instruction will be of most value. Many children enter the accuracy stage sometime in kindergarten or first grade, although a few children may not enter this stage until second grade.

The purpose of having children learn phonics is to allow them to decode unfamiliar words by taking advantage of the alphabetic nature of the English language. Once a new word is decoded or identified, it need not be the subject of phonics analysis again, but should become part of the child's store of sight words—words recognized instantly, without any conscious analysis.

Children in the automaticity stage are able to identify many words by sight without having to go through phonics analysis. Because they can read so many words quickly and accurately, they can devote most of their attention to comprehension or understanding of the text. Research suggests that many poor readers can decode words accurately but are reading much too slowly and laboriously (Campbell & Ashworth, 1995). The answer for these students is not further phonics instruction but an approach such as repeated reading (Samuels, 1979), in which they gain automaticity by learning to read quickly and smoothly.

As this brief overview suggests, phonics instruction plays a critical but temporary role in children's development as readers. The timing of phonics instruction is critical. Phonics instruction is most beneficial when children are in the accuracy stage of word identification development. It is of little use in the awareness stage, when children are not yet tracking print, or in the automaticity stage, when children need to learn to read quickly and free up attention for comprehension.

Given this research background, we can address three questions often raised about phonics:

- How much emphasis should be given to phonics?
- Should all children be given phonics instruction?
- How should phonics be taught?

Emphasis on Phonics

Should phonics be the most important element in the beginning reading curriculum? Clearly, phonics has its place. However, phonics cannot be the sole focus of the readers' workshop. An overemphasis on phonics gives students a misleading picture of what reading is all about. Reading is the process of constructing meaning from text, not just accurate word calling. Phonics instruction must be balanced with instruction in other aspects of reading, including ownership, reading comprehension (see Experience-Text-Relationship Lessons, this chapter), vocabulary development (see article in this chapter), and voluntary reading (see article in chapter 5).

Phonics for All Children?

In response to the second question, research has established that not all children require phonics instruction. Durkin (1966) and others studied children who learned to read before going to school. These children were able to discover for themselves the systematic relationships between letters and sounds in English. Nevertheless, the majority of children, who do not come to school already reading fluently, can probably benefit from instruction in phonics, particularly if skills are taught in meaningful contexts within the readers' workshop and the writers' workshop. In most classrooms, phonics instruction can begin in kindergarten, when children can be taught initial consonant sounds, and can conclude in second grade. In the second grade and above, instruction shifts from a focus on phonics to strategies for dealing with multisyllabic words and acquiring new vocabulary.

Some children will need little instruction in phonics, while others will require a great deal. Because of these differences, many phonics lessons will be given to selected children in a *flexible skills group*. Children in a flexible skills group are placed together because of their need for instruction in particular skills. For example, a group of children may need instruction in initial consonant sounds already known to others in the class. The teacher gathers this group together for a lesson, perhaps while other children are engaged in activities at learning centers. The group is flexible because its membership changes over time, depending on the children's needs and the skills to be targeted in the lessons.

How to Teach Phonics

The third question is that of how phonics should be taught. In general, research supports the approach of teaching students to decode by analogy (see article on Decoding by Analogy in this chapter). This approach appears effective for children who experience difficulty learning to read, as well as for normally developing readers (Gaskins, Gaskins, & Gaskins, 1991). Certain enhancements to this approach are needed for students who experience extreme difficulty with decoding. These children benefit from extra instruction that enables them to analyze and retain the correct spelling of words that must be stored in memory. A full description of the instruction needed is presented in Gaskins et al. (1996-1997).

There is some evidence that many children start out by analyzing words sound by sound, letter by letter, taking an approach known as phonemic segmentation (Ehri & Robbins, 1992). An effective way of promoting phonemic segmentation is through the writers' workshop. When children are drafting, they can be encouraged to say words slowly and to write down all the sounds they hear. By inventing their own spellings for words, children learn how letters go together to form words in the English language. They can learn the conventional spelling of these words when the time comes for them to edit their writing.

There is no evidence that a single approach to phonics or beginning reading instruction will work best with all children in all situations (International Reading Association, 1999). Teachers must decide for themselves when and how they will teach phonics, based on the needs of their students and their own understandings of effective literacy instruction.

References

Adams, M. J. (1990). *Beginning to read: Thinking and learning about print.* Cambridge, MA: MIT Press.

Campbell, J. R., & Ashworth, K. P. (Eds.). (1995). *A synthesis of data from NAEP's 1992 integrated reading performance record at grade 4.* Washington, DC: Office of Educational Research and Improvement, U.S. Department of Education

Durkin, D. (1996). *Children who read early: Two longitudinal studies.* New York: Teachers College Press.

Ehri, L. C., & Robbins, C. (1992). Beginners need some decoding skills to read words by analogy. *Reading Research Quarterly, 27* (14–26).

Gaskins, I. W., Ehri, L. C., Cress, C., O'Hara, C., & Donnelly, K. (1996–1997). Procedures for word learning: Making discoveries about words. *The Reading Teacher, 50* (4), 312–327.

Gaskins, R. W., Gaskins, J. C., & Gaskins, I. W. (1991). A decoding program for poor readers—and the rest of the class, too! *Language Arts, 68* (3), 213–225.

International Reading Association. (1999). *Using multiple methods of beginning reading instruction.* Newark, DE: International Reading Association.

Samuels, S. J. (1979). The method of repeated readings. *The Reading Teacher, 32,* 403–408.

Stahl, S. A. (1997). Instructional models in reading: An introduction. In S. A. Stahl & D. A. Hayes (Eds.), *Instructional models in reading* (pp. 1–29). Mahwah, NJ: Erlbaum.

Chapter 5

STUDENT-DIRECTED ACTIVITIES IN THE READERS' WORKSHOP

Student Ownership

Students who have ownership of literacy have positive attitudes toward literacy and make literacy a part of their everyday lives (Au, Scheu, & Kawakami, 1990). In readers' and writers' workshops, students' ownership of literacy is the overarching goal of the curriculum. Teachers strive to develop students' ownership of literacy, just as they seek to improve students' ability to comprehend text and to decode words.

In a balanced literacy program, the affective side of students' literacy development, including ownership, is considered to be as important as the cognitive side. Skills and proficiency remain important considerations. However, too often students who have acquired reading and writing skills do not put these skills to use, except when the teacher requires them to do so. These students have the skill but lack the will to read and write.

Attitudes and Habits

Ownership involves students' attitudes toward literacy and their habits of using literacy. Students who have a positive attitude toward literacy understand that it can be used to accomplish real-world tasks and to enrich their lives. Students who have the habit of using literacy incorporate reading and writing into their daily routines at home as well as at school. For example, they may read in their spare time, keep diaries, write notes to friends, and make to-do lists. These students have the will as well as the skill to use literacy, and they see reading and writing as personally meaningful activities.

While the concept of student ownership is powerful and useful, it is also complex. Dudley-Marling and Searle (1995) suggest that ownership has to do with students having responsibility for their own learning and control over their lives in school. Shannon (1995) argues that language is not property and so cannot be owned in the sense that land or a car can be owned. From this point of view, ownership of literacy is not an individual matter but a matter of participating in a community of language users, with the responsibility of respecting a diversity of voices and looking after the well-being of all within the community.

Fortunately, while student ownership is complex, it is also observable. Teachers can recognize actions within the readers' and writers' workshop, and at other times of the day, that indicate students are developing ownership of reading. The assessment checklist in Figure 5.1 lists items that teachers may observe. The form includes space for teachers to note dates and write comments.

FIGURE 5.1   OWNERSHIP CHECKLIST

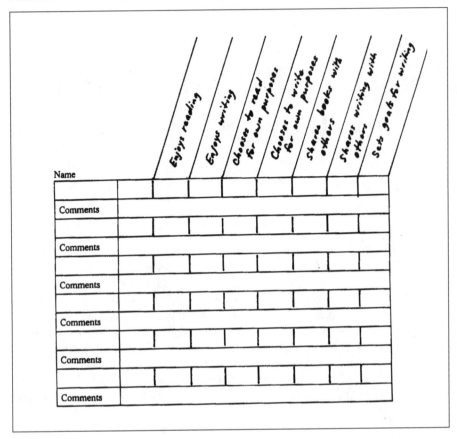

Examples of ownership of reading and writing include the following. Bobby shows that he enjoys reading by picking up a book to read in his spare time. As he reads silently, he seems to be chuckling to himself. Near the end of the writers' workshop, Akiko shows that she enjoys writing by asking if she can stay in at recess to finish a notebook entry. Barbie, a second grader, reads a picture storybook aloud to her kindergarten buddy, demonstrating that she can share books with others. Douglas indicates that he chooses to write for his own purposes when he decides to compose a letter to his cousin during the writers' workshop. Jeff demonstrates that he can share his writing with others by asking Matt to listen to his draft.

Teacher Responsibility

Teachers new to the concept of ownership sometimes have the mistaken view that students must be allowed total free choice during the readers' workshop, always choosing the books they want to read and even having the option of not reading. Developing student ownership should not be equated with a hands-off approach. While it is important for students to have choices, it remains the teacher's responsibility to guide students to make informed choices. For example, it does not detract from student ownership for teachers to provide systematic, guided discussions of literature. Students may not have chosen on their own to read a book such as *The Giver* by Lois Lowry (1994). Yet the teacher may decide that reading and discussion of this thought-provoking book in a small group will promote students' higher-level thinking.

Ownership, like other aspects of literacy, is learned. One of the most powerful sources of student ownership is the classroom teacher who is an avid reader and writer (see Carroll, Wilson, and Au (1996) for a description of how two teachers shared their literacy with students). Teachers can let students know about the books they are reading for their own enjoyment. They can speak about their favorite authors and their own tastes and preferences as readers. Teachers serve as models of ownership by showing how important literacy is in their own lives.

References

Au, K. H., Scheu, J. A., & Kawakami, A. J. (1990). Assessment of students' ownership of literacy. *The Reading Teacher, 44* (2), 154–156.

Carroll, J. H., Wilson, R. A., & Au, K. H. (1996). Explicit instruction in the context of the readers' and writers' workshops. In E. McIntyre & M. Pressley (Eds.), *Balanced instruction: Skills and strategies in while language* (pp. 39–63). Norwood, MA: Christopher-Gordon.

Dudley-Marling, C., & Searle, D. (Eds.). (1995). *Who owns learning: Questions of autonomy, choice, and control.* Portsmouth, NH: Heinemann.

Shannon, P. (1995). Dialectics of ownership: Language as property. In C. Dudley-Marling & D. Searle (Eds.), *Who owns learning: Questions of autonomy, choice, and control* (pp. 142–152). Portsmouth, NH: Heinemann.

Children's Books Cited

Lowry, L. (1994). *The giver.* New York: Bantam Doubleday Dell.

Literature Discussion Groups

Students meet in literature discussion groups to converse about books they are reading in the readers' workshop. Although the teacher may help the group get started, or stop by to observe the group, the students themselves take control of the discussion. Literature discussion groups usually consist of four to six students who meet several times a week for sessions of about 20–30 minutes.

If you refer back to the continuum of strategies described in chapter 4, you will see that literature discussion groups are an advanced form of instruction. In literature discussion groups, in contrast to the ETR lessons given for guided discussion (see article in chapter 4), students lead their own discussions of literature. Literature discussion groups give students the chance to develop independence in exploring their own responses to literature.

Book Clubs

Book clubs are a form of literature discussion group developed by Taffy Raphael, Susan McMahon, and their colleagues (McMahon & Raphael, 1997; Raphael, Goatley, McMahon, & Woodman, 1995; Raphael & McMahon, 1994). Book clubs give students the chance to engage in natural conversations about books, just as adults do. Many adults enjoy discussing books with friends. Among adults, conversations about books do not begin with questions such as "Who was the main character?" Instead, adults discuss their feelings about the book, interesting points, and issues raised.

Raphael et al. (1995) were interested in student-led rather than teacher-led literature discussions. Student-led discussions increase students' opportunities to talk about books, since a teacher can only meet with one small group at a time. Student-led discussions also require students to develop their own ideas, instead of relying on the teacher. However, it takes time and effort on the part of the teacher to help students develop the skills to successfully lead their own literature discussions.

Overview

To create book clubs, the teacher divides the class in to small groups of four to six students, taking into account such factors as how talkative students are, how well they get along with others, and so on. At the beginning of the school year, book clubs may be conducted by having all students in the class read the same book. Then, once students have become familiar with the routine, the teacher can have them choose from three books, all of the same genre or centered on a common theme. By offering a choice of books, the teacher will be able to offer easier and more difficult selections, to accommodate the differing levels of reading ability in the class. For example, if the genre is fantasy, students might choose from *Tuck Everlasting* (Babbit, 1975), *The Giver* (Lowry, 1994), and *A Wrinkle in Time* (L'Engle, 1962). *Tuck Everlasting* is a shorter book that will be easier for poor readers to handle, but that still offers much to think about and discuss.

A typical day in a book club classroom begins with a teacher read aloud and mini-lesson. The mini-lesson may deal with a literary element (such as flashbacks), a strategy (such as making inferences), or an issue related to effective participation in book clubs (such as asking open-ended rather than yes-no questions). Following the mini-lesson, there is time for students to read their novels and prepare written responses, on their own or with a partner. After this preparation time, students meet in book clubs with their peers. The final event is community share, a time for students in the different book clubs to share their ideas with the whole class. Descriptions of each of these components is provided in Raphael, Pardo, Highfield, and McMahon (1997).

Improving Discussion Skills

When students are just beginning to work in book clubs, their conversations are often stilted and superficial. Students read the entries they have written in their reading logs but do not respond to one another's ideas. They spend considerable time negotiating how the discussion should proceed, as shown in the following interaction in which group members were trying to get Joshua to share.

Ken:	Your turn, Joshua.
Joshua:	I don't got nothing to read.
Ken:	You gotta tell about, go, you gotta tell about your picture. Talk!
Eva:	You copycat [referring to his log entry].
Ken:	Talk!
Mei:	Tell us about your picture. (Raphael & McMahon, 1994, p. 105)

Fortunately, situations like that illustrated in the transcript above do not continue indefinitely. Over time, students learn how to interact with one another around ideas in the literature. This process is speeded up if teachers make audio or videotapes of book club discussions and have students analyze what went well and what could be improved. Over time, conversations flow more freely, involve all students in the group, and delve deeply into issues raised by the literature. Students' writing in response to literature also increases in range and depth. Here is an example of a conversation held in mid-February in a fifth-grade class. The students in this book club were responding to an episode in *Number the Stars* (Lowry, 1989), a novel set in Denmark during World War II. In this episode a German soldier playfully touched a child's head, because the child reminded him of his sister.

Crystal:	If you were in Annemarie's place, um what would you feel if someone was touching your sister?
Ken:	I'd tell him to leave her alone.
Helena:	But they were scared. You see, they had a gun to your back, what would you do? It was probably real steel or something.
Ken:	I'd say "leave her alone" and then I'd go hit him. I'd sock 'em all!
Richard:	What happens if they shot you with the gun?
Ken:	If they shot me?
Richard:	Yeah.
Randy:	But they had a gun. You shouldn't do that, you should just stand there . . .
Ken:	I'd risk my life for my sister, yeah.
Crystal:	I would.
Helena:	I would.
Richard:	It depends which sister I am talking about here. (Raphael & McMahon, 1994, p. 114)

As this conversation shows, these students have learned how to share their responses to literature with one another. They know how to express agreement or disagreement, invite the ideas of others, and even share a joke.

To promote thoughtful discussions of literature, teachers help students develop the skills needed for effective participation. Teachers guide students in listening to audio-tapes of their book club discussions to identify strengths and areas needing work. They teach students to observe one another's behavior during book clubs and to provide constructive feedback. They set aside time for students to evaluate their own contributions to book clubs. Teachers also provide instruction to improve students' reading comprehension ability. For example, they give lessons to help students understand the sequence of events and cause and effect relationships. They teach students about literary elements, such as character development and theme, and about the features of different genres of literature. Students are encouraged to compare and contrast books within and across themes.

Written Responses to Literature

After students read each chapter in the book, they write their responses in reading logs (see Written Responses to Literature, chapter 4). Students represent their ideas in various forms, including pictures and webs as well as words. Teachers often provide students with a question to think about. In addition, they create menus which give students ideas for writing. Throughout the year, the teacher and students add to this menu. A sample list of options for writing, suggested by Raphael and McMahon (1994), is shown in Figure 5.2. At times students might engage in typical comprehension activities in their logs, for example, creating maps to show all the characters in the story, charts to keep track of the sequence of events, and questions for their peers to discuss. After participating in book club discussions, students use their reading logs to summarize key points and to consider what they have learned.

Figure 5.3 shows an example of a student's written response to *Maniac Magee* (Spinelli, 1990). The student has chosen to record the titles of the three chapters and to write about predictions, wonderful words (similar to Sparkling Jewels, see chapter 4), and special story parts. At the bottom of the page, the student has copied and answered two prompts (questions written by the teacher). This written response shows that the teacher allowed students to write about topics of their own choice, but also focused their attention on what she judged to be important issues in the novel.

Book clubs are an effective approach to literature discussion groups. Teachers who have used these approaches find that students need considerable guidance at the beginning of year, but gradually take control of the discussions as the year goes on. Literature discussion groups promote thoughtful involvement with literature and increase students' engagement and ownership during the readers' workshop. Book clubs can also be an effective approach for integrating literature with a content area, such as social studies. For an example, refer to Pardo (1998).

Teachers may wonder when to use a particular type of lesson or discussion group during the readers' workshop. Mini-lessons (chapter 4) should be used when the teacher wishes to provide systematic instruction in a particular strategy or skill, either to the whole class or a small group. Experience-Text-Relationship lessons (ETR, chapter 4) should be used when the teacher wants to provide students with close guidance to foster comprehension of a story or novel. Grand conversations (chapter 4) should be used when the teacher wants to be present with a small group to facilitate discussion, but without the structure of ETR lessons. Literature discussion groups (book clubs) should be used when the teacher feels students can read the text with comprehension on their own and can benefit from the chance to develop their own interpretations and questions.

FIGURE 5.2   READING LOG ENTRY POSSIBILITIES

GETTING READY FOR BOOK CLUB: *WHAT I CAN DO IN MY READING LOG?*

BOOK/CHAPTER CIRTIQUE

Sometimes when I'm reading, I think to myself, "This is absolutely GREAT!!!" Other times I think to myself, "If I were the author, I sure would do this differently." In my log I can write about things the author did really well and things he or she might want to do better.

ME & THE BOOK

Sometimes what I read about a character or an event makes me think of things in my own life. I can write in my log and tell about what the character or the event or other ideas made me think about from my own life.

AUTHOR'S CRAFTS AND SPECIAL TRICKS

Sometimes authors use special words, paint pictures in my mind with words, make me wish I could write like they do, use funny language, write dialogue that is really good, and many other things. In my log, I can write examples of special things the author did to make me like the story.

SPECIAL STORY PART

I can mark the page number so I can remember where to find it. Write the first few words, then "..." and the last few words so I can remember what I want to share. Then I can write about why I thought it was interesting or special.

SEQUENCES

Sometimes events in the book might be important to remember in the order they happened. I can make a sequence chart in my log and share it with my group, explaining why I thought it would be important to remember.

CHARACTER MAP

I can think about a character I really liked (or really didn't like, or thought was interesting). The map can show what I think the character looked like, things the character did, how the character went with other characters, what made this character interesting, and anything else that I think is important.

WONDERFUL WORDS

I can find some really wonderful words—words that are new, crazy, or descriptive, ones I might want to use in my own writing, ones that are confusing, or whatever. Write down the word or words and share them with my Book Club group. I might want to write a short note about why I picked the word, so that I can remember later. I might also want to write the page number where I found the words so that I can find it again.

PICTURES

Everytime I read, I end up with some kind of picture in my head about the story, if I just think about parts I like. I can draw in my log and share my picture with the group. I have to remember that when I draw a picture, I need to write a little about why I drew it so that I can remember where the picture came from, what made me think about it, and why I wanted to draw it.

FIGURE 5.3   LITERATURE RESPONSE JOURNAL EXAMPLE

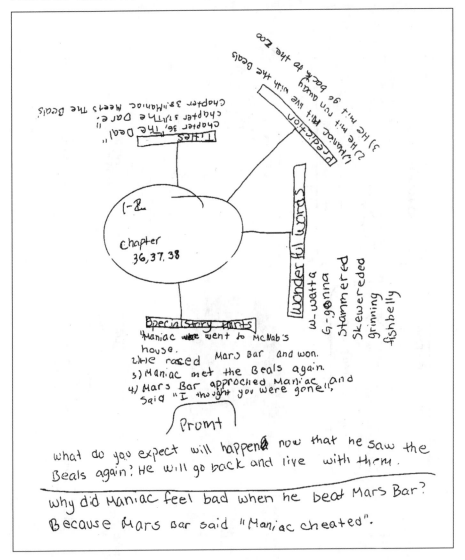

References

McMahon, S. I., & Raphael, T. P. (Eds.). (1997). *The book club connection: Literacy learning and classroom talk.* New York: Teachers College Press.

Pardo, L. (1998). Criteria for selecting literature in upper elementary grades. In T. E. Raphael & K. H. Au (Eds.), *Criteria for selecting literature in upper elementary grades* (pp. 219–238). Norwood, MA: Christopher-Gordon.

Raphael, T. E., Goatley, V. I., McMahon, S. I., & Woodman, D. A. (1995). Promoting meaningful conversations in student book club. In N. L. Roser & M. L. Martinez (Eds.), *Book talk and beyond: Children and teachers respond to literature.* Newark, DE: International Reading Assocation.

Raphael, T. E., & McMahon, S. I. (1994). Book Club: An alternative framework for reading instruction. *The Reading Teacher, 48* (2), 102–116.

Raphael, T. E., Pardo, L., Highfield, K., & McMahon, S. I. (1997). *Book club: A literature-based curriculum.* Littleton, MA: Small Planet Communications.

Children's Books Cited

Babbit, N. (1975). *Tuck everlasting.* New York: Farrar, Straus and Giroux.

L'Engle, M. (1962). *A wrinkle in time.* New York: Dell.

Lowry, L. (1989). *Number the stars.* Boston: Houghton.

Lowry, L. (1994). *The giver.* New York: Bantam Doubleday Dell.

Spinelli, J. (1990). *Maniac Magee.* New York: Scholastic.

Book Talks

A book talk is a brief, tantalizing introduction to a book, intended to interest others in reading that book. Book talks play an important part in the development of a community of readers during the readers' workshop. Whether presented by teachers or students, book talks are a way of sharing books and the love of reading.

Ms. Baxter, a first-grade teacher, blends book talks with reading aloud. One day, she began the readers' workshop by reading *The Wheels on the Bus* (Kovalski, 1987) aloud to her students. After the children had responded to the book, Ms. Baxter gave a book talk:

> Some of my favorite books are books like this one, based on a favorite song or rhyme. Here's one called *Peanut Butter and Jelly* (Westcott, 1987), and it has funny illustrations, too. If I show you a picture from this book, I think you'll see what I mean.

Ms. Baxter opened the book so the children could see the picture of the elephants crushing the peanuts. She concluded her book talk by placing *Peanut Butter and Jelly* on the chalk rail and encouraging the children to read it on their own or with a partner.

Book Talks in Upper Grades

Mr. Ortega's fifth-grade class was in the process of completing a unit on the westward expansion. He took the opportunity to encourage his students to read books depicting this period in American history. He had selected four books, varying in difficulty. *My Prairie Christmas* (Harvey, 1990) and *The Chickenhouse House* (Howard, 1991) were easier, while *Justin and the Best Biscuits in the World* (Walter, 1990) and *The True Confessions of Charlotte Doyle* (Avi, 1990) were more challenging. Mr. Ortega related these books to themes explored in previous class discussions, such as the importance of a family sticking together in the face of new challenges. Then he read a short passage to give students the flavor of each book. He ended by saying that two copies of each book would be on the wire book rack. He told students they might want to find a buddy. That way, a pair of students could read the same book and talk it over.

In deciding which books to feature, teachers can think about their goals for students as readers at that time of year. Early in the year, the goal may simply be to encourage students to enjoy reading. In this case, teachers might select titles known to be popular with students at that grade level. Later in the year, teachers might have the goal of broadening students' horizons as readers. Now teachers will give talks about books that students are not naturally choosing for themselves. For example, if most of the students are reading humorous and realistic fiction, the teacher might give talks about fantasy, featuring books by Lloyd Alexander, or talks about nonfiction, such as books by Carolyn Arnold.

Student Book Talks

After teachers have given book talks on a number of occasions, they can invite students to give book talks. Students can be prepared through a whole-class discussion on the features of an effective book talk. Students need to understand that the purpose of a book talk is to share a favorite book in a way that will entice others to read it. Students' ideas can be listed on a chart. For example, students may have noticed that the teacher read an exciting part of the book aloud, or showed them an interesting illustration, but did not give away the ending.

At the beginning of the week, the teacher might meet with a group of three or four students. The students review the reading logs listing the books they have read independently. They may choose a book from their logs, or they may recall another favorite. The teacher can ask students what they particularly liked about these books. Then the teacher has students think of how they could give book talks to convince other students to read these books. A planning form for book talks is shown in Figure 5.4. Students can discuss their plans with the group, then rehearse their book talks with a partner.

FIGURE 5.4   BOOK TALK PLANNING FORM

1. What I will say to get the audience's attention

   _____

   _____

2. What I will say to introduce myself (optional)

   _____

   _____

3. Title and author

   _____

   _____

4. Why I liked the book (special features)

   _____

   _____

5. Quick summary (don't give away the ending) OR favorite part

   _____

   _____

   _____

   _____

   _____

   _____

   _____

A good time for scheduling book talks might be immediately before or after sustained silent reading. The students giving the book talks can sit in the author's chair. The audience can be reminded to follow the same procedure used when students read their published books. For example, students can say something positive about the book talk and ask questions.

After all interested students have had the chance to give a book talk, the teacher can put up a sign-up sheet. Two or more students can be encourage to give book talks every week. Students can be reminded to tell the class when they have enjoyed reading a book featured in a talk by one of their classmates.

Children's Books Cited

Avi. (1990). *The true confessions of Charlotte Doyle.* New York: Orchard.
Harvey, B. (1990). *My prairie Christmas.* New York: Holiday.
Howard, E. (1991). *The chickenhouse house.* New York: Atheneum.
Kovalski, M. (1987). *The wheels on the bus.* New York: Dutton.
Walter, M. P. (1990). *Justin and the best biscuits in the world.* New York: Knopf.
Westcott, N. B. (1987). *Peanut butter and jelly.* New York: Dutton.

Paired Reading

In paired reading, also known as partner reading, two students read books together. Paired reading provides students with both academic and social support for reading and may be used beginning in kindergarten and continuing through the upper grades. The approach is especially useful when texts are too difficult for some students to read on their own, but not so difficult that close teacher guidance is required. Paired reading is a step in moving students toward independent reading.

Students may engage in paired reading in order to prepare for a teacher-led or student-led discussion (see Experience-Text-Relationship Lessons and The Impact of Wells and Eeds: Grand Conversations, chapter 4, and Literature Discussion Groups, this chapter). Paired reading may also be used to promote voluntary reading with younger children or struggling readers, who are not yet independent enough as readers to benefit from sustained silent reading.

Forming Pairs

Different procedures are used to form the pairs of readers, depending on the purposes for paired reading. If the purpose is to give all students access to the literature, the teacher may match an able reader with a struggling reader. The teacher can ask the able reader either to help the struggling reader decode and understand the text, or to read the text aloud to the struggling reader. If the purpose is to give students practice in decoding text, the teacher may pair students with similar levels of reading ability. In this case, the students will share in the work of reading the text, because one will not find the task much easier than the other. Students may be allowed to choose their own partners, or to change partners, after they have had some experience with paired reading.

Reading the Text

Teachers can discuss with students different ways of reading in pairs. Often, students take turns reading a page or a paragraph of the text, so the reading is evenly divided. If an able reader is paired with a struggling reader, the able reader may read two or three paragraphs, while the struggling reader reads just one.

Students can be asked to help one another during paired reading without giving away the answers. Teachers can teach students to give one another hints about how to figure out an unknown word. Hints can be worded as questions and written on a chart for the students' reference.

- What word might make sense here?
- What is the first letter in the word?
- How is the last part of the word spelled? Do you know any words with the same spelling pattern?

Students can be told that their job during paired reading is to become better readers, and that this is best accomplished by helping their partners figure out the words, not telling them the answers.

Teachers can encourage students to pause occasionally to discuss the text. They can be asked to talk about their feelings about the text, what they understand, and what is puzzling them.

Role Sets

MacGillivray and Hawes (1994) use the term role sets for the frameworks that students negotiate during paired reading. In their study of a first-grade classroom, they discovered that the most common role set was coworkers. In this role set, students worked together to choose the book and shared in the reading. In the second role set, fellow artists, students performed for one another, showing how well they could read. The third role set, which seemed to be the most common, was that of teacher/student. The child assuming the role of teacher used many traditional teaching behaviors, such as asking the other child to "repeat after me." In the fourth role set, boss/employee, the child acting as the boss took control and made all the decisions. Fortunately, this role set was only observed with one pair of children.

The findings of MacGillivray and Hawes (1994) highlight the importance of discussing with students appropriate ways to work together during paired reading. They suggest that students role play how they can help a partner without upsetting that person, and what they can say to a partner when their feelings get hurt. Teachers might wish to set aside time every so often for a class evaluation of paired reading. During the evaluation, teachers and students can cite examples of the positive and negative behaviors they have observed, and the class can brainstorm solutions to problems.

References

MacGillivray, L., & Hawes, S. (1994). "I don't know what I'm doing—they all start with *B*": First graders negotiate peer reading interactions. *The Reading Teacher, 48* (3), 210–217.

Voluntary and Independent Reading

Voluntary reading is reading that people do on their own because they want to read. A term formerly used for voluntary reading was recreational reading, denoting the reading that people do in their free time. Voluntary reading differs from independent reading, which is reading students do on their own but not necessarily because they want to. For example, teachers may give students the assignment of reading a textbook chapter; students read the chapter independently but not voluntarily. Both voluntary and independent reading are important parts of the readers' workshop.

Voluntary reading occurs when people read because they want to enjoy the experience of reading, adopting what Rosenblatt (1978) calls the aesthetic stance (see The Impact of Louise Rosenblatt: Reader Response Theory, chapter 2). Voluntary reading, an important part of ownership of literacy (see article in this chapter), is a habit that can bring students pleasure throughout their lives. Teachers can do much to encourage voluntary reading, including reading aloud (see chapter 4), sharing their own literacy with students (see The Impact of Shelley Harwayne: Teachers as Readers, chapter 4), and giving book talks (see article in this chapter).

Sustained Silent Reading

Sustained silent reading (SSR) is a time when students, the teacher, and anyone else in the room sit quietly to read books of their choice. SSR goes by a number of different names, including "drop everything and read" (DEAR), "our time to enjoy reading" (OTTER), "sustained, uninterrupted reading for fun" (SURF). Teachers should allow time everyday for SSR. SSR may last for only 10 minutes in a first-grade class and for 20 minutes or more in the upper grades. For capable readers, SSR is a time for independent reading. For children who cannot yet read on their own, partner reading may be substituted for SSR (see Hong, 1981, for other suggestions).

SSR is not the same as voluntary reading; the teacher has scheduled this event, and students do not have the option of doing anything but reading. However, SSR is a means of encouraging students to develop the habit of daily reading. Because students choose the books they will read, they have the opportunity to develop their own tastes and preferences as readers. SSR is also a means of increasing the amount of reading students do everyday, an important step toward becoming a capable reader (Fielding, Wilson, & Anderson, 1986).

SSR seems to work best in classrooms where students have time to engage in social interactions around their reading (Manning & Manning, 1984). After SSR, teachers may have students discuss their reading with a partner, or volunteers may tell the whole class about their books. As students listen to one another, they can get ideas about books that they might like to read in the future. SSR, when accompanied by social interaction around books, contributes to the building of a community of readers.

Matching Students with Books

Some students are avid readers who know how to find books they will enjoy. However, some students have yet to develop their own tastes as readers. These students need the teacher's help, first to identify books that match their interests, and second to locate these books. Teachers may start by having brief individual conferences with these students, to discover their hobbies and interests. A sample questionnaire is shown in Figure 5.5. Teachers can then recommend specific titles or get ideas from the school librarian. Children's Choices is a project of the International Reading Association (IRA) that identifies recent titles found to be popular with students. The list is published annually in *The Reading Teacher* or can be obtained through IRA's web site (www.reading.org).

Most teachers work collaboratively with students to establish rules for SSR. "No talking, no walking" is a common rule. Examples of other rules are that students may get up just once to look for another book, or that they may do paired reading only in a particular corner of the room. In a fifth-grade classroom, SSR occurred right after recess. The rule was that students had to have their books for SSR ready at their desks before they could go out to recess.

To reinforce the habit of daily reading, many teachers have students do some reading on their own every night. Students choose the books they will read, and they make entries in a reading log listing the title, author, and pages read each night. Parents may be asked to discuss the reading briefly with the child and to sign next to the reading log entry. A sample independent reading log form is shown in Figure 5.6.

Of course, teacher-assigned activities that compel students to read are not the same as voluntary reading. Nevertheless, these activities may get students involved with books they enjoy and lead them toward becoming lifelong readers. A fifth-grade student revealed in an interview that he became a reader because his third-grade teacher insisted that he read everyday during sustained silent reading. After faking it for a several days, he decided that he might as well read. Soon he found a book he actually did enjoy, and eventually he became an avid reader.

FIGURE 5.5   INTEREST QUESTIONNAIRE

Interest Questionnaire

Name _____ Date_____

1. What are some things you enjoy doing with your family?

2. Do you have any hobbies?

3. What sports or games do you enjoy?

4. Do you take lessons in art, dancing, or music?

5. Are you a member of a club or group, such as a choir or a scout troop?

6. Do you have any pets?

7. If you could take a trip anywhere in the world, where would you go?

8. Is there a famous person you especially admire?

9. What do you think you would like to be when you grow up?

10. Do you have a favorite book? What makes that book your favorite?

11. Is there a certain kind of book you especially enjoy reading? (If necessary, give examples, such as realistic, adventure, mystery, factual books.)

FIGURE 5.6 INDEPENDENT READING LOG

Independent Reading Log

Name_____

Date	Title & Author	Rating (1–5)	Type of Book	Interesting Words	Page

References

Fielding, L., Wilson, P., & Anderson, R. C. (1986). A focus on free reading: The role of tradebooks in reading instruction. In T. E. Raphael (Ed.), *Contexts of school-based literacy* (pp. 149–160). New York: Random House.

Hong, L. K. (1981). Modifying SSR for beginning readers. *The Reading Teacher, 34* (8), 888–891.

Manning G. L., & Manning, M. (1984). What models of recreational reading make a difference? *Reading World, 23* (4), 375–380.

Rosenblatt, L. (1978). *The reader, the text, the poem: The transactional theory of the literary work.* Carbondale, IL: Southern Illinois University Press.

Connections to Home and Community: Extending the Reading Community

We know that parent involvement has a positive effect on student achievement. So as teachers plan their readers' workshops, they will want to find ways to include students' families and even other community members to support children's reading and reading-related activities.

Background

Recent research has shown that parental engagement at home (e.g., helping children organize their time, monitoring children's homework, discussing schoolwork, and reading to children) has a strong positive influence on children's academic performance (Finn, 1998). Best of all, home factors over which parents have control (such as their child's attendance at school, the amount of television watching permitted, and the variety of reading materials in the home) has been shown to account for most of the differences in average student achievement (U. S. Dept. of Education, 1994).

Procedure

Suggestions for communicating with parents as part of the readers' workshop structure have been made in chapter 3. Here, we look at ways parents (and other family members) can become more actively involved in reading with their children.

Some parents want to work directly in the classroom as teachers' aides or classroom tutors. These parents will benefit from gaining a deeper understanding of readers' workshop and how it helps students achieve literacy. For other parents, spending time at their child's school is not an option. Their work schedules, home environment, or language barriers may keep them away from school. Therefore, it is important to help all parents learn good ways of promoting reading at home.

The best ideas are often the basic ones. When parents ask how to help their child be a better reader, teachers can assure them that the most important activities do not require a lot of training. Teachers may want to use part of the class newsletter early in the school year to send home a list of suggestions such as the following:

- Read to your child, every day if possible. Don't stop when he or she gets older.
- Let your child see you reading and know you like reading. Be a good model for literacy. It is especially important for boys to see adult males reading. Otherwise, they may think of reading as an activity only females enjoy.
- Provide books, magazines, and other materials for your child to read. You don't need to buy books, although it's great if you do. Visit your local library, and make it a frequent, fun family event.
- Provide a good environment for reading (a quiet, comfortable, inviting spot). If this cannot be done at home, look for alternatives—a relative's or friend's house, a quiet place at the park, or the library.
- Talk with your child about what he or she is reading, and tell your child about what you are reading.
- Encourage your child's reading efforts and praise accomplishments.
- Limit television viewing and encourage reading, writing, listening to story audiotapes, and other literacy activities in its place.

Many parents appreciate ideas on what books to read with their child. The teacher can compile a list of suggested readings—perhaps monthly for younger readers and quarterly for older ones—and post it, send it home, or print it in the class newsletter. Students can put together a list of class favorites and distribute it. Some public libraries have lists of children's choices, award-winners (e.g., Newbery, Caldecott), and books by topic or genre. Sometimes these lists are published in the form of bookmarks, a format that keeps the suggestions handy. Teachers can suggest resources such as *The Read-Aloud Handbook* (Trelease, 1995), and they can send home book order forms from the book clubs for students that many publishers have. In the last newsletter of the school year, teachers can include information about library summer story reading hours and related activities for children.

A backpack program developed by Richgels and Wold (1998) has shown success in building home-school literacy connections. In this program, the teacher selects three books of a single genre or type (e.g., alphabet books, fantasy, comedy, adventure) at three reading levels—independent, instructional, and challenging. The teacher also prepares supporting materials for the backpack—a letter to parents describing the program, a response journal, writing and drawing materials, hand puppets, and a materials checklist. The teacher explains to her students that they can decide which kind of reading they want to do at home with the backpack books—"read to me" (for challenging books), "read with me" (for in-between books), or "listen to me read" (for easy books). The backpacks are sent home overnight, so that each child has a turn to enjoy backpack home reading once every four to five weeks.

Within the classroom, parents as volunteers can be a valuable resource. Parents who are avid readers may enjoy reading aloud to the whole class, small groups of children, or individuals. They can also serve as listeners for students needing extra support as they read, such as beginning readers, second language learners, and students with special needs. When students do follow-up projects for the books they are reading (e.g., dramatic productions, art activities, writing), parent volunteers can help organize and monitor some of the groups as the teacher works with others.

For some parents, however, reading is a difficult activity. They may not be native speakers of English, or they may have had trouble learning when they were in school. Programs such as the Partnership for Family Reading (Handel, 1992, 1999) have shown good results in teaching parents to become stronger readers and supporters of literacy with their children. In this program, parents attend a series of workshops, each of which features a high quality children's book, a reading strategy (e.g., making predictions, generating questions, relating the reading to personal experience), practice using the strategy with a partner, group discussion, preparation for reading to children at home, and book borrowing. A program such as this can be a good foundation for strengthening the connections among the school, the home, and the community.

Whatever their level of involvement, parents should be praised for their efforts at helping their child by providing a supportive home environment. They should be encouraged to continue that support, even as the child gets older and more competent as a reader. Time spent in reading independently tends to drop off dramatically by fourth or fifth grade. Parents need to understand their role in encouraging lifelong reading habits in their children and helping develop positive attitudes about literacy.

References

Finn, J. D. (1998). Parental engagement that makes a difference. *The Reading Teacher, 55* (8), 20–24.

Handel, R. D. (1992). The partnership for family reading: Benefits for families and schools. *The Reading Teacher, 46,* 116–126.

Handel, R. D. (1999). *Building family literacy in an urban community.* New York: Teachers College Press.

Richgels, D. J., & Wold, L. S. (1998). Literacy on the road: Backpacking partnerships between school and home. *Reading Teacher, 52* (1), 18–29.

Trelease, J. (1995). *The read-aloud handbook, 4th ed.* New York: Penguin Books.

U. S. Dept. of Education. (1994). *Strong families, strong schools: Building community partnerships for learning.* Washington, DC: Author.

Troubleshooting: What About Struggling Readers?

Every teacher hopes for the ideal classroom where all students come to school well-prepared and eager to learn, where no student faces learning difficulties that cannot be overcome in the course of the school year. Unfortunately, few teachers will have this experience. In most every classroom, there will be one or more children who find learning to read difficult. Teachers of the readers' workshop will need to consider how best to work with these students.

Past Efforts at Helping Struggling Readers

At one time, teachers were expected to teach students with a wide range of reading abilities. With the advent of federal programs such as Title I of the Elementary and Secondary Education Act in 1965 and PL 94–142 of the Education of Handicapped Children Act in 1975, large numbers of special reading teachers began to be hired in elementary schools across the country. At that time, federal and state policy experts felt that hiring specialists would be more cost-effective than upgrading the skills of existing classroom teachers to deal with reading difficulties and federal mandates.

Although it was not necessarily the intent of this legislation, especially of Title I, to replace regular classroom instruction, the result was that many low-performing students completely moved out of the classroom for reading instruction. Critics pointed to the fragmentation of these students' educational experience, and large-scale studies of Title I showed little or no positive effects (Walmsley & Allington, 1995). Federal efforts are being made to redesign and improve the program, with a move away from supplementing classroom instruction and toward improving the ability of schools to serve struggling readers better. For special-education students, the trend has been toward "mainstreaming," moving students out of self-contained classes and resource rooms back into regular classrooms with special-education teachers coming with their students to support them and the classroom teacher.

Effective Practices in Working with Struggling Readers

Given that most teachers will find themselves with some students who have difficulty reading, what are effective ways of working with them? Not surprisingly, the structure of the readers' workshop, the teaching strategies, and the student-directed activities that are at the heart of literature-based instruction create ideal conditions for these students to learn. Struggling readers benefit from flexible grouping, where they are not relegated to the bottom group permanently. They benefit from strong cross-curricular connections, where what they learn during reading instruction is applied to other subjects like science and social studies. Author studies, genre studies, and thematic units help them see their reading experiences in a larger context.

Struggling readers need to know how to choose books for themselves. Bomer (1999) advocates working with students to help them identify a book that is comfortable for them to read independently, and then asking them to use it as a template for choosing similar books on their own. He also recommends coaching students in "read along" conferences during independent reading. In this type of conference, the teacher follows along while the student reads until the student gets stuck. The teacher then offers strategies, a few at a time, for decoding and making sense of the text.

Struggling readers also need opportunities to explore good literature, even if they can't read all the words independently. They benefit from hearing good stories read aloud, which "significantly improves children's vocabulary and reading comprehension, and results in greater complexity and sophistication of syntax in both oral and written language" (Meek, quoted in Sloan, 1991, p. 108). They benefit from paired reading and participation in literature discussion groups, where they can tackle harder material with support from their classmates. And most importantly, they benefit from solid instruction in small group reading lessons, where comprehension, interpretation, and personal connections are emphasized and decoding skills are taught in context.

Struggling readers need strategies to help them monitor their comprehension and to do something when they don't understand what they are reading. Cooper (1997) identifies "fix-up" strategies that good readers use: rereading, reading ahead, raising new questions, revising predictions, evaluating what is being read, and looking up words when the text doesn't make sense. He advocates teaching readers to "stop and think" periodically about whether or not they understand the text. If it doesn't make sense, readers need to apply some of the fix-up strategies listed above.

Equally important is what does not help struggling readers. They do not need to spend time learning skills in isolation, which they tend not to connect to real reading and generally fail to apply. They are hurt by being kept away from challenging, high-level reading discussions, which teachers may reserve for more able readers because they mistakenly believe that poor readers are also poor thinkers. They do not benefit from slower-paced instruction, which causes them to get even further behind. In fact, when instruction is paced too slow, many students lose interest in what is being taught (Cooper, 1997).

In addition, struggling readers are not helped when their reading materials, especially in the content areas, are so simplified that the students miss out on complex content and ideas. The lack of exposure to the content they are expected to know, just because they cannot read the information, widens the gap between these students and their classmates. Students can work with a partner or a group to understand a more challenging piece of reading, and they can get information from other media (e.g., audiotapes, videotapes, speakers, hands-on activities) to supplement their reading.

Beyond these basics, the key for helping struggling readers appears to be giving them more time in instruction with high expectations of success. Richard Allington has studied the problems of poor readers for over 25 years. He and his colleague Sean Walmsley state, "We have good evidence that children with low scores on readiness assessments can learn to read along with their peers, but only when provided substantially larger amounts of more intensive instructions than is normally available" (Allington & Walmsley, 1995, p. 6).

Consider a beginning reader who has difficulty decoding words. The teacher could set up a flexible skills group that included this child and others who would benefit from additional practice in decoding by analogy. The teacher might begin by asking the students to bring a book they are reading independently and point to some words that are hard for them to read. She would then choose some that fit commonly used patterns (see Decoding by Analogy, chapter 4) and teach those. Students would be asked to look for other words that fit these patterns as they continued reading independently, and to share their findings with the group the next time they met. The group could continue to meet for several sessions, with students taking on greater responsibility for using the decoding strategy on their own.

Another type of problem is the older student who is capable of reading but does not read fluently, dislikes reading, and rarely chooses to read. In this case, the teacher could enlist the help of the student's peers to choose him as a partner for paired reading and to help him find books he might enjoy reading. The teacher could use any information she has about this child's interests to recommend books to him (e.g., a beginning of year interest inventory, a letter from his parents describing home interests, topics he has written about in the writers' workshop). She should be sure he knows strategies for choosing books (e.g., look at the cover and read the blurb on the back of the book, read the first few paragraphs, ask friends for recommendations, ask the librarian for books about a topic you like, read more books by an author you like, read books that have won awards or have been chosen by other children as favorites). She could show him how to find books that are accompanied by a tape recording. In addition, the student may benefit from an individual or small group mini-lesson on avoiding unproductive reading habits (e.g., word-by-word reading, subvocalizing, using a pencil or finger to track reading unless the text is highly technical or you are looking for a particular fact).

Working with struggling readers is a challenge, but to see them achieve on a par with their peers is one of teaching's greatest rewards. The additional effort a teacher makes to reach these students can change their lives significantly. To be successful with struggling readers, teachers and schools need to change the conventional practices of the last 30 years that placed these students outside the classroom for instruction.

References

Allington, R. L. & Walmsley, S. A., Eds. (1995). *No quick fix: Rethinking literacy programs in America's elementary schools.* New York: Teachers College Press.

Bomer, R. (1999). Conferring with struggling readers: The test of our craft, courage, and hope. *New Advocate, 12* (1), 21-38.

Cooper, J. D. (1997). *Literacy: Helping children construct meaning.* Boston: Houghton Mifflin.

Sloan, G. D. (1991). *The child as critic: Teaching literature in elementary and middle schools, 3rd ed.* New York: Teachers College Press.

Walmsley, S. A., & Allington, R. L. (1995). Redefining and reforming instructional support programs for at-risk students. In R. L. Allington & S. A. Walmsley, (Eds.), *No quick fix: Rethinking literacy programs in America's elementary schools* (pp. 19–44). New York: Teachers College Press.

SECTION 11:

THE WRITERS' WORKSHOP

Chapter 6

OVERVIEW OF THE WRITERS' WORKSHOP

Writers' Workshop in Mrs. Sally O'Brien's Kindergarten Class

Sally O'Brien introduced the writers' workshop on the first day of school. To begin their first workshop, Mrs. O'Brien used a mini-lesson to share a story she wrote that told how she felt about coming to school that day, and she asked the students to respond to her story. Next she invited the children to write their own stories. Soon everyone was busy with paper, crayons, and pencils expressing themselves through pictures, letter-like marks, letters, and an occasional recognizable word. To begin other workshops throughout the year, Mrs. O'Brien's mini-lessons have focused on such areas as invented spelling, picture details, and publishing techniques. Often, at the end of the workshop, Mrs. O'Brien invites the children to share their stories from their special Author's Chair and their classmates listen and respond.

During the school year, Sally O'Brien has observed and assessed her students' growth as writers in a variety of ways. She has also helped them become aware of their own growth. Before the end of September, Mrs. O'Brien placed a "We Can Do" chart on the bulletin board. From time to time the class has talked about specific writing goals, often as a result of mini-lessons, and Mrs. O'Brien has added new goals to the chart. When students consistently meet a goal, they write their names on the chart beside that goal. Now, in May, most of the children plan, draft, edit, and publish their own stories. The process has become familiar and comfortable.

On this day, the children sit together on the floor. Their teacher reads the book, *It's My Birthday, Too!* (Jonell, 1999), and then asks the children to think how it is like some of the books they have written. The children know a great deal about authors, how they write and what they write, because they have examined and discussed a large number of picture books this year. They talk easily and relate their own family stories to the book during this mini-lesson.

Next Mrs. O'Brien takes a status of the class (see Figure 11.5). She speaks briefly to each child about what he or she will be doing before the children are dismissed to get their writing folders. Some children will begin new stories, some will continue with a story in progress, some will reread to check their work, and some will be publishing their pieces.

There is a buzz of activity as the children work—they all have an important message to communicate through writing. A developmental range is evident—a few children draw pictures and print random letters, a few children have several pages of traditionally spelled words—but most children use consonants correctly at the beginning and ending, and often in the middle, of words. Many are aware of vowels and experiment with their use.

Children confer with one another as they spontaneously read aloud, question, and provide assistance. They freely use the many resources available in their classroom. Word lists, which they have contributed to and have illustrated, hang from a chart stand. This "dictionary" is well used. They refer to print on wall posters, and books and materials in the library center.

While the children work, Mrs. O'Brien confers with them informally. She provides support for selecting new topics, asks what children plan to do next, and encourages their independence.

Children check their pieces against a chart before publishing.

Are you ready to publish?

   1. Name?

   2. Does it make sense?

   3. Good pictures?

   4. Title?

   5. Date?

This reminder gives children a purpose for rereading their work. One area in the classroom has a variety of materials useful for publishing so that children can select what they need independently.

Children share their publications with their classmates in different ways. There are individual and group authored books in the classroom library, bulletin board displays, and a special Author's Chair where students sit to read their published pieces. Today, as the class gathered together at the end of writers' workshop, Melissa sat in this chair to share "My Pet" (see Figure 6.1). Her classmates listened attentively to her soft but confident voice. After Melissa shared, Mrs. O'Brien said, "Children, let's tell Melissa what we thought about her story." Melissa smiled shyly in response to the students' enthusiastic comments.

Mrs. O'Brien plans to help Melissa try a variety of sentences in future pieces, and she will include Melissa in a small group mini-lesson on *-ing* endings. She also thinks the class could benefit from a lesson to discuss story titles.

Children's Book Cited

Jonell, L. (1999). *It's my birthday, too!* New York: G.P. Putnam's Sons.

FIGURE 6.1   KINDERGARTEN STUDENT'S WRITING PIECE

Writers' Workshop in Mr. Marcus Jamal's Second-Grade Class

Though most of his students began second grade with some writing experience, Marcus Jamal gave careful thought to launching the workshop. He wanted to establish classroom routines, focus on important strategies, and assess his students' facility with the writing process. Mr. Jamal began the first workshop by sharing a piece of his own writing. He talked about why he had decided to write about his daughter and asked his students to comment on his piece.

Mr. Jamal usually begins each workshop with a mini-lessons. Some deal with procedures, some with skills, others with author's craft. There have been lessons, for example, on ideas for publishing, revising procedures, topic selection, using punctuation, examining the writing techniques of published authors, and assessing writing. These lessons have been in direct response to the needs of the students as shown through their writing and their conversations about their writing, and to Mr. Jamal's own writing goals for second-grade children.

Mr. Jamal begins the writers' workshop with a large-group meeting. His mini-lesson invites the children to explore the leads in several familiar trade books, and they reflect upon the leads of their own stories. Mr. Jamal uses his Status of the Class form (see figure 11.5) to review what each child is working on, and to see who needs special help.

After the lesson, students leave the large group to collect their writing folders and begin their work. A few children begin new stories. They meet as a group to confer and plan. Other children work on drafts, composing and revising, a few are editing, some are working on final publications.

Two pairs of children have requested conferences and have gone to designated corners of the room to share their stories. Mr. Jamal consistently emphasizes the meaningfulness of conferring by asking, "What do you need help with?" "Did you have a helpful conference?" As the children work, Mr. Jamal confers with them briefly, modeling writing conversations. As he listens, reflects, and encourages, he often leaves Post-its with the children to remind them of their conversation ideas. He makes notes on his Status of the Class form using these anecdotal notes to evaluate his instruction and students' progress and to plan further instruction.

Students' writing folders (see Figure 7.1) contain a form entitled "Things I Can Do When I Write" on which they list their personal goals. Some of these are class goals such as "I choose topics I know a lot about" and "I check for capitals and periods." Other goals are personal, such as "I tell my story to someone before I write" and "I use paragraphs to organize my stories." Another form is stapled into the writing folders on which the children list the titles of their published stories. For example, Kevin's form shows that he has published five personal pieces this year.

Mr. Jamal has designated a time later in the day when children share their writing. Students write their names on a list at the front of the room to indicate they would like to share. Three children's names are listed today. One is a finished publication, two are pieces-in-progress. James' name is one of those listed. He plans to share "My Brother, The Pig" (see Figure 6.2).

FIGURE 6.2   SECOND-GRADE STUDENT'S WRITING PIECE

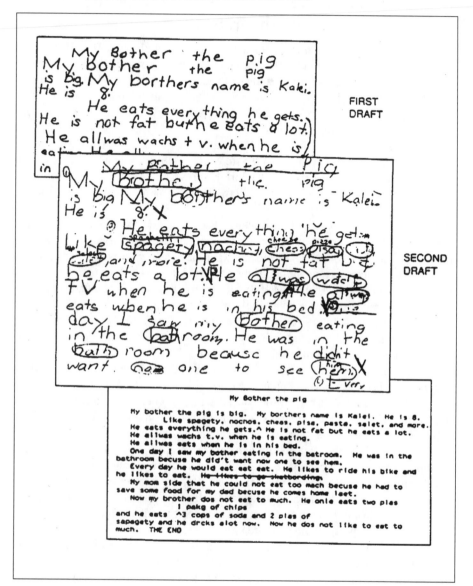

Writers' Workshop in Ms. Brenda DeRego's Fourth-Grade Class

Mrs. DeRego and her class participate in a regular writer's workshop. Throughout the year they have worked to identify writing topics that are meaningful and special to them. Mrs. DeRego's questions to students have been, "Why is that so important to you?" "What is the main thing you want people to know about your grandmother?" A look at the students' publications in the classroom library reveals their personal involvement and concern for audience.

During the second semester, the class engaged in a theme study focused on preservation of the environment. As a part of the study each student chose a topic to research. Mrs. DeRego expected the students to report their research in some written form. She helped them build upon the connections between report writing and the familiar process of their personal writing.

Mrs. DeRego often spoke of the students "becoming experts" on their topics in the same way they were experts on their personal experiences. They began with a K-W-L form (see figure 4.14) on which they listed what they already knew about their topics and what they wanted to find out. Students read, used their K-W-L form to make notes of interesting information they had learned, conferred with one another, asked more questions, and repeated the cycle in their goal to become experts.

Their talk greatly enhanced this stage of the process. During a variety of groupings— large group, small groups, interest groups, informal conversations—the children shared the interesting information they found. Their talk helped to clarify their thinking, allowed for sharing of their developing strategies and skills, and further strengthened the classroom community of learners.

A variety of resources helped students answer their questions and gain additional information. Mrs. DeRego's mini-lessons on notetaking supported their work. When the children felt they were "full" of information, they began a draft of their reports. Mrs. DeRego guided the students through several mini-lessons to think of how they could organize their information. Some children liked using a category chart to organize the information they found. On their charts they organized their information into categories such as animal's description, family life and reproduction, home/habitat, food and eating habits, interesting facts. They found their charts provided them with logical support for paragraphing their reports.

Children shared their report drafts during large group and peer conferences. They received feedback about what their classmates were learning and what was most interesting about their pieces. The children worked to add facts, and to present their information in ways that would appeal to their audience. After revising, the children checked their own pieces for mechanics, had an editing conference with a classmate, then signed up for an editing conference with their teacher. The children chose a variety of ways to make their information public.

Paul decided to study an endangered animal, the wolf. He wrote his report from the perspective of a wildlife biologist which added further interest to his piece (see figure 6.3). Today, Paul shared his completed report with his classmates. He told them that his next piece of writing will be a poem about wolves.

FIGURE 6.3   FOURTH-GRADE STUDENT'S WRITING PIECE

Paul B.
5-18

I Speak For The Wolves

"Hey, hold it. What are you shooting at?" "I'm shooting at that damn wolf who stole one of my favorite chickens," screamed the angry farmer in disgust. "Well, you had better listen up because I'm David the worlds most famous, smartest, and best wild life biologist and I speak for the wolves because I can understand what they say. People think of wolves as "big bad wolves." Well, I have news for you and those people, they absolutely never ever kill a human unless there are hunted or cornered. They are at risk all over North America, Russia, and Central Asia. Now they are extinct over most of Western Europe, although still found in some Eastern European countries.

It's habitat is mostly mountains and open country. They eat mostly large animals like reindeer, moose, and caribou. Wolves produce or give birth to about 5-9 cubs born 7 weeks after mating, usually spring. The young cubs are sexually mature at 18 months old.

Wolves usually hunt at night, they may have formed this habit to avoid man. The Tasmanian wolf already has become extinct. They are not part of the wolf family, they are part of the pouched family called marsupials. Wolves may become extinct UNLESS people start putting wolves into game reserves and learn that they only attach the sick. They don't attack sheep or cattle or even humans or whatever people say they do. It is more of a possibility that a bear or cougar would attack sheep or cattle and humans than a wolf.

This country's population is finally learning something the Indians and Eskimos have known all along: when wolves prey upon larger game they actually improve the herds. Many people do not know hat wolves will acually hunt for mice and small rodents as well as for big game animals. Wolves are larger and more powerful than a german Shepard witch it resembles. "Oh, and for your information that wolf over there is not the one who took your chicken it's that coyote over there at the edge of the feild that did it." "Oh, thank you" said the stunned, shocked, and impressed farmer.

The Impact of Donald Graves:
The Process Approach to Writing

It was the first day of kindergarten. Tandy picked up her pencil and began to write in her own way, by drawing a picture of her family. Her teacher came by to offer encouragement and to help Tandy write an *M* for *mommy*. In the past, most teachers did not believe that kindergartners and first graders could compose. Today, educators know that young children can express their ideas in writing when they are given daily experiences with the writers' workshop and the process approach to writing.

In 1983, Donald Graves published *Writing: Teachers & Children At Work,* a book that became the standard reference for teachers interested in the process approach to writing. This groundbreaking book opened teachers' eyes to the fact that even kindergarten children could be authors, selecting topics and composing their own texts. Graves' ideas inspired teachers to create writers' workshops in their classrooms, providing students with the opportunity to engage in the full process of writing. The terms often used to describe the writing process are planning (including topic selection and rehearsal), composing or drafting, revising or rewriting, editing, and publishing. Instruction focuses on teaching students to move pieces of writing through this process, although this movement is not a straightforward one. For example, a writer might abandon a piece during drafting, or put a piece aside for a while before deciding to revise it. Students learn traditional skills (such as grammar, spelling, and punctuation) as part of editing their writing to make it understandable to others, but these skills are no longer seen as the core of writing instruction. Teachers attend first to the message students are trying to communicate, then later address the surface features such as spelling.

Raising Expectations

In *A Fresh Look at Writing*, Graves (1994) notes several shifts in his thinking. He describes his present approach as more assertive, because he believes that more is now known about when teachers can step in and teach. Mini-lessons, focused on issues evident in children's writing, play a central role in teaching. Graves suggests that teachers need to raise their expectations for students and teach more about writing at every grade level. For example, he recommends that more attention be given to the teaching of spelling in first grade, because his observations show that children need and can make use of that knowledge. The idea of high expectations extends to having students expect more of themselves.

Graves (1994) describes why he added the word *nudge* to his vocabulary as a teacher of writing. A nudge is a "slight push in the right direction" that prevents students from stalling and failing to improve as writers (p. 93). Nudges might include having a student describe a character in more detail or substitute verbs that describe action more precisely. When giving a nudge, the teacher does not dictate changes to the student but suggests that he or she experiment with the suggested approach. Graves carries "nudge paper" around. A sheet of nudge paper, which can hold 5 to 10 minutes of writing, is handed out when it seems the nudge has been effective and the student is ready to experiment.

Conditions for Learning

Graves places less emphasis on methods of teaching than on conditions for learning. Time is a first condition. Unfortunately, the trend is toward fragmenting the school day into smaller and smaller bits of time (Graves, 1999). Rather than jumping from one thing to another, Graves argues for solid blocks of time when students can become totally absorbed in learning. Students should write a minimum of four times a week, for at least 35 to 40 minutes, beginning in first grade. Daily writing puts students in what Graves (1994, p. 107) describes as a "constant state of composition" in which they are alert to moments in their lives that can feed their writing. Choice, another essential condition, can be challenging for students, particularly those unaccustomed to selecting their own topics. But choosing a topic is made easier if students write every day and have the time to think about possible topics. Graves puts limits on the concept of choice. Students should choose their own topics, but they must produce. If students are in a rut or making bad choices, topic assignments may be helpful or even necessary.

Demonstrations are another condition for learning. Graves points out that students have few opportunities to see adults write. Teachers can make aspects of the writing process clear to students through demonstrations using their own writing. For example, the teacher can put a draft of her writing on an overhead transparency and demonstrate revision, showing how she uses carets to add words and circles and arrows to move a sentence to another spot.

The writing classroom provides students with a highly structured, predictable environment. Besides knowing they will write everyday, students learn basic procedures to follow at writing time, such as going to a corner of the room for a peer conference, as well as methods for dealing with difficulties, such as checking the word wall when unsure of how to spell a word (see Decoding By Analogy, chapter 4). The teacher contributes to the orderliness of the environment by walking among students to hold brief conferences and monitor the room. When problems arise (such as the noise level being too high), the teacher engages students in discussion to solve the problem.

Graves (1994) stresses the importance of teachers leading students toward independence in writing. Children should be taught to read their own work, so they learn to see for themselves what needs improving. Teachers seek to shift responsibility for writing where it belongs—with the students themselves. The gradual release of responsibility, consistent with Vygotsky's thinking (see chapter 1), is a recurring theme in Graves' writing. He recommends that teachers try to understand the processes students use as they think, learn, and write. As teachers develop this understanding, they help students gain an awareness of their mental processes. With encouragement, students can take control of their own learning. Then improvement in writing becomes less a matter of teachers pushing students and more a matter of students moving themselves forward, because they know where they want to go.

Teachers as Learners

To teach writing effectively, Graves (1994) suggests, teachers begin by putting themselves in the position of learners. In particular, they are learning about their students as people. This can be accomplished by listening closely to what students say, by trying to see the world through their eyes, and by accompanying them on walks through their neighborhoods. Students soon reveal themselves as multidimensional and knowledgeable of topics with which the teacher may be unfamiliar.

> Jon read his draft about bows and arrows to his fourth-grade class and when he finished, several of his classmates made comments and asked him questions. His teacher raised her hand and he called on her.

She asked, "Does a forty-pound bow weigh forty pounds?"

"No," answered Jon. "It takes forty pounds to pull it back. Mine's backstrung. Do you know what that means?"

"No," confessed Ms. Kinzie.

"A backstrung bow has more power. A ten-pound backstrung bow has twenty pounds of power." (Hansen & Graves, 1986, p. 807)

In this example, the teacher was comfortable with the fact that Jon knew more about bows than she did. She encouraged him to show his expertise and to teach others through his writing and oral responses. Students, like adults, will write well and at length when they care about the topic and know a great deal about it.

Teachers face the challenge of helping students to see that they have knowledge and experiences worth writing about. Often, students believe that good writing comes only from exciting or unusual events. As Graves (1994) notes, "Writing comes from the events of our daily lives, from what appears at first glance to be trivial" (p. 36). Teachers can help students to become aware of how writing can and should grow from their everyday experiences. Graves points out that this can be accomplished through mini-lessons. For example, in one mini-lesson the teacher might show students how she has written a piece based on an everyday experience. In another mini-lesson, the teacher might show how fiction can grow from everyday situations familiar to students, such as conflicts between siblings.

When students feel confident in writing about a topic, their voice comes through in their writing. Graves (1994) writes,

Voice is the imprint of ourselves on our writing. It is that part of the self that pushes the writing ahead, the dynamo in the process. Take the voice away and the writing collapses of its own weight. There is no writing, just word following word. Voiceless writing is addressed "to whom it may concern." The voice shows how I choose information, organize it, select the words, all in relation to what I want to say and how I want to say it. The reader says, "Someone is here. I know that person. I've been there, too." (p. 81)

Through the work of Graves and other advocates of the process approach to writing, teachers have come to recognize the importance of concepts such as voice and audience for even the youngest writers. These concepts do not remain mysterious but become understandable to students through teachers' demonstrations. For example, to communicate the concept of voice, the teacher can show students two pieces, one written with voice and the other without, and have students discuss the differences between the two.

In the process approach, teachers show respect for students' ideas and writing. However, as Graves points out, they also do a great deal of teaching, often through demonstrations, to provide students with knowledge, strategies, and skills. With consistent nudging, they see that students make steady progress toward becoming effective writers.

References

Graves, D. (1983). *Writing: Teachers and children at work.* Exter, NH: Heinemann.

Graves, D. (1994). *A fresh look at writing.* Portsmouth, NH: Heinemann.

Graves, D. (1999). *Bring life into learning: Create a lasting literacy.* Portsmouth, NH: Heinemann.

Hansen, J., & Graves, D. (1986). Do you know what backstrung means? *The Reading Teacher, 39* (8), 807–812.

Chapter 7

STRUCTURING THE WRITERS' WORKSHOP

Setting Up Your Classroom

Writing, by its nature, is a "messy" task. A well organized, predictable workshop environment can heighten a writer's productivity. As writers ponder, seek feedback from peers, shuffle and reshuffle text, it is important that they know where to go for ideas and how to gain support from colleagues, and that they have the necessary tools at their fingertips.

Background

Before a teacher ever meets her students, she must organize herself and the classroom environment. A teacher's beliefs about writing will determine the classroom's emotional and physical climate. Regie Routman (2000) notes that a teacher's beliefs are greatly influenced by her own literacy practices. She suggests that teachers explore their own personal practices by listing what they do as writers, and then consider how these practices affect their teaching. When doing so, teachers should consider, "If this is what I do as a writer, what does that mean for the students in my classroom? Am I providing them authentic opportunities to use writing?" Teachers should be able to articulate their beliefs and explain how these beliefs support their classroom practices.

Routman (2000) suggests this list of practices which can guide the way we structure and arrange our classrooms for writers' workshop:

- Establish a safe, caring, well-organized, risk-taking, collaborative classroom
- Demonstrate writing
- Promote writing across the curriculum
- Discuss outstanding literature in many forms and genres
- Use a variety of resources, for example, books, technology, peers, librarians
- Provide useful feedback, response, and evaluation
- Provide opportunities for oral, written, and artistic responses
- Share, celebrate, and publish meaningful work
- Guide and support students in becoming independent, joyful, lifelong learners (p. 25–26)

Procedure

Practices such as those suggested by Routman suggest an environment that is meaningful, collaborative, and interactive. They imply that students feel ownership for their learning.

Teachers, therefore, will want to organize their classrooms so that children can move around easily and talk with one another as they go about their writing (see Figure 3.1). Teachers usually cluster student desks to form groups of four or five. Some teachers, especially those with large numbers of students, may designate areas along the classroom edges where students can engage in peer conferences without disturbing others. A place where students can comfortably come together as a whole group is very important. An area rug may signal the spot where children will gather in a circle at the beginning and often at the end of writers' workshop. A special chair (see Author's Chair, chapter 9) is included from which student authors share their writing with classmates.

Some teachers set aside a special area where students can edit their work. This might be two or three desks placed together or a small table with helpful references nearby. Teachers may arrange a place where students can publish their final pieces of writing. They will take care to select and organize the publishing materials so that students can work with little adult guidance or supervision. Children's access to computers allows additional opportunities to edit and to publish.

Teachers also plan ways for students to share their writing throughout the classroom. Bulletin boards and displays of many kinds highlight students' meaningful writing pieces. Student publications are placed alongside commercially published books in the classroom library. Students' written messages, observational notes, and letters are prominent and testify to their use of writing for genuine purposes. Kindergarten teachers provide paper and pencils for many purposes such as making grocery lists in the housekeeping center and for labeling creations and making signs near the building blocks.

Throughout the school year, teachers conduct mini-lessons to help students learn to work within the environment they have set up. One of the first lessons may be to set the tone for a calm, purposeful workshop by showing children how they will be expected to leave their desks, perhaps one cluster at a time after pushing in their chairs, to sit quietly on the carpet. Other lessons will deal with routines such as the use of writing folders and other materials (see Materials in this chapter), getting ideas for writing, responding to teacher conferences, seeking peer assistance, sharing, and responding to one another's writing.

It is important that students become comfortable with the physical arrangement of their classroom and with the patterns for operating within it. Having a familiar, predictable environment provides support for their exploration of the new and unpredictable waiting to be discovered within their writing experiences.

Reference

Routman, R. (2000). *Conversations: Strategies for teaching, learning, and evaluating.* Portsmouth, NH: Heinemann.

Materials

Having the right materials at hand is important to all writers. Special materials can generate inspiration. When teachers set up their writers' workshops they try to assure that supplies are varied, in abundance, and accessible to all students.

Background

In *How Writers Write* (Lloyd, 1987) authors of children's books speak of their work as writers. They emphasize how important it is for them to have specific materials. Beverly Cleary prefers a certain kind of ballpoint pen and yellow legal pads. Lloyd Alexander feels more connected to his words when using a typewriter than he does with a word processor. Jack Prelutsky has a pen and pad of paper that he can use underwater because he often gets ideas while in the bath.

Procedure

A good way for teachers to decide what materials their students may need is to think through the experiences offered during writers' workshop. Such reflection will help them generate a list of supplies needed to carry out the workshop. Teachers can then determine how items will be acquired. They will likely place orders for some classroom materials, others will be brought in by students, some will be on hand, and some may be items that are recycled or "give-aways."

To start with, paper and pencils are key tools. For kindergarteners large pieces of plain paper are appropriate. Children can take their paper to the floor to write with large pencils or markers. First-grade children usually begin the year with plain paper or with paper that is lined at the bottom and plain at the top to accommodate their writing and drawing. As first graders rely less on drawing, teachers may offer them small books made by stapling several lined sheets of paper between construction paper covers.

As children mature some teachers prefer that they use composition tablets or spiral notebooks; others prefer loose paper. Teachers of older children may designate one color of writing paper for drafts and another color for final pieces. Special types of paper often inspire students. Teachers can make available books of different sizes from very small to large, paper from adding machine rolls, computer paper, index cards, etc. Recycled paper with one blank side is great for students' drafts. Often businesses are willing to save their used paper which sometimes comes in interesting sizes and textures.

Standard pencils work well on any paper, but having a variety of implements adds interest. Colored pencils, markers of differing sizes, ballpoint pens, even crayons and paints can be just right for some children.

As students revise their writing, they will find certain materials helpful. Young children can add to their stories by taping another sheet of paper to the end. Or, they may want to staple on a "spider leg" by cutting a strip of paper to add information missing from the middle of a story. Of course, a staple remover is handy when they change their minds.

When editing their stories, students will need dictionaries and word lists at the appropriate levels of difficulty, and some students may have access to a computer's speller. Grammar and punctuation books are often useful resources for older students. Lists telling what to look for when editing are good reminders to students. For younger children, a posted list may ask that they edit for their name, date, and story title. When students gain more skills, a list, either general or specific to each individual, can go into their writing folders to check against when editing.

Students need folders to accommodate their writing. Many teachers have students keep two folders, one a working folder (see Figure 7.1–7.4) and another for storing completed works. If young children use large-sized paper, they will need large folders as well. Bankers boxes or specially designed wire holders provide good storage for students' folders at the end of writers' workshop. Evaluation portfolios (see Setting Up a Portfolio System, chapter 11) are a special kind of folder and teachers need to consider what form they take. Some teachers use regular file folders, some use notebook binders, some like students to design their own.

FIGURE 7.1 CONTENTS OF A WRITING FOLDER

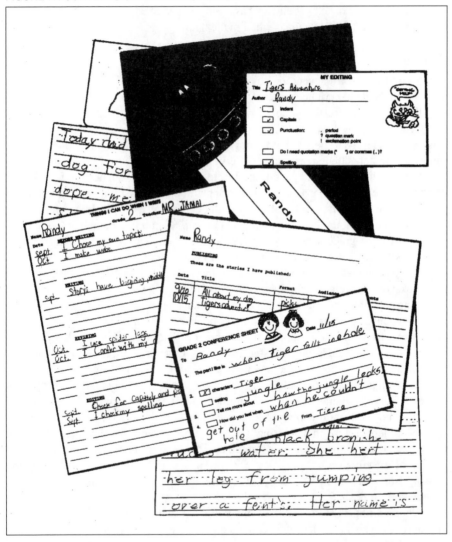

FIGURE 7.2   FORM FOR STUDENTS TO LIST PERSONAL WRITING SKILLS

THINGS I CAN DO WHEN I WRITE

Name_____ Grade_____ Teacher_____

Date   BEFORE WRITING

_____   _____

_____   _____

_____   _____

_____   _____

_____   _____

WRITING

_____   _____

_____   _____

_____   _____

_____   _____

RIVISING

_____   _____

_____   _____

_____   _____

_____   _____

EDITING

_____   _____

_____   _____

_____   _____

_____   _____

_____   _____

FIGURE 7.3   FORM FOR STUDENTS TO LIST PUBLISHED STORIES

Name _____

Publishing
These are the stories I have published:

Date	Title	Format	Audience	Comments

FIGURE 7.4   FORMS FOR STUDENT CONFERENCES AND EDITING

GRADE 2 CONFERENCE SHEET

To _____   Date _____

1.   The part I like is _____

      _____

2.   ☐ characters _____

      ☐ setting _____

3.   ☐ Tell me more about _____

4.   ☐ How did you feel when_____

                              From _____

MY EDITING

Title _____

Author _____

☐   Capitals

☐   Punctuation: . period
                      ? question mark
                      ! exclamation point

☐   Do I need quotation marks ("   ") or commas (,)?

☐   Spelling

Students enjoy publishing their stories in different formats throughout the year. A first publication may be the child's final draft stapled into a construction paper cover or a story neatly printed on paper with a special border. As the school year continues students will like to publish books that are cut into different shapes, folded accordion style, or with pop-up features. They will find it interesting to use a variety of art media to illustrate their books such as crayons, markers, watercolors, poster paints, and "findings" to create collages. Wallpaper samples can be glued over cardboard to make attractive book covers. Paper is placed between and the spine is stitched with dental floss. Students find that special title and dedication pages add a professional touch to their publications.

Other materials contribute to an effective writers' workshop. Rubber stamps and pads allow students to date their writing and mark it "unedited," "revised," or "draft." An overhead projector, transparencies, and markers aid mini-lesson presentations. Computer word processing programs, discs, and printer helps ease the publishing of student writing as does access to a photocopier.

In setting up their classrooms, teachers consider how materials can best be organized to promote student independence, thoughtfulness, and productivity. Open, labeled shelves may house writing materials so that children can access them easily. Teachers usually plan mini-lessons early in the year to focus on managing materials. Young children need to learn how to use the stapler and staple puller. Older students can more easily spot their writing folders in the storage box when each is unique in color or design. If general-use materials are located in various places throughout the room, congestion is eased as students move around to get the supplies they need.

It is a good idea to prepare forms needed for writers' workshop prior to the start of the school year. Frequently forms are used for status of the class, peer conferences, editing reminders, to list possible topics, and the titles of stories students' have published.

Reference

Lloyd, P. (1987). *How writers write.* Portsmouth, NH: Heinemann.

Scheduling

Many teachers emphasize that time is one of the most important elements in an effective writers' workshop. Donald Graves (1991) and others emphasize that predictable, abundant time is essential if students are to become intensely absorbed in their writing. Teachers will need to examine their schedules and the demands placed upon their instructional time. They may need to do some "creative juggling" in order to present their students with the "luxury" of time to write.

Background

Lucy Calkins (1991) discusses the reasons that predictable, abundant time is so important to young writers. First, if students know that they will be writing tomorrow morning, they can anticipate and plan while they are away from their desks. These students often speak of their experiences: "Last night when me and my family had a flat tire, I thought that would be a good thing to write about today." Students also begin making plans for themselves such as arranging for peer conferences or jotting down notes that they can develop later. Second, Calkins emphasizes that students must have long blocks of time in order to develop and expand their ideas, draft, revise, share—to become completely absorbed with a piece of writing. This need is often contrary to the pace running through many schools due to mounting demands that leave the curriculum fragmented and make interruptions the norm.

Procedure

The ideal classroom schedule would include an hour-long writers' workshop every day. Many teachers have been able to manage this by thinking more broadly about the curriculum. They know that the writers' workshop encompasses all the language arts so they may find ways to incorporate their curriculum requirements within it. For example, instead of teaching grammar and punctuation as separate subjects, they note the skills their students are to acquire and present them as mini-lessons. Then they support their students' use of those skills as they write. Some teachers bring theme or content unit study into the workshop by taking a month or two during the year when children may write about related topics. This writing often takes the form of research report writing for older students (see Writing Aross the Curriculum, chapter 7, and Classroom Description, chapter 6). In some classrooms the workshop time is segmented. For exmple, teachers may include the mini-lesson and time for students to work on writing in one block; sharing takes place at another time later in the day.

There will be teachers who will find it impossible to accommodate the ideal schedule: kindergarten teachers whose students attend school half day, upper-grade teachers with 45 minute time blocks, teachers who feel that other obligations must be met. They will want to consider how sustained writing time can be allocated for shorter blocks of time. They may plan a workshop which meets three days a week for half a year, or daily for a few months. Fewer, concentrated workshops are of more benefit to students than experiencing writing only once or twice a week (see Figures 3.2, 3.3, and and 3.4 for examples of classroom schedules).

References

Calkins, L. (1991). *The art of teaching writing*. Portsmouth, NH: Heinemann.

Graves, D. (1991). *Build a literate classroom*. Portsmouth, NH: Heinemann.

Grouping

During writers' workshop it is frequently efficient and productive for students to work together in flexible groups. Flexible groups are in contrast to whole-class and individual writing activities. The groups may be made up of two, three, or more students who meet just once or they might come together over the course of several writers' workshops. The purpose of the groups is to accommodate students who share specific interests, concerns or instructional needs and may or may not include the teacher.

Background

J. David Cooper (1997) discusses several types of flexible groups that are appropriate to the writers' workshop. He notes that there is overlap among the groups. *Interest groups* bring together students with similar interests to work collaboratively or to share writing—for example, a few students who have chosen to write about their pets. *Strengths and needs groups* may benefit from a teacher's mini-lesson, or students of similar strength may work together to complete a specific task such as editing. *Mini-lesson groups* are not always based upon specific needs. They may be formed because the teacher wants to introduce the children to something new or to review a previous lesson such as use of adjectives in descriptive writing. *Discussion groups* might meet so that students can present and discuss writing in process. *Project groups* give students, often of differing abilities, an opportunity to contribute to one product—for example, a display highlighting their research on dinosaurs.

Donald Graves (1991) notes the benefit of flexible groups for the presentation of mini-lessons and suggests that the instructional focus of the small-group lessons be determined by either teachers' observations or by students' requests. He also suggests that some students be required to attend the sessions, while other students may choose to participate.

Procedure

As noted above, the topic of any whole class mini-lesson can be the focus of a flexible group lesson. After a skill has been introduced and reviewed within the large group and students have had opportunities to practice the skill in their own writing, teachers will observe a time when most students can independently apply the concept. Yet, there may be a few students not using the skill who could benefit from additional support. For example, first-grade teacher Sally O'Brien noted that a few of her students ignored the convention of spacing between words. They ran most of their inventively spelled words together. Lack of spacing became a problem when these student authors tried to reread the pieces they had composed. Mrs. O'Brien found it more efficient to work on spacing with these children in a small group rather than instruct each child individually.

A third grade teacher, when reviewing her students' writing folders, may discover that a few of them could benefit from a mini-lesson on the mechanics of dialogue and decide to form a group based upon this need. She might begin the next workshop by saying,

> Today, during writers' workshop, I will meet with a small group to work on
> using quotation marks. We will get together at 9:00. On the board I have
> written the names of those I want to attend. If your name isn't there, and you
> feel you could use some help, you may add your name to the list.

Students may initiate help from their teacher. For example, while conferring two fourth-grade students found they were unhappy with the characters in their fiction pieces. They were interested in learning techniques to make their characters appear more real. What could they do? They went to their teacher, Ms. DeRego, for instructional guidance. She pointed out that a few other students were also writing fiction pieces and suggested that she offer a mini-lesson the next day for the two students and any others who wished to attend. Then she encouraged these students to meet on their own during subsequent workshops to discuss their progress.

Some teachers record their mini-lessons in a notebook (see Mini-lessons, chapter 8). They find it helpful to indicate which students have participated in the flexible group sessions along with comments about the students' understanding of the skill. This reference serves teachers as they assess students' development as writers and aids in their planning of further instruction.

Flexible small groups provide teachers with an efficient, effective means of instruction and give students a way to learn from one another. Their structure allows students the opportunity to form communities of learners to support and remind one another as they practice the focus of lessons. These groups are another way to assist students as they grow and develop as writers.

References

Cooper, J. (1997). *Literacy: Helping children construct meaning.* Boston: Houghton Mifflin Company.

Graves, D. (1991). *Build a literate classroom.* Portsmouth, NH: Heinemann.

Selecting Literature

Good literature is as important to a strong writers' workshop as it is to a readers' workshop. As children enjoy and explore the imaginative, artistically created books of professional writers their appreciation of literature grows. When children value and take ownership of fine literature, those works can serve to arouse and nurture their own writing development.

Background

Shelley Harwayne (1992) notes that she and her colleagues continually explore the question, "How does the literature we read inform the literature we write?" (p. 2) She offers some of their responses:

- Sharing literature can help establish a supportive classroom community. Books whose themes involve respect and caring for one another, listening to one another, and celebrating one another's differences are certain to raise issues about cooperation and getting along together. These elements are necessary in a writers' workshop where respect for one another's efforts and response to other's work is essential.

- Sharing literature can cultivate a delight in language. Books with rich language, new and interesting words, playful language, and precise words provide stimulus for writers as they shape and revise their texts.

- Listening to literature that is read, recited, and performed well helps children develop a keen and critical ear for language. As students are given many, diverse listening opportunities they become better able to listen to their own writing so that their ears are part of the revision process.

- When children become familiar with a wide variety of literature they are able to make numerous connections to their own lives. They see possibilities within their own experiences and interests for topics they, too, might develop as writers.

Procedures

Teachers need to become familiar with a large body of children's literature appropriate to the age level and interests of their students. They will want to carefully select good literature that is well suited to the particular goals and purposes they have in mind.

Teachers find that reading aloud every day with their students builds the foundation for a cohesive literary community within their classrooms. When children have shared literary experiences they can express their thoughts and feelings as "insiders" who speak a common language. For example, on the first day of school, to deal with her first graders' beginning-of-the-year jitters, one teacher shared Denys Cazet's (1990) *Never Spit on Your Shoes*. Thereafter, when students found an activity a little long or tedious a young voice frequently spoke up to quote a line from the story: "Is it time for lunch yet?" "Thanks for inviting me, but I really must be going home now." The class would chuckle, then move on with the task at hand. Other books to nurture a classroom community might highlight cooperation such as Lisa Campbell Ernst's *Zinnia and Dot* (1992) and Laura Rader's *The Turnip* (1996).

Appreciating the differences among people is the focus of Barbara Corcoran's *The Potato Kid* (1989), Ingrid Slyder's *The Fabulous Flying Fandinis* (1996), and Mary

Hoffman's *Amazing Grace* (1991). Diane Stanley's *The Conversation Club* (1990) emphasizes the importance of attending to what others say. Teachers will discover other appropriate titles as they browse in libraries and bookstores and talk with colleagues. Guides to children's literature list books of these kinds under headings such as "human relationships," "friendship," and "social issues."

As teachers and students share literature, they delight in the expressive language they encounter. Children come to realize what an important tool words are for writers. Teachers of very young children know the pleasure their students take in reciting phrases like "Fee, fi, fo, fum, I smell the blood of an Englishman" and "trip trap, trip trap, over the rickety, rackety bridge." Older students are intrigued with the nuances of related words such as glance, stare, glimpse, sight, spy, gaze, gape, and ogle. Katie Wood Ray (1999) suggests that teachers carefully select literature through which students can study the craft techniques employed by familiar authors (see Author Study in this chapter). She suggests that through guided study and reflection, students will come to understand that authors deliberately choose words and arrange them carefully to produced a desired effect such as, "Stir it. Stick it. Dig it. Dance it. Gooey, gloppy, mucky, magnificent mud" (Rey, 1996).

Some authors create a rhythm through their patterning of sentences as Mem Fox (1997) did when she wrote: "Joys are the same, and love is the same. Pain is the same, and blood is the same. Smiles are the same, and hearts are just the same." Often teachers create class lists and encourage students to create personal lists of "sparkling jewels" (see Author Study, this chapter and Vocabulary Development, chapter 4) to serve as resources for their writing. In some classrooms distinctive names are given to authors' techniques as they are studied (e.g., Same-sound Starts, See Saw sentences). As each technique is studied it is listed on a chart along with an example, and the chart is posted for reference during the writers' workshop.

Children are most attentive to literature that is read, recited, and performed well. Teachers can learn to share literature interestingly and effectively by attending to and emulating the techniques of those they admire. They may want to talk with their students about people they know who read aloud well, consider what those people do, and practice the techniques they note. Children will also benefit by hearing literature presented by good storytellers and recorded by professionals on audio tapes. Children's experiences in listening to literature will have application within the writers' workshop when they listen to their classmates' writing as well as to their own words. Their listening experiences will guide students to present their own pieces in appealing and unique ways to capture the attention of their audience.

Literature can give students ideas for topics. To encourage children to make connections, teachers often ask questions like, "Where do you think the author got his idea for this book?" or initiate discussions about the author's dedication or remarks the author shares about writing a book. Resulting conversations may prompt children to recall events or interests in their lives that could become topics for stories. Over time, children will discover that most stories involve lived-through experiences common to many people; it is the author's perceptions and expression of those experiences that create a unique story.

References

Harwayne, S. (1992). *Lasting impressions: Weaving literature into the writing workshop.* Portsmouth, NH: Heinemann.

Ray, K. W. (1999). *Wondrous words*. Urbana, IL: National Council of Teachers of English.

Children's Books Cited

Cazet, D. (1990). *Never spit on your shoes*. NY: Orchard Books.
Corcoran, B. (1989). *The potato kid*. NY: Atheneum.
Ernst, L. C. (1992). *Zinnia and Dot*. Bergenfield, NJ: Viking.
Fox, M. (1997). *Whoever you are*. Ill. by L. Staub. San Diego: Harcourt Brace.
Hoffman, M. (1991). *Amazing Grace*. Bergenfield, NJ: Dial Books.
Rader, L. illus. (1996). *The turnip*. Bergenfield, NJ: Viking.
Rey, M. L. (1996). *Mud*. San Diego, CA: Harcourt Brace and Company.
Slyder, I. (1996). *The fabulous flying Fandinis*. Bergenfield, NJ: Cobblehill.
Stanley, D. (1990). *The conversation club*. NY: Aladdin.

FIGURE 7.5   STUDENT'S STORY DEDICATION

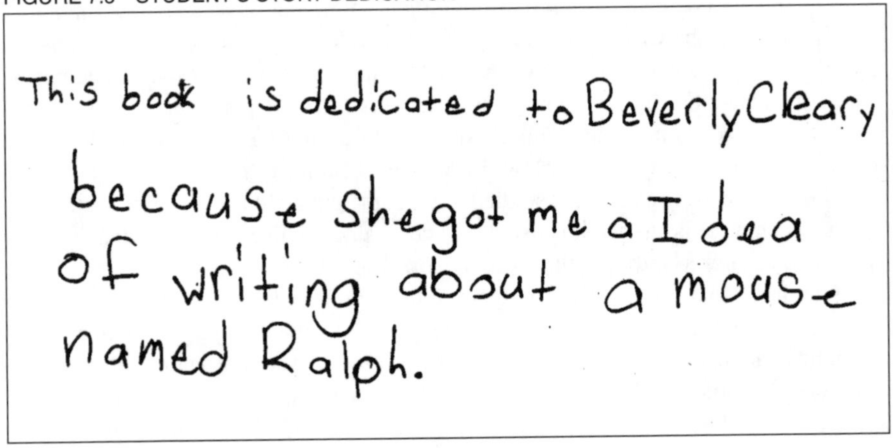

This book is dedicated to Beverly Cleary because she got me a I dea of writing about a mouse named Ralph.

Author Study

The best way for students to learn the craft of writing is to deliberately apprentice themselves to authors whose work they admire. Students who "read like writers" (Smith, 1988) notice the way things are written and reflect upon the author's style or technique. When students attend to the techniques of other writers, and borrow from the styles of authors they admire, their learning increases and their individual expression is enhanced.

Background

In *Wondrous Words,* Katie Wood Ray (1999) describes how teachers can help students more deliberately examine particular ways in which authors practice their craft. Ray suggests that initially teachers work with the class as a whole, guiding them to explore pieces of literature; eventually students will become independent, examining authors' skill within their personal reading. First it is necessary for readers to gain the habit of noticing craft in text and identifying craft features, speaking of them in terms that have meaning for the group (e.g., "striking adjectives," "super ellipses"). Teachers should choose familiar literature, books students have shared together as readers. The teacher selects portions from the text containing elements of craft useful for students. Students should have access to the text so they can really study and be involved with the words.

Next, the teacher engages the students in a predictable line of thinking:

The Five Parts to Reading Like a Writer

1. *Notice* something about the craft of the text.
2. *Talk* about it and *make a theory* about why a writer might use this craft.
3. Give the craft a *name*.
4. Think of *other texts* you know. Have you seen this craft before?
5. Try and *envision* using this crafting in your own writing (Ray, 1999, p. 120).

Ray (1999) points out that writing is something you do, not something you know. It is the doing that is important. When writing is thought of in this way, we understand that an author crafts her work through a series of intentional moves. Students need opportunities not only to recognize craft, but to explore their knowledge in intentional, individual ways within their own writing.

Procedure

Second-grade teacher Marcus Jamal introduced his students to Ray's (1999) "Five Parts to Reading Like a Writer" through his morning message (see Morning Message, chapter 8). After reading one of his messages and discussing its content, Mr. Jamal asked his students what he had done as a writer to make the message easy to read or to make it interesting. In early responses students noted such things as, "You put spaces between your words." "You put a question mark at the end of that sentence." After each response Mr. Jamal asked, "Why do you think I did that?"

Soon children began commenting on things such as the structure of the message and Mr. Jamal's choice of words. When the students pointed out the message's greeting and salutation Mr. Jamal commented that letters written to others usually follow a common structure. He then asked if students remembered seeing letters written by other people. Students talked of letters they had received or written in the past, and one student retrieved the book *We Are Best Friends* (Aliki, 1982) from the class library showing a letter written by one of the story characters. Together the class compared the structure of that letter with the morning message.

Later students began commenting on Mr. Jamal's use of language. One day they focused on his words, "fun-filled Friday." They decided he chose those words because they are fun to say and make his writing more interesting. The class termed this technique "same-sound starts." Mr. Jamal wondered aloud if other authors might use "same-sound starts," too. Together they returned to a favorite read aloud, *The Elephant's Child* by Rudyard Kipling (1983), savoring once again phrases like "oh best beloved" and "the great, gray-green greasy Limpopo River." Mr. Jamal suggested to his students that they be on the lookout for other authors' use of "same-sound starts" during readers' workshop. He provided children with Post-its to mark the examples they found. Later, he asked the students to choose their favorite examples. Then the children came together and sitting in a circle, they read aloud in turn their selected favorites. This served to get the sound of many interesting-sounding words and phrases out in the classroom for all to appreciate.

Mr. Jamal asked students to consider how "same-sound starts" might make their own writing more interesting. He recalled the writing of a few students and offered some alliterative suggestions. For example, Rachel's story about her dream life as a princess, began: "There once was a princess and she was pretty. Her name was Rachel." He asked her to consider: "There once was a pretty princess named Rachel." He asked all students to imagine using this feature in their own writing. Soon "same-sound starts" became a writing feature noted, used, and celebrated in this classroom.

Over the year, Mr. Jamal maintained three charts which highlighted crafting techniques they studied as a class. The charts were titled "Story Structures," "Sparkling Jewels," and "Interesting Punctuation." Book titles, by published and class authors, were listed as examples for the techniques on each chart. The "Story Structures" chart included, in part, Letter Texts with *Dear Mr. Blueberry* (James, 1991), *Dear Brother* (Asch, 1992), and *Dear Dad* (student authored) as examples: Repeated Sentences with *When I Was Young in the Mountains* (Rylant, 1982), *The Sky Was Blue* (Zolotow, 1963), and *When I Went to Disneyland* (student authored) as examples; and Conversation Texts with *The Day Jimmy's Boa Ate the Wash* (Noble, 1980), *I Am the Dog, I Am the Cat* (Hall, 1994), and *To the Mall, Mom* (student authored) as examples; The "Sparkling Jewels" chart included such techniques as Same-Sound Starts, Made-Up Words, and Great Verbs. The "Interesting Punctuation" chart listed items such as The look out, here it comes colon, The let me tell you dash, and Parentheses secrets. Students loved discovering how authors used colons, dashes, parentheses, and other punctuation and often experimented with these marks in their own pieces. All charts were ongoing and served students as reminders and references.

Mr. Jamal used the charts frequently as a focus for his mini-lessons. In choosing elements of craft for study, Mr. Jamal's prime consideration was their accessibility and usefulness for his students. He needed to imagine his students putting the techniques to use in their own writing. Through ongoing assessment of his students, he was continually able to offer suggestions encouraging their exploration of craft, helping them develop the importance of not just writing—but of writing well.

References

Ray, K. W. (1999). *Wondrous words*. Urbana, IL: National Council of Teachers of English.

Smith, F. (1988). *Joining the literacy club: Further essays into education.* Portsmouth, NH: Heinemann.

Resource

Fletcher, R., & Portalupi, J. (1998). *Craft lessons: Teaching writing K–8.* York, ME: Stenhouse Publishers.

Provides specific craft lessons in three sections for teachers of grades K–2, 3–4, 5–8. Each lesson discusses a particular element and why it should be taught, suggests how to teach the element, and offers resource material to exemplify the element for students.

Children's Books Cited

Aliki. (1982). *We are best friends.* New York: Greenwillow Books.

Asch, F. (1992). *Dear brother.* NY: Scholastic.

Hall, D. (1994). *I am the dog, I am the cat.* New York: Dial.

James, S. (1991). *Dear Mr. Blueberry.* New York: McElderry.

Kipling, R. (1983). *The elephant's child.* New York: Harcourt Brace Jovanovich.

Noble, T. H. (1980). *The day Jimmy's boa ate the wash.* New York: Dial.

Rylant, C. (1982). *When I was young in the mountains.* New York: Dutton.

Zolotow, C. (1963). *The sky was blue.* New York: HarperCollins.

Forms of Writing

We all use writing for many purposes. Writing helps us make sense of our world; it helps us remember and communicate our understandings and beliefs. The form our writing takes is influenced by our needs, purposes, and interests.

Background

People use writing to record events, explain, hypothesize, persuade, invite a response, predict, command, amuse, narrate, invent, inform, find out, reflect, summarize, or comment, and they select a form of writing to best suit the purpose of their expression. The forms available to us are many and diverse: lists, diaries, commentaries, reviews, autobiographies, letters, notes, minutes, reports, charts, recipes, brochures, captions, instructions, applications, advertisements, signs, notices, plays, poems, jokes, riddles, menus, editorials, questionnaires, and so forth.

Rebecca Lukens' discussion of genre is as applicable to the writers' workshop as it is to the readers' workshop (see Genres, chapter 3). Forms of writing, like literature genres, share common characteristics. And, as she suggests with literature, classifications are useful as teachers and children examine and discuss the elements of different text structures. Figure 7.6 shows the common forms of writing usually studied and used by elementary school students.

It is important and logical that these forms of expression find authentic purpose within the life of the classroom. Writing in which students engage must connect with the curriculum and be addressed to real audiences. It is the teacher's role to help students understand the characteristics of a form before expecting them to use the form effectively. In order to write well in a particular genre or form, students need first to spend time reading and studying that form. Teachers will want to build a file of well-written pieces in a variety of forms by both professionals and students. These pieces will serve as models during mini-lessons when teachers guide students to identify and compare the distinctive elements of a particular form and then apply their knowledge to their own writing.

Procedure

During the writers' workshop teachers will want to provide opportunities for students to gain familiarity with many forms of writing so that they develop a variety of means for expressing their thoughts and ideas. Often young children begin the school year writing about experiences from their lives in the form of reports or personal narratives (see Topic Selection, chapter 8), but personal narratives are appropriate for all grade levels. Mr. Jamal asks his second graders to write about an experience they shared with a special friend. To guide his students' writing in this form, he shares a piece of his own writing along with picture books such as *Some Birthday* by Particia Polacco (1991) or *Tar Beach* by Faith Ringgold (1991). As his students examine the stories of others, they reflect upon what the author did to make his story interesting—uncovering craft elements such as author's choice of language, leads, dialogue, and text structure. As students draft their stories, Mr. Jamal frequently asks individuals to share what's working well. This gives all students examples of what makes this form of writing successful.

Letter writing and note writing are forms that have many purposes in elementary classrooms. They can be used to share information, persuade, record events, invite a response, find out, inform, and amuse as well as express social courtesies. Children's letter writing frequently begins with note writing, sometimes surreptitiously. Ms. DeRego legitimizes this form by placing a container of note paper in the classroom and encourages students to communicate with one another through a message board or their mail boxes. If children need Mr. Jamal's attention while he is working with a small instructional group, he asks that they use notes to communicate with him. Teachers demonstrate the structure and function of this form by corresponding with students. The Morning Message (see chapter 8) provides a good model. Teachers may also write personal notes to children to congratulate, thank, and make suggestions.

In mini-lessons teachers can examine the purposes for which people write letters and share some of their own recent correspondence. This might include, for example, a letter to the children's parents, a birthday greeting to a relative, a letter of complaint to a local store, or an e-mail message to a friend. After discussing letter writing possibilities, children can decide to whom they would like to write and for what purpose. Within this context, the clarity and style of each student's message becomes very important (How is the style of a business letter different from that of a friendly letter, from that of an e-mail message?), as well as conventions such as spelling and punctuation. Older children especially, might use graphic organizers to plan the content of their letters using events from their lives to inform, and possibly amuse, their letter-receiving audience.

Poetry is another form that elementary age children find enjoyable and accessible. Routeman (2000a) and others who have worked with young children in writing poetry recommend that teachers regularly include poetry in their read aloud times. After children are familiar with a great many poems the teacher should ask, "What do we know about poetry?" When recording children's responses, the teacher may find his students believe the words must rhyme. It is difficult for young children to write meaningful poetry that rhymes, but they can be very successful composing free verse. Teachers will want to explore examples of free verse with students such as those by poets Paul Fleischman (1985), Carl Sandburg (1999), and those collected by Routeman (2000b), and then demonstrate how a poem may be created. A teacher may share the composing of his own poem; he may engage the whole class in creating a poem about a common experience or a classroom pet. When teachers share a great variety of poetry, demonstrate poetry writing, and share and discuss children's work, they will find poetry chosen as a favorite form by many of their students.

Personal narratives, letter and note writing, and poetry are just a few of many forms that teachers will want to offer children. Teachers should decide which forms to introduce and then provide systematic instruction to enhance and support student's efforts. When children have opportunities to explore a wide repertoire of possibilities, they are likely to discover further options and expand their writing experiences. They will frequently find ways to imaginatively blend writing forms to create their own unique pieces (see Figure 6.3, a research report written in the style of a personal narrative).

Reference

Routman, R. (2000a). *Conversations: Strategies for teaching, learning, and evaluating.* Portsmouth, NH: Heinemann.

Resources

Graves, D. (1998). *How to catch a shark and other stories about teaching and learning.* Westport CT: Heinemann.

Graves encourages teachers to examine their own learning histories. By doing so they can help students access the power of their own stories.

Routman, R. (2000b). *Kids' poems: Teaching children to love writing poetry*. New York: Scholastic.

Routman has collected a variety of poems written by children that she presents in a series of four books for grades K–4. Each book presents the rationale for teaching poetry and instructional plans to guide teachers.

Fleischman, P. (1985, 1988). *I am phoenix: Poems for two voices* and *Joyful noise: Poems for two voices*. New York: Harper & Row Junior Books.

Two books of free verse for reading aloud, one about birds, the other about insects.

Sandburg, C. (1999). *Poems for children nowhere old enough to vote*. New York: Random House, Inc.

Poetry recently discovered by Sandburg scholars provides a fresh look at familiar objects such as pencils, chairs, and clocks.

Children's Books Cited

Polacco, P. (1991). *Some birthday.* New York: Simon & Schuster.

Ringgold, F. (1991). *Tar beach.* New York: Crown Publishers.

FIGURE 7.6   A DIAGRAM OF FORMS OF WRITING

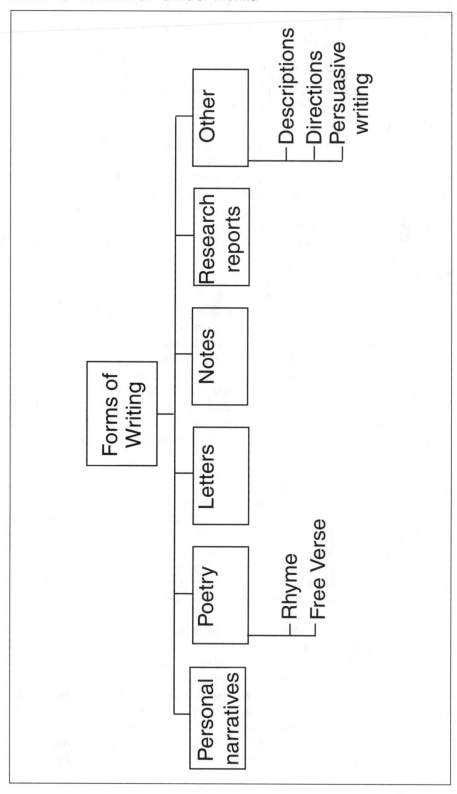

Writing Across the Curriculum

In a balanced literacy program, students' writing is not limited to the scheduled writers' workshop. Throughout this text we have discussed the role of writing in the readers' workshop. However, writing can serve as a tool across other curriculum areas such as math, science, and social studies. Many teachers have also discovered ways to bring content subjects into their writers' workshop.

Background

Gail Tompkins (1994) suggests that writing across the curriculum can benefit elementary students in at least three ways: (a) it encourages learning of content area information; (b) it develops writing fluency, strategies, and skills; and (c) it activates critical thinking skills. Writing contributes to learning because through writing students develop greater knowledge of the subject. When students write in all curriculum areas, they write more easily and the writing makes their thinking more concrete. As students write they discover, organize, classify, connect, and evaluate information.

Procedure

Many teachers have students use content journals to record information and communicate their learning as they explore a variety of content areas and theme studies. (This is different from personal writing in journals as discussed in chapter 9.) The journals may be purchased composition tablets or simply paper stapled together between construction paper covers. Students regularly use their journals to review and interpret problems they have solved and record and reflect upon information discussed or material they have read. Sometimes teachers ask students to use their journals to respond to specific prompts or questions. Open-ended questions such as, "What did we do? What did we find out?", will encourage reflection on a math lesson or a science experiment. Students may be asked to use their journals to explain how they worked through and solved a math problem.

Before beginning a social studies or health lesson teachers may ask students to do a "quick write" to focus on information they already know about the subject. The teacher may set a timer, and for 5 or 10 minutes everyone considers "What do you know about slavery?" prior to a social studies discussion or "What is junk food?" to begin a study of nutrition. Paired with the focus question might be a second question, "What would you like to learn?" At the conclusion of the study students return to their journals to consider "What new things did you learn?" "What would you still like to know?" Journals provide students with a concrete record of their growth as learners. Students' journal entries give teachers a means to evaluate student learning as well as the effectiveness of their instruction (see Figure 7.7).

Constructing visual organizers such as charts and webs to record information is a valuable strategy for students to develop. A K-W-L form (see Figure 4.14) can be used to record information about students' selected topics. Teachers, of course, will need to introduce each strategy by modeling it and then support students as they work together to practice it (see K-W-L, chapter 4). Once students are comfortable with the strategy, they should be encouraged to use it independently as they pursue their topics of study.

Forms of writing such as journals, charts, and webs can be thought of as first-draft writing. They will not move through the five phases of the writing process. It is unlikely that they will be revised or edited. The writing serves as a tool for thinking and learning.

As teachers review their students' drafts, they may want to attend to important misunderstandings about content, but mechanics or spelling will be of little importance.

FIGURE 7.7   STUDENT'S SCIENCE JOURNAL ENTRY

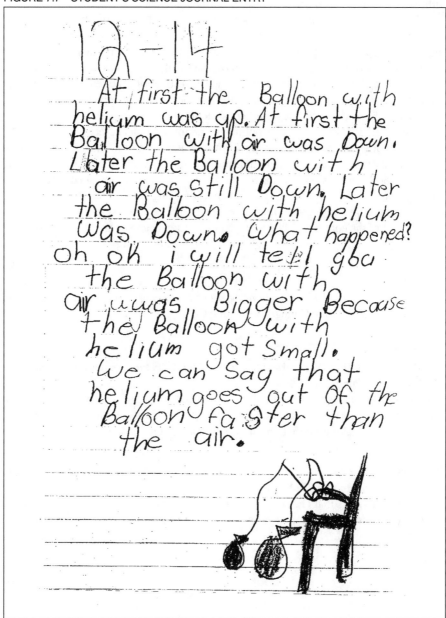

There are times, however, when students' informal writing will be developed further and the writing process will be utilized. When students prepare research reports, they will go through the writing process. The informal writing in which students engage helps them develop expertise about their research subjects as they record and clarify information. This writing can be thought of as the topic selection and rehearsal part of the process. It informs their informational writing in much the same way that lived-through experiences inform their personal writing. Once students are knowledgeable about the subjects of their reports, they will draft, confer, revise, and edit. They will work to make their pieces interesting for their audience.

For example, a class may explore a theme such as nutrition. As a part of the study, students will pursue individual interests by selecting topics such as carbohydrates, the digestive system, the importance of legumes. As the children become "experts" on their subjects through a variety of resources, they will make notes, organize information, and record their reflections. During their investigations the teacher will present mini-lessons on strategies such as using the Internet to find information, note taking, organizing information into categories, constructing webs, writing an interereisting lead, and selecting a distinctive form for publishing an informational piece.

Once students have gathered enough information, organized it, and selected a focus for their writing, they will begin drafting. Conferences will be held with peers and their teacher. Revisions will be made. Pieces will be edited, published, and shared. During times in the school year when students are engaged in content-related writing, this writing usually becomes the focus for the writers' workshops. Writing becomes an integral part of the content study and the content study becomes an integral part of the writers' workshop.

Reference

Tompkins, G. E. (1994). *Teaching writing: Balancing process and product, 2nd ed.* New York: Macmillan College Publishing Co.

Resources

Duthie, C. (1996). *True stories: Nonfiction literacy in the primary classroom.* York, ME: Stenhouse Publishers.

Duthie encourages a balance between fiction and nonfiction in primary-grade classrooms. She suggests teachers capitalize on children's curiosity about the real world and offers ideas for making nonfiction an integral part of the readers' and writers' workshops.

Harvey, S. (1998). *Nonfiction matters: Reading, writing, and research in grades 3–8.* York, ME: Stenhouse Publishers.

Harvey suggests that children's nonfiction writing often lacks the voice shown in their other forms of writing. She offters many practical ways for teaching children to write nonfiction well.

Connections to Home and Community:
Extending the Writer's Audience

Children's ownership of writing is nurtured within an extended community. Teachers of writers' workshops need to ensure that students encounter many, meaningful settings to encourage and support their efforts as developing writers.

Background

Au, Mason, and Scheu (1995) note that the sense of membership in a literate community often begins with the classroom as children work together to explore topics, share, and refine their pieces, and assess and reflect upon one another's growth as writers. Teachers recognize, however, that for children to develop into life-long readers and writers, it is necessary that they find purposes for literacy beyond the classroom and that their efforts in reading and writing be supported by those people most significant in their lives.

Reggie Routman (2000) emphasizes the value of inviting families to become members of the classroom community. Many parents were exposed to a very different model of writing when they were in school and do not understand the goals of a writers' workshop. It is important that parents gain an understanding of the learning process and know how to observe their children's involvement and growth. To profitably extend their students' writing community, teachers should seek opportunities which extend into an ever-expanding community and explore a variety of ways to encourage family participation and support.

Procedure

Teachers often begin the school year by connecting with the families of their new students. They may invite parents to share information about their child's interests and literacy development. Some teachers outline their goals for the year and explain how classroom activities will address those goals. They may also suggest ways that parents can participate in the classroom program. Such information might be conveyed through a letter, phone call, or home visit. A questionnaire may ask parents about children's reading and writing at home as well as activities that occupy their free time. Such forms of communication express teachers' interest in students and their families, and help inform their instructional planning.

Most schools organize meetings early in the school year when parents visit their child's classroom and meet the teacher. These meetings offer teachers an opportunity to discuss and enlist support for their curriculum. During the meetings teachers often propose ways that parents might participate in, and enhance, their children's writing experiences. Their suggestions may include:

- *Celebrate your child's writing.* After sharing a new publication with his/her classmates, your child will check out the piece from our classroom library to take home. Please enjoy it as a family and use the comment sheet in the book to write a positive response. We will invite you to join us later this year for an Author's Brunch when students will share their favorite pieces of writing.

- *Encourage your child to use writing for real purposes.* Communicate with him/her through notes placed in a lunch box or school bag and ask that s/he leave notes for you. Have him/her write reminder lists such as "Things I need for my science project." Often notes you send to school can be composed by the child. Your signature at the bottom will verify that you've read and endorsed the message.

- Provide materials. Our beginning writers need books for publishing their stories. We'd like volunteers to make blank books so that we can have a supply on hand. If you have a source for paper (wallpaper, blueprint, blank on one side) we can probably put it to use.

- *Join our writers' workshop.* (Your suggestions will depend upon students' ages and abilities These are some examples.) Our beginning writers need help editing and publishing their pieces. You can type or print the children's stories as they read to you from pieces they've revised and edited. Our writers could use support with revisions of their stories. Share your own writing with us. Show us how you use writing in your own life.

Teachers often communicate with parents and share the news of the classroom through regular newsletters. A newsletter may be written exclusively by the teacher, by students, or as a combined effort. Teachers may use newsletters to discuss students' classroom writing experiences, to showcase students' writing, to recommend books for home reading, and to share classroom events. One newsletter format contains general information that goes to all families as well as a blank area where students write personal news (see Figure 7.8). In some classrooms, rotating committees are in charge of each week's newsletter.

Beyond the Family

Teachers should consider ways for students' writing to extend into other communities as well. Often a classroom of older students "buddies up" with a classroom of younger children. Children enjoy exchanging notes with their buddies. A dialogue journal passed back and forth between two children from different classrooms fosters their relationship and provides a meaningful purpose for writing. Pen pals and key pals (for those with e-mail access) serve this purpose as well. Some teachers arrange for "in school" as well as "distant" writing pals.

Teachers will continually discover ways to extend children's use of writing. They might encourage students to publish their works more widely, perhaps through a web page, in the local newspaper, or in a children's magazine. Children can write the memos and letters needed for field trips and to pursue themes of study. To culminate a unit of study, students' learning might be shared in brochures written for a specific group in their community.

When teachers demonstrate and encourage a broad application of writing, they find their tone contagious. Soon they will find their students actively joining the pursuit to explore and expand opportunities to use writing for purposes that have relevance and meaning for them.

Reference

Au, K. H., Mason, J. M., & Scheu, J. A. (1995). *Literacy instruction for today.* New York: HarperCollins College Publishers.

Routman, R. (2000). *Conversations: Strategies for teaching, learning, and evaluating.* Portsmouth NH: Heinemann.

Resource

Morrice, C. & Simmons, M. (1991). Beyond reading buddies: A whole language cross-age program. *The Reading Teacher*, 44 (8), 572–577.

FIGURE 7.8   STUDENT TO PARENT NEWSLETTER FORM

Monday:	**Date:**
Tuesday:	**Date:**
Wednesday:	**Date:**
Thursday:	**Date:**
Friday:	**Date:**

Troubleshooting: What About Pacing?

The curriculum demands of the elementary school are great and growing greater. Teachers frequently begin the school year wondering, "How can I possibly cover all that?" To "get through everything," many teachers often find themselves racing from one subject to the next pulling their students along behind. They sample broad topics (e.g., mammals, drugs, transportation, families) and try various forms of writing (e.g., poetry, persuasive, fiction, informational report), but they haven't the time to pursue any area in depth. The curriculum is "covered," often concealing more than is revealed.

We know the importance of students' active involvement in learning, but involvement is difficult when students lack time to pursue their interests in depth. It is a struggle for teachers to keep the pace moving so they can "get to everything" and still grant students opportunities to inquire and investigate at length. This issue is as true of the writers' workshop as it is of other subject areas.

Examine Your Curriculum

Lucy Calkins (1994) encourages us to consider our curricula in terms of both depth and breadth. She recommends narrowing our focus within areas of study so that students can probe more deeply and meaningfully. Because schools' curricula are usually presented in broad concepts, teachers often plan their instruction to be broad based. Calkins points out that broad concepts inherently reside within more limited issues and subject areas. She believes we can trust that as students delve deeply into their studies, they will encounter and deal with a broad range of concepts.

Calkins (1994) suggests that teachers review their curricula to identify those areas best suited for deep inquiry and those better served by more cursory coverage. Teachers can then schedule longer time segments over several weeks for students to explore some subjects in depth and shorter blocks to focus on more limited curriculum requirements. For example, a first-grade teacher may choose to spend considerable time exploring the role of families, but give just incidental attention to the investigation of holidays. It is important for teachers to make choices about which areas will have greater pay off for student learning and spend more time on those areas.

Within the writers' workshop teachers may want students to experience a range of forms and genres, or the school curriculum may specify the variety to be taught. Some kinds of writing might benefit from in-depth study; others may need only a short amount of attention or be addressed within the longer studies. Teachers need to make choices and set priorities. Knowledge of students and their needs should guide teachers' decision making.

One Teacher's Solution

Jack Wilde (1993), a teacher in Hanover, New Hampshire, provides a model for teacher planning. He paced the variety of experiences offered within his writers' workshop, allotting ample time for students to pursue each one in depth. Wilde explained that there is not sufficient time within the school year to focus on every genre or form in depth. He felt he needed to make some decisions. Based upon his own experiences as a writer and knowledge of his students, he set goals and made plans. Wilde wanted his students to experience enough variety in the writing forms they worked with to discover at least one with which they were at ease. He hoped that each student could find his or her own voice within a particular genre or form. Wilde acknowledged that a degree of student ownership was lost when he chose to center blocks of the workshop time on specific kinds of writing. Some, he knew, would argue that students should be supported in discovering that voice on their own during free writing exploration. Wilde learned from experience, however, that with such an open approach opportunities can be lost. Too often people will not risk the unfamiliar. A student may never discover the power of his persuasive voice unless he is expected to write in that form. So, Wilde chose to ask his students to try specific genres and forms to learn what they might offer them. As students explored, he provided help and support, choices and challenges.

Wilde selected five specific kinds of writing on which to focus: personal narrative, fiction, poetry, persuasive, and informational. Over the course of the school year, each type of writing was studied during the writers' workshop. Several weeks were devoted to each study—for example, four weeks for poetry, ten weeks for the informational report. Students were expected to publish a piece of each of the five types after having taken it through the writing process. As students were immersed in their writing, Wilde offered a variety of specific mini-lessons to support their efforts. Because all students were focused on the same type of writing, Wilde's lessons could be more precise and students' support for one another was more focused.

As students shaped their pieces, they explored many broad concepts. They examined character motivation in their fiction pieces and rhyme, rhythm and word choice in their poetry. Other concepts cut across their work—leads and endings, embedding information, metaphors, flashbacks. They made choices about their topics and ways to express their ideas. Wilde encouraged students to present their informational pieces in a variety of forms or genres such as interviews, diaries, stories, or scripts.

Wilde's approach shows that it is possible to "cover" the curriculum and still give students opportunities to engage in meaningful, in-depth exploration. If pacing is an issue, Wilde presents a good model to consider. Teachers will do well to examine their goals and curricula, decide how goals can be met with in-depth studies whenever possible, and allocate extended time to those investigations.

References

Calkins, L. M. (1994). *The art of teaching writing*. Portsmouth, NH: Heinemann.

Wilde, J. (1993). *A door opens: Writing in fifth grade*. Portsmouth, NH: Heinemann.

Chapter 8

TEACHER-DIRECTED ACTIVITIES IN THE WRITERS' WORKSHOP

The Impact of Donald Graves: Teachers As Writers

Graves (1990) believes that successful teaching within the writers' workshop begins with teachers' explorations of their own literacy.

Teachers like Nancie Atwell, Mary Ann Wessells, and Linda Rief have convinced me that, to encourage literacy among children, attention to teachers' literacy has to come first. The children in their classrooms went beyond the usual kinds of writing that accumulate in writing folders to write about challenging material because they asked big questions of themselves. Moreover, these same teachers saw their personal and professional lives change because they changed their own reading and writing patterns. (p. 21)

A possible starting point for change is teachers' explorations of their own backgrounds as writers. Graves suggests that teachers reflect on their history as writers, recalling any teachers who had affected them positively or negatively. For example, Graves remembers a sixth-grade teacher who lost patience with his handwriting, as well as a high-school teacher who encouraged him to become a writer with the advice that he write and rewrite. Such memories serve to remind us of the powerful effects teachers can have on students as writers, even years later.

Guidelines Based on Experience

These memories can guide teachers' work in the future. By thinking back on what helped them as learners, teachers gain insights about how they can be better teachers of writing. Here are some guidelines Graves (1994) derived from his own experiences:

- *Take a writer seriously.* Mrs. Dower, my high school English teacher, believed me when I said I wanted to be a writer.

- *Help writers to have high expectations.* Mrs. Dower took me seriously by asking me to do more work. The extra work was proof that she believed in me.

- *Demonstrate a life with high expectations.* Don Murray, along with Mrs. Dower, helped me to have high expectations because he expected much of himself. Both of them revealed their own hunger for learning. (p. 13)

To teach writing effectively, Graves (1990) argues, teachers must see themselves as writers. He recognizes that one of the barriers to this goal is the limited time teachers have to write. Graves recommends making a commitment to write for 10 minutes every day. To fit this 10 minutes into a busy life, he suggests "piggybacking" writing onto existing routines. For example, a teacher may start the writers' workshop with 10 minutes of sustained silent writing and choose to write at that time. Or there may be 10 minutes in the evening before going to bed. The hardest part, Graves notes, is finding that first 10 minutes.

The reason many adults do not write is because they believe they have nothing to say. Graves points out that writing grows from daily life and events that may appear at first to be trivial. He notes that his topics for writing usually come from an everyday occasion that raises a question in his mind, such as why the dog is trembling or why going through Customs causes a sense of guilt. In Graves' view, the writer can start by trying to capture the details of that moment, describing the appearance of the trembling dog or the feeling of going through Customs. Daily life presents us with many such moments, which Graves calls "literate occasions," that may be captured in writing. When in doubt about a topic, Graves recommends returning to close observation and careful listening. Knowing that one is going to write creates an alertness to everyday life and attention to its details.

Many teachers are familiar with the notion that good writers use a "show not tell" approach in their work. The writer might state, "Nick's shoulders slumped" rather than "Nick felt discouraged." Graves (1999) suggests that teachers experiment with such concepts to deepen their insights about writing. For example, to understand how to convey character through writing, he suggests choosing a person you know well and listing all the ways that person reveals herself (for example, chuckles and shakes her head when reading the newspaper).

Writers' Struggles

When teachers write in the manner recommended by Graves, they come to a better understanding of themselves as writers and of the struggles that all writers face. This understanding helps them to be more effective in helping their students grow as writers. Teachers who are writers can use their own writing as the basis for mini-lessons. For example, a teacher can demonstrate revision, showing how she added details, moved paragraphs around, or experimented with different leads. Teachers can read their writing aloud to the class and invite students to offer advice for improving the piece. Teachers who share their struggles as writers with students show that they are living writers' lives. Students know that they are not being asked to try anything as writers that their teachers have not already tried themselves.

Graves (1990) writes, "Although as teachers your professional lives are centered in the children, you first need to read, write, listen, and learn for yourself" (p. 124). He believes that excellent teachers have an insatiable desire to learn. Because they see themselves as learners, interested in exploring life's big questions, they can inspire their students to use listening, reading, and writing to learn.

References

Graves, D. (1990). *Discover your own literacy.* Portsmouth, NH: Heinemann.

Graves, D. (1994). *A fresh look at writing.* Portsmouth, NH: Heinemann.

Graves, D. (1999). *Bring life into learning: Create a lasting literacy.* Portsmouth, NH: Heinemann.

Morning Message

The morning message or daily message is often a part of the writers' workshop. It is an activity used by teachers to share information of interest with the class. The morning message can serve many purposes such as developing comprehension, introducing and reinforcing vocabulary, developing word reading strategies, and introducing and reinforcing writing conventions. It also provides an effective means for teachers to model their own literacy as members of the classroom community.

Background

Doris Crowell, Alice Kawakami, and Jeanette Wong (1986) described how the morning message contributed to children's literacy development in Mrs. Wong's kindergarten classroom. The school day began with the children gathering on the carpet for "morning business." As a part of this routine, Mrs. Wong wrote a message while the class watched and tried to read along. After the message was written, the children read it aloud as a group. Their attention focused first on comprehension. The children commented on the information contained in the message and asked questions. They used context combined with their knowledge of word and letter cues to determine some of the words.

To encourage their understanding of phonetic elements and writing conventions Mrs. Wong asked questions such as, "Does anyone see a word that begins with the same letter as Kimo's name?" Or, when ending a sentence she might comment, "I'm putting a period here to show this is the end of a sentence." As students became more aware of print conventions, Mrs. Wong encouraged their observations by asking what they noticed. Then she elaborated upon their findings. When a girl circled the *s* at the end of *books* and said "plural" the teacher helped the group clarify that "plural" meant more than one. In this kindergarten, Mrs. Wong used the morning message to model writing and to encourage her students' active participation in constructing meaning from text.

Procedure

Teachers at a variety of grade levels use written messages as part of their morning routines, though some teachers find they fit better in another part of the day such as just after recess or lunch. They usually allow 5 to 10 minutes for the activity.

Before his students arrive in the morning, second-grade teacher Marcus Jamal prints a message on the board to greet them and remind them of a special event. Mr. Jamal uses a message as part of the students' daily routine along with putting their belongings away, turning in notes and homework, and sharpening pencils.

Once those responsibilities are finished the students gather on the carpet for their morning meeting. During this meeting they discuss the content of the message, and then Mr. Jamal turns to an instructional focus. In this example (see Figure 8.1) the class noted the word variants *poems* and *poetry,* talking about similarities in appearance and meaning. The students added the words *poem* and *poet,* and Mr. Jamal introduced them to *poetic.* He helped students see how the words are related. He invited the children to note other words of interest. The students also noted that as an author he chose to write his message in two paragraphs and discussed the reasons for his choice.

FIGURE 8.1   MORNING MESSAGE

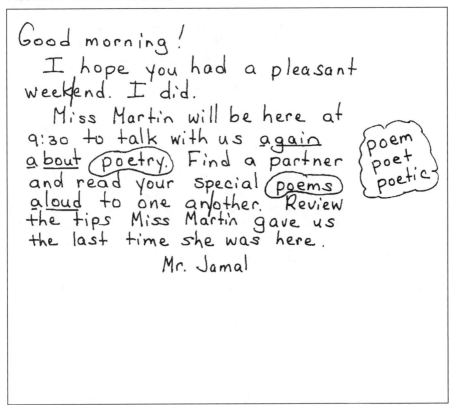

Another teacher may use an overhead projector, thinking aloud as she composes her message in front of the students. The children read to themselves, and then they all read the message aloud with the teacher. Their discussion also begins with the message's meaning, and then the teacher directs their attention to elements of text. She may ask, "Why did I put a capital letter here?" "What is the reason for this period?" "What is the difference between this word (e.g., here) and this one (e.g., hear)?"

Upper-grades teachers often use written messages to communicate activities and scheduling information, provide reminders, and connect with students on a personal level.

> *Happy Groundhog's Day! Who knows? Did Phil see his shadow? Is spring on its way or are we condemned to 6 more weeks of brrrr...?*

> *Group A, like Phil, will be heading underground today. They go to band practice at 1:45. (Check your shadows on your way back to class.)*

After his students are settled at their desks, the teacher would likely speak briefly about Groundhogs Day, perhaps making connections with news reports they had heard or read before school that morning. The teacher might choose to focus on paragraphing and ask why he had written his message in two paragraphs. He might also review the use of parentheses and ask that students take note of any they discover during times of independent reading.

Teachers who make written messages a part of the school day speak of how much their students value their communications. They also speak of how valuable the messages are in terms of instruction. Daily messages provide a means for teachers to model their own literacy as well as to reinforce skills within a meaningful context.

Reference

Crowell, D. C., Kawakami, A. J., & Wong, J. L. (1986). Emerging literacy: Reading-writing experiences in a kindergarten classroom. *The Reading Teacher, 40* (2).

Mini-Lessons

Mini-lessons are the key instructional component of the writers' workshop. Whole-class mini-lessons usually begin the workshop and may be 5 to 20 minutes in length. Small-group and individual lessons may occur throughout the workshop. Nancie Atwell (1998) finds that mini-lessons offer her an opportunity to present herself as the "grown-up" who has inside knowledge about writing and understands the needs of her particular group of students. Mini-lessons may focus on workshop procedures, literary craft, or conventions of writing. The topics of mini-lessons are guided by teacher observation of student need, curriculum guidelines, or by student request.

Background

Lucy Calkins (1986, revised 1994) first introduced the idea of mini-lessons. She compared mini-lessons with "well-timed tips from experts" (p. 167). It is when people are deeply involved in a project or topic that they value and benefit from the instruction of someone more knowledgeable. This is applicable, as well, to children involved in a writers' workshop. It is because they are deeply involved in their writing that lessons aimed at helping them improve are meaningful.

Calkins (1986, revised 1994) pointed out that the purpose of a mini-lesson is to "add information to the class pot" (p. 170). Seldom does a lesson call for all children to practice the concept immediately. Perhaps a small number of students will have use for the information at the time it is presented, but it is out there in the classroom. For some students it may resurface in their minds when they need it; other students will have it recirculated for them as classmates talk about the concept during conferences and sharing sessions.

Procedure

It is helpful to use Atwell's ideas for categorizing mini-lessons (see Figure 8.2). To introduce the writers' workshop, a teacher's first mini-lesson will likely deal with the strategy of topic selection (see Topic Selection in this chapter). An important purpose for this lesson is to help students understand that writers think about, or rehearse, their writing prior to sitting down at their desk. Another purpose is for students to understand that the best writing comes from things we have experienced and know well (see Selecting Literature, chapter 7). Students should see that the ordinary things in life can be viewed and related with interest and freshness. Teachers will explain the importance of these ideas to writers by sharing examples from the work of published authors. Teachers may also share how they go about choosing writing topics using their own writing as an example. Teachers will then ask students to apply information from the lesson, perhaps by jotting down some topic ideas and talking through them with a partner. Next, students will select a topic and begin writing.

FIGURE 8.2 MINI-LESSONS

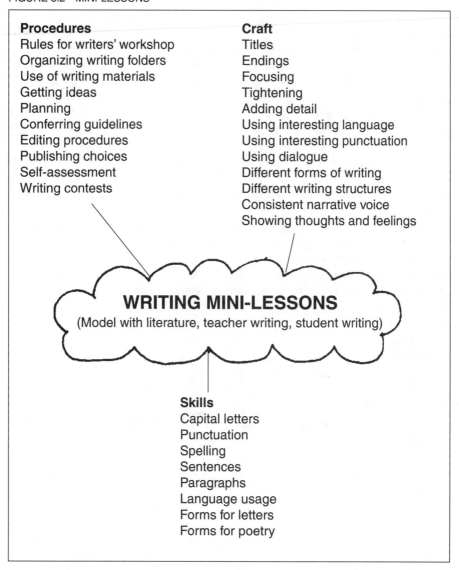

Procedures
Rules for writers' workshop
Organizing writing folders
Use of writing materials
Getting ideas
Planning
Conferring guidelines
Editing procedures
Publishing choices
Self-assessment
Writing contests

Craft
Titles
Endings
Focusing
Tightening
Adding detail
Using interesting language
Using interesting punctuation
Using dialogue
Different forms of writing
Different writing structures
Consistent narrative voice
Showing thoughts and feelings

WRITING MINI-LESSONS
(Model with literature, teacher writing, student writing)

Skills
Capital letters
Punctuation
Spelling
Sentences
Paragraphs
Language usage
Forms for letters
Forms for poetry

Also on the first day teachers will want to explain some of the writers' workshop procedures (see Setting Up Your Classroom, chapter 7). They will point out why procedures and organization are important to the workshop. They may explain the choices of materials available (see Materials, chapter 7) and how they expect students to use them. They will want children to know what to do with their writing each day and will probably explain the use of the folders in which students will keep their work. They may use themselves and their own writing as examples, or they may have writing and folders of former students to share. As students use the procedures over time, teachers will solicit feedback to check on students' understandings and to note the effectiveness of their individual planning and organizational styles.

Teachers will prepare lessons to begin most workshops throughout the year. Because they are familiar with the skills and strategies appropriate for students at their grade levels and guided by benchmarks (see Establishing Grade Level Benchmarks, chapter 11), they will plan lessons to address those concepts. As teachers interact with their students and their writing, they will note specific needs that can be addressed by mini-lessons. They will decide whether to present those lessons to the whole class, small groups, or to individuals (see Grouping, chapter 7). They will also encourage students to initiate their own lesson topics and be alert to students who could present lessons themselves.

This chapter and others provide numerous examples of how mini-lessons might support students' growth in writing. In preparing lessons, it is helpful to consider this three-part plan: (a) help students recognize the concept and understand its importance or usefulness, (b) share related information and provide examples, (c) ask students to consider ways they might use the information. The examples used in mini-lessons should be drawn from professionally authored children's literature (previously read to or by students), or writing done by the students or teacher.

Donald Graves (1991) suggests a helpful procedure for teachers planning mini-lessons. He recommends that they use overhead transparencies to present their lessons. An ongoing list of the lessons can be recorded on a classroom chart and the transparencies filed into plastic sleeves and placed into a three-hole binder. Teachers will have their lessons for future reference, and their students will have resources to use when they want to review a concept.

References

Atwell, N. (1998). *In the middle: New understandings about writing, reading, and learning.* Portsmouth, NH: Heinemann.

Calkins, L. M. (1986, revised 1994). *The art of teaching writing.* Portsmouth, NH: Heinemann.

Graves, D. H. (1991). *Build a literate classroom.* Portsmouth, NH: Heinemann.

Shared-Writing Lessons

Teachers and students sometimes work together to compose a piece of writing within the writers' workshop. During these shared writing experiences, teachers and students "pool" their expertise as they collaborate on a piece of text, together exploring both the writing process and the ways in which written language functions.

Background

Pinnell and Fountas (1998) define three types of collaborative writing. *Language experience* is an approach in which teachers record exactly what individual students say as they dictate their ideas and experiences. This approach is frequently used with beginning writers with the purpose of showing that writing is language written down. Teachers of older students may act as scribes to demonstrate important aspects of composition, sentence construction, or punctuation.

During *shared writing* the teacher also acts as scribe; but unlike language experience, students work collaboratively as a group to negotiate topics, text structure, and word choice. Often, the teacher's ideas are heard as she thinks aloud to help students notice something important about the writing. The teacher's support and encouragement allow students to engage in writing experiences that they are unlikely to manage on their own.

Interactive writing, like shared writing, is an approach in which students and teacher compose a text together. Though the text's meaning is of prime importance, the teacher also has planned to engage children in exploring specific aspects of words, such as hearing consonants and consonant clusters or in listening for word parts in longer words. During interactive writing, teacher and students often "share the pen" throughout the writing experience. Children may write word parts or whole words while the teacher fills in the rest. The teacher's intent is to provide enough instructional support so that students learning will be extended.

Through shared experiences, students gain new options to explore in their independent writing; and because they do not have full responsibility for transcribing, their minds can be more open to the creative and reflective. Also, the texts they create provide excellent materials for shared reading experiences (see Shared Reading, chapter 4).

Procedure

Often teachers combine elements of shared and interactive writing as they compose with students. They find that students of any age can benefit from such collaborative experiences. Topics are diverse, as well. Literature often provides a good stimulus as the class retells a story, creates an innovation based upon a familiar text, or composes a different story ending. Topics can come from informational studies such as science observations and experiments, journal entries, and reports. Letters of many kinds, such as thank you notes and newsletters, can be opportunities to share a writing experience. Of course, collaborative writing presumes a common experience so that everyone may participate.

Kindergarten teacher, Sally O'Brien often has students share in the writing of the morning message. During a study of farm life, her students experienced the hatching of chicken eggs inside a classroom incubator (see Readers' Workshop in Mrs. Sally O'Brien's Kindergarten Classroom, chapter 2). The day the eggs began to hatch, Mrs. O'Brien helped her students add Leanne's comment to that day's message: "Leanne heard a little peep." First, Mrs. O'Brien talked with the class about how Leanne's sentence would add more information to the message and make it more interesting. Mrs. O'Brien knew that many of her students were able to write most of the letters and words in this sentence. Her goals at this time in the year were to help students attend to spacing between words, to say words slowly to hear all their sounds, to use available references for spelling words, and to become aware that capital letters and periods denote sentences.

First she asked the students to say Leanne's sentence together. Then she asked if anyone knew how to write Leanne's name. Most children's eyes went to the chart which they used to record attendance each morning. Leanne came to the board and wrote her name as Mrs. O'Brien asked students why she used an upper-case *L*. They talked of the need to start both names and beginnings of sentences with capital letters. Hans wrote an *h* to begin "heard" while Leanne placed her hand after her name to remind them that spaces are needed between words. Then the group said "heard" slowly listening for all its sounds. They recognized the need for an *r* and a *d*, which Hans printed after Mrs. O'Brien wrote the *ea*. All children said, "a is the letter a." and their teacher wrote it. Brian pointed out that "little" appeared elsewhere in the morning message and came to the board to copy it into their new sentence. The children heard three sounds in "peep." As Cheri wrote them, Mrs. O'Brien noted the need for a second *e* to "make the word look right." "And what goes at the end of the sentence?" A period was added and the children joined in reading their completed sentence and then the entire message.

Throughout the writing, Mrs. O'Brien was careful to keep the momentum going and not focus on too many details. She also noted each child's level of participation. Her observations informed her later work with individual children and with small groups.

Fourth-grade teacher Brenda DeRego also looks for opportunities to share writing with her students. After their return from a visit to the Weather Bureau she began, "We learned so much information today, and I know many of you will want to use some of it in your individual projects. Let's put our heads together and see how much we can recall." As students began sharing, Ms. DeRego helped them organize their information by offering, "I hear some categories. I'm going to make a diagram here at the side to list our main topics. Then we can organize our thoughts better." If a student offered something that was unclear the teacher said, "Let's listen to that idea." She repeated the statement, giving students an opportunity to clarify the thought. Other times, she encouraged students to recall and use more precise and technical vocabulary. "Who remembers? Is Beau describing a tornado or a hurricane? What is the difference?" Will someone get a piece of chart paper to begin a listing of different types of weather. Let's see if we can work out the spellings for these two words by thinking about each syllable. Do we know other words that can help us with the spellings of these two?"

It is important to note that while the teacher's voice is important during shared writing experiences, that voice should not overshadow those of the students. The teacher's role is to encourage sharing and guide the learning of all participants.

Reference

Pinnell, G., & Fountas, I. (1998). *Word matters: Teaching phonics and spelling in the reading/writing classroom.* Portsmouth, NH: Heinemann.

Resource

Button, K., Johnson, M. J., & Furgeson, P. (1996). Interactive writing in a primary classroom. *Reading Teacher, 49* (6). The authors show how phonics and other linguistic patterns can be taught to beginning readers within the context of meaningful text.

Topic Selection

Writers write best about topics they know and care about. All people have ideas, interests, memories, and concerns. Teachers should help students identify things that are significant in their lives and support students' exploration of the possibilities within those topics throughout the writers' workshop.

Background

Donald Graves (1994) is firm in his view that it is a teacher's role to show students how to select topics from the ordinary events in their lives and expand them into a variety of writing forms. Children need guidance and support to find significance within ordinary subjects. Otherwise their writing will likely be broad brush "all abouts," focused on big events like a trip to Disneyland or a retelling of someone else's movie or television drama.

Graves suggests that teachers regularly demonstrate how writing topics are chosen by sharing their own thinking during mini-lessons. The lessons will help children learn of the possibilities for writing within one's experiences. These lessons may also model what Katie Wood Ray (1999) describes as "envisioning possibilities for writing" (p. 59). She suggests that when writers consider a variety of text structures, they see that one topic has the potential to become many very different pieces. It is a mistake, she believes, that once a piece is published, the writer thinks she needs a new topic to begin writing again.

Teachers can also expect students to verbalize their own topic selection. Students should anticipate that a teacher conference will include questions such as, "What is your piece about?" "How did you choose this topic to write about?" "What will you do with this piece? Who might you share it with?" and be prepared to respond.

Graves points out that students who can count on a regular writing time, and know they are in charge of the content, will discover ideas for writing throughout the day. When they think, "I could write about that," rehearsal or planning is often integrated into the process. Rehearsal may take the form of daydreams, sketches, notes, lists of words or diagrams, and conversations as students reflect on their subjects—or a thought (e.g., "The kids will really like this story."). If teachers assign topics, they limit opportunities for children to practice the important skills of both choice and rehearsal. Instruction should help students examine the events of their lives and envision the many possibilities for exploring those events through writing.

Procedure

Teachers often begin a first writers' workshop with a mini-lesson to show how they might select topics for writing. They brainstorm in front of their students a list of topics they could write about—setting up a new aquarium, decorating a cake for a friend's birthday, concern for a sick aunt, shopping with a daughter. They share briefly and descriptively about each topic explaining that these are ordinary things, but things they know and care about. Then they ask the children, "What are some things you could write about?" As the children share, the teacher asks questions to help students consider their subjects in more detail. "What did you do at the beach?" "How did you make the sand castle?" Teachers find that after lessons like this, children can choose a topic and begin writing. As children draft, their teacher will talk with them individually about their choices. Teachers have found, too, that one lesson is not enough. Mini-lessons concerning topic generation need to continue throughout the year as do their individual, topic-related conferences.

As children become more confident and fluent, teachers will want to help them bring greater focus to their writing. To support students, a teacher will again plan mini-lessons using her own writing to show how she limits her focus to one aspect of an experience. The teacher would begin by showing children how she does this herself by brainstorming a list of subtopics within a larger topic. For example,

Shopping with my daughter:

- going to the mall
- our conversation in the car
- finding a place to park
- choosing a T-shirt
- my sore feet

lunch

- which restaurant?
- our funny waiter

She would explain that she didn't tell about her shopping trip from beginning to end, instead she limited the story to her daughter's difficulty in selecting just the right T-shirt.

Lessons like this will help children learn that when writers focus their topics it is possible to include more description and detail, and stories become more interesting. As good literature is shared in the classroom, children will gain from thinking about the text from the perspective of a writer. How do you think the author choose his topic? Do you think he told everything about his experience? What was his focus? Ongoing lessons such as these will help students become more deliberate about their own choice of topics.

It is also effective to plan mini-lessons in which children share their sources of topics. They can be asked to tell where and when they thought of the idea. What did they do to remember the idea? Some students find it helpful to keep a notebook (see The Impact of Lucy Calkins: Notebooks, chapter 9) for noting story ideas. Some keep paper and pencil beside their beds. As children share ideas about topic selection, they soon begin to "borrow" topics from one another. They may also be nudged to think about writing at times and in ways they might not have discovered on their own. As children share, teachers can extend their thinking by helping them envision possible structures for their writing (see Author Study, chapter 7). Teachers who give students regular time to write, and offer accessible models for expressing their ideas, find most students highly engaged and energized during writers' workshop.

However, teachers sometimes find a need to use mini-lessons for dealing with problematic issues concerning topic selection. Occasionally, there is a child who cannot think of anything to write about. Suggesting strategies such as looking around the room or out the window of the classroom—or writing over and over "I cannot think of anything to write"—will usually spark an idea. There are some children whose writing simply retells someone else's story—a video or television show. Teachers need to help them understand that this is inappropriate unless it carries some personal significance. Other children need help in seeing that writing about a future event such as, "What I will do at my friend's birthday party." is unlikely to produce a good story. Writers usually have many more interesting things to say about events they have experienced than those they are anticipating.

Another common issue is the child who continues to repeat the same story over and over again. As we discussed earlier, there are many possibilities for writing differently about one topic, and the teacher needs to help children explore those possibilities. Children should recognize that improvement in their writing should be apparent over time and that repeating the same story is unlikely to help them grow and improve as writers. It is reasonable to say, "It's time to try something different. Do you need my help in doing so?" (see Troubleshooting: What About Struggling Writers?, chapter 9).

References

Graves, D. H. (1994.) *A fresh look at writing*. Portsmouth, NH: Heinemann.

Ray, K. W. (1999). *Wondrous words*. Urbana, IL: National Council of Teachers of English.

Spelling Strategies

What do you do when you don't know how to spell a word? Your response to this question most likely revealed at least one of your spelling strategies. Spelling knowledge and strategies are important in the writers' workshop. As teachers, we must help our students develop a repertoire of strategies in order for them to become independent, competent spellers.

Background

In the past the common strategies suggested to children for spelling unknown words were, "Ask the teacher." and "Look it up in a dictionary." Sandra Wilde (1997) acknowledges that seeking out resources to provide unknown spellings is a useful strategy, but she suggests that teachers make a decision that they not be a resource for their students except in special cases. Instead of providing the word, teachers should usually respond, "What do you think? or "Where might you look?" By responding in this way, teachers will "create a useful vacuum in which . . . other strategies can develop, as well as eliminate a dependency that can delay growth in self-reliance" (p. 79). Also, looking in a dictionary is often not the most efficient strategy. Use of a dictionary requires sophisticated knowledge and often takes a lot of time.

Wilde notes that children easily acquire a great deal of knowledge about spelling patterns and letter sounds as they read, but instruction is needed to help them develop and select useful strategies that integrate the knowledge they have gained. Teachers should help their students address the question, "What do I do when I want to write a word I don't know how to spell?" by offering strategies they can use independently. Wilde suggests four strategies arranged in order from least to most sophisticated. These are;

- use a placeholder or invent phonetically
- use knowledge of spelling patterns and/or meaning
- try variations, ask someone, or use a textual resource
- memorize the word (optional)

The first two strategies work well for younger students who do not yet know a lot of words. They are fast. The next two are of increasing value as students mature as writers. They are more accurate. However, all writers will find occasions for employing each of the strategies—even adult writers.

Procedure

The strategies Wilde (1997) proposes provide useful guidance to teachers as they work with students on writing and spelling. The ways they approach the specific strategies will depend upon students' age and development.

Writers use the strategy of *invented* or *placeholder spelling* in order to get their ideas down quickly. Beginning spellers often use strings of letters which may not represent the sounds in their words at all, or they may write a few letters which correspond to the sounds they hear. Though this is the least sophisticated of all the strategies, it is a very useful one for young writers. But, it can be helpful for mature spellers as well. Teachers of older children might use a mini-lesson to demonstrate the use of placeholder spelling in their own writing, perhaps with the name of a country, city, or person. They want students to understand that when they have the need to use difficult words and they don't want to interrupt their train of thought, it is helpful to create a word of about the same length with some correct letters. The context of the piece will support their understanding of the word when they return to reread it, and then they can take the time to seek out the correct spelling

As young children gain more experience with reading and writing, their strategies will begin to incorporate their *knowledge of spelling patterns and meaning* as they consider, "How have I seen this sound (or word) spelled before?" "What do I know about the meaning of this word that can help me spell it?" This kind of thinking often operates at an unconscious level as most young writers quickly gain knowledge about the words they read and write frequently. Teachers will want to focus instruction on students' conscious use of word wall and glue words (see Decoding by Analogy, chapter 4) as aids for their spelling.

Children need to understand that there are times when it is appropriate to "draft-spell" and times it is appropriate to check that their spellings are conventional. When writers move their work toward publication, correct spelling becomes very important. They will want to proofread carefully—a process of monitoring and revising. Teachers can provide lessons that show students how to proofread—how to scan their work for surface errors. When proofreading, students must learn to slow down their reading in a conscientious way in order to focus carefully on each word. To do so, teachers can demonstrate techniques such as reading aloud, pencil pointing at each word, or reading from the bottom to the top of the page. As students proofread, they should mark the words they believe to be spelled incorrectly. In order to correct a misspelled word, they may use the common strategy of *trying variations* of the word by writing it several times and then deciding which spelling looks correct or determining some possible spellings and selecting the correct one. For young children this may be circling three words on the page they believe incorrect or "Have-A-Go" (see Figure 8.3) in which they try at least two spellings for each word, and then determine what is correct. More advanced spellers can be expected to work toward 100% accuracy.

As students proofread, they may *ask someone* to provide words they don't know how to spell. As noted before, it is best to discourage student's reliance on the teacher, but discussing spelling options with peers is a good strategy to develop. Then the result is more likely to be a collaboration. To help students gain the skills needed for working together, teachers' mini-lessons can demonstrate how students should think through the spelling of a difficult word or how to consult with a student editor. For such lessons, teachers often use one child's unedited draft (with permission), making an overhead transparency and duplicated copies for all students. Students can work first as pairs, later exchanging their ideas as the teacher marks the copy on the overhead. When beginning spellers are ready to take a piece to publication, the teacher usually serves as the final editor, but only after the child has taken responsibility for editing himself.

Dictionaries usually come to mind when we think of *using textual resources*. Instead of purchasing a copy of the same dictionary for every student, most teachers prefer having a variety of resources available. They will want to have dictionaries at a variety of levels (e.g., picture, elementary, adult) and of different kinds (e.g., personal and rhyming), thesauruses, a variety of glossaries, map references, word charts (e.g., with glue words and rimes, commercially and class produced), reference books on a variety of content topics, and computer spell-checks. Teachers' instruction should support students' use of these resources through regular mini-lessons. When planning lessons, teachers will consider the development and needs of their students as well as the skills recommended for their grade level. Periodically, teachers will want students to evaluate their use of proofreading strategies during the writers' workshop.

Wilde (1997) notes an optional fourth strategy to be *memorizing words*. Sometimes there are words that students use often and consistently misspell. In some classrooms students decide together that everyone will work to memorize three to five words each week. These words may be self-selected by each student from their personal writing, from a unit of study in which the class is involved, or from words not yet mastered on a list of most-frequently occurring words. Whatever the origin of the words-to-be-memorized lists, the words selected should be ones that have value for the students—words they do not know how to spell and words that are used frequently by them in their writing

Jan Turbill (2000) speaks of the need for students to develop a "spelling conscience." Children who have a spelling conscience have learned a variety of spelling strategies and know when and how to use them appropriately. They are able to not only read-like-a-writer, but read-like-a-speller as well.

It is also important that students be aware of their progress as spellers. From time to time teachers will want to focus students on the number of words they know how to spell correctly. Comparing a current writing piece with one done earlier is a clear way for students to see that their knowledge of correct spellings has increased. Teachers should also help students articulate the strategies they use to spell words correctly, explaining why they chose a particular strategy and noting its effectiveness.

References

Wilde, S. (1997). *What's a schwa sound anyway?: A holistic guide to phonetics, phonics, and spelling.* Portsmouth, NH: Heinemann.

Turbill, J. (2000). Developing a spelling conscience. *Language Arts, 77* (3), 209-217.

FIGURE 8.3   HAVE-A-GO

Have-A-Go		
First Spelling	Tries	Correct Spelling

Vocabulary Development

The purpose of vocabulary development activities in the writers' workshop is to enable students to use more precise and memorable language in their own writing. Often, students give few details and use the same words over and over again in their writing. The events in their lives are described in superficial terms such as "good" or "fun," while their friends and relatives are "nice."

Vocabulary development mini-lessons center on examples of distinctive language in works of children's literature. These lessons resemble vocabulary development activities during the readers' workshop in having the initial purpose of making students aware of interesting words and phrases in literature. They differ in having the additional purpose of helping students to incorporate interesting words and phrases in their own writing. Peter Lancia (1997), a second-grade teacher, found that his students did borrow language patterns and vocabulary from works of children's literature introduced in class.

Collecting New Words

Collecting new words, an approach appropriate for all grades, is shown in this example, based on *Miss Nelson is Missing!* by Harry Allard (1977). The teacher begins by reading the story aloud to the children. When the students discuss the story, the teacher notes the topics of particular interest to them. In this case, the students are likely to be fascinated by one of the characters, Miss Viola Swamp. The teacher has the students make a web of memorable words and phrases related to the topic of interest. For example, students make a web with the words and phrases the author used to describe Viola Swamp: *unpleasant voice, real witch, wicked*. The students may also add words of their own: *mean, cruel, ugly*. The teacher completes the lesson by asking the students to be looking for words that might be added to the list in the future. She reminds them that they may come across such words when they read new books. Later, when students suggest new words, the teacher adds them to the chart. Periodically, the Collecting New Words lesson is repeated with other books. Children can also be invited to make their own lists or webs of vocabulary words.

Author's Craft Lessons

Students need to be reminded that good writing is not just a matter of substituting an uncommon word, such as *humongous*, for a common one, such as *big*. Teachers may conduct lessons to show students how an author uses language to create specific effects. For example, in *Encounter*, Jane Yolen (1992) describes Columbus' landfall in the New World from the perspective of a Taino boy. Students can learn from this text how the effective use of vocabulary goes beyond using uncommon words. Yolen describes the Europeans' gift of bells in the following way:

> And they gave hollow shells with tongues that sang *chunga-chunga*.

The teacher can have students identify phrases in *Encounter* that they find striking. These phrases are written on the board. Students can then discuss how Yolen has used words effectively. For example, in the sentence above, students may notice that Yolen does not use the word *bells* but substitutes words for objects the boy would know: *shells* and *tongues*. She writes that the *shells sang*, instead of that the *bells rang*. She invents a word for the sound the shells made. In concluding the lesson, the teacher asks the students to think about ways that they might improve their own writing by following the author's example.

The writers' workshop provides many opportunities for vocabulary development that build upon lessons for collecting new words and studying the author's craft:

- In mini-lessons, the teacher calls students' attention to new words and phrases that have been added to the new words charts. She asks students if they have come across other words that might be added. She reminds students to refer to charts for ideas to improve their own writing.

- In individual conferences with students, the teacher can praise students for using interesting vocabulary in their drafts. She can encourage students to revise their writing to make their language more precise and descriptive. She can refer students to works of literature that might help them with particular issues they are facing in their writing (Harwayne, 1992).

- During the Author's Chair (see article in chapter 9), the teacher can call the group's attention to the distinctive use of language in pieces written by student authors.

References

Harwayne, S. (1992). *Lasting impressions: Weaving literature into the writers' workshop.* Portsmouth, NH: Heinemann.

Lancia, P. J. (1997). Literary borrowing: The effects of literature on children's writing. *The Reading Teacher, 50* (6), 470–475.

Children's Books Cited

Allard, H. (1977). *Miss Nelson is Missing.* Ill. by J. Marshall. Boston: Houghton Mifflin.

Yolen, J. (1992). *Encounter.* Ill. by D. Shannon. San Diego: Harcourt.

Teacher Conferences

In the writers' workshop, conferences provide teachers opportunities to talk briefly with individual students about their writing. Children share information about their topics and what they are trying to accomplish. Their teachers' comments, questions, and suggestions help children see their writing from a fresh perspective. When a conference ends, students should have a better sense of where their writing is going and what to do next.

Background

Donald Graves (1991) points out that we often view teaching as correcting. When teachers approach student conferences with this philosophy, conferring is difficult. Each conference, then, becomes a lengthy affair as the teacher checks a child's piece, word by word, finding errors for correction. Graves reminds us that skill work should take place at other times, such as during mini-lessons or during special editing conferences before a piece is taken to publication. While children are in the process of drafting their works, conferences have the benefit of putting both teacher and child in touch with the child's writing.

Graves (1991) offers some essential elements to be found in good conferences:

1. *Hearing the child's voice.* This is a time for both the child and the teacher to hear the child. The teacher listens and follows the child's lead.

2 *Considering plans.* Knowing one's intent enables the piece to move forward. The teacher might ask, "What will you do next?"

3. *Extending thinking.* The teacher should make suggestions to move the child into his "zone of proximal development" (see The Impact of Lev Vygotsky: Constructivism, chapter 1).

4. *Proposing solutions and new problems.* The teacher supports the child's resolution of problems and poses new issues for consideration (p. 93).

Procedure

Conferences may take place at students' desks as the teacher moves around the classroom, at the teacher's desk, or at a special conference table. Teachers usually find the flow of the workshop is smoother when they are the ones who do the moving. Also, their conferences tend to be shorter. As teachers circulate about the room, they often carry a clipboard for recording conferences, Post-its to make notes for the students, and a small chair or stool to pull up beside each author. They vary their movement pattern throughout the classroom so that children always feel the need to be prepared. And, as teachers talk with students, they expect that other students may be listening and learning from the conversation.

Teachers should think of conferences as being about two minutes in length (though some may last only a few seconds). During a conference the child will show the teacher what he knows and gain a better sense of where the piece is going. The teacher should project a sense that, "You know your subject and your plans for your piece. I want to hear about them so that I can support and help you." Children will come to anticipate questions such as, "How is it going?" "What is your piece about?" "What do you plan to do next?" Students know that their teacher expects a response and will wait, patiently, for their reply. Teachers should be less concerned with what they will say in a conference than in being an attentive listener. They should also remember that every issue cannot be addressed in one conference. They need to be selective, realizing that there will be other days for other things.

As teachers confer with students they will note those who can clearly and succinctly talk about their writing. When Marcus Jamal approached Edward's desk and asked, "How is it going?" Edward responded, "I'm working on my story about my cousin's birthday party. I'm trying to add more detail about the fun games we played." Mr. Jamal asked Edward what he had written about the games so far. Edward read, "When Lori hit the piñata lots of candy came out. I grabbed a big bunch. Then we blew up balloons. Mine got bigger and bigger and then it popped. All the kids laughed. I got a prize." Mr. Jamal commented that he could tell the party was a great one and that he felt sure the class would enjoy Edward's story.

Mr. Jamal was pleased to note that Edward was considering information from a recent mini-lesson in which Marcus had shown how he used "spider legs" to extend his own writing to make it clearer and more interesting. Mr. Jamal talked with Edward about why he thought adding more details about the games would be a good idea. He suggested Edward choose one of the games and get a good picture of what that game was like. Edward chose the piñata, and Mr. Jamal encouraged him to talk about some of the detail he might include. "Where was the piñata located and what did it look like? What did all the children do when Lori broke it? What did Lori do?" Mr. Jamal then "nudged" (see The Impact of Donald Graves: The Process Approach to Writing, chapter 6 for a discussion of the "nudge paper") Edward to add some of this information about the piñata game to his piece and suggested he might want to think about adding more about the other party games as well. He said he would check back later to see how it was going. Mr. Jamal made a note of the conference on his Status of the Class form (see figure 11.5).

Teachers' conferences around students' drafts usually proceed as Mr. Jamal's did. They discuss what the child is doing, offer encouragement, suggest how he might become a better writer (perhaps leaving a note as a reminder), and record the content of the conference and their intent to follow up with the student.

Students who have finished pieces they want to publish can benefit from an editing conference. Teachers often find it works well to designate one writers' workshop each week for this purpose. Before conferring with the teacher, students should be expected to edit their own work and then to meet with a peer for further editing assistance. The responsibility students are expected to assume for themselves will depend on their grade and developmental levels. During an editing conference, the teacher will review the student's writing, then choose to teach two or three specific skills which will best serve the child's needs, for example inserting periods at the end of each sentence or capitalizing the first, last, and important words in a title. The student can then use the skills to edit her piece and add the skills to an ongoing list of editing skills for which she is responsible.

During conferences, teachers serve as listeners and guides for their students. As children explain their intentions and discuss their problems, they often discover clarification for themselves. At other times the teacher's support will help students uncover solutions or reveal new challenges. It is the teacher's role to listen, reflect, determine what responsibilities students can accept, and decide whether or not they know what to do next. Conferring teachers need to remember that their goal is not to fix everything in a child's piece of writing, but to help students develop the strategies needed to assume increasing independence for the improvement of their own writing.

Reference

Graves, D. H. (1991). *Build a literate classroom*. Portsmouth NH: Heinemann.

Resources

Anderson, C. (2000). *How's it going: A practical guide to conferring with student writers*. Portsmouth NH: Heinemann.
A conference should be viewed as a conversation between writers. Anderson shows how teachers can structure their conversations to first, learn about the work the child is doing as a writer and, second, to help the child become better at that work.

Thomason, T. (1998). *Writer to writer: How to conference young authors*. Norwood, MA: Christopher-Gordon.
Each of fourteen short chapters introduces a different facet of the writing conference or the philosophy and classroom practice to support it. Thomason believes teachers should assume the role of coach—demonstrating, guiding, mentoring, and encouraging their students as they work to craft each piece of writing.

Troubleshooting: What About Conventional Spelling?

It is common to hear public complaints about a decline in literacy standards within today's schools. Invariably, the evidence for such a decline is "Kids today can't spell," followed by the recommendation, "It's time to go back to the basics." Wendy Bean and Chrys Bouffler (1997) note that "spelling looms large in the 'public' perception of what it means to be literate." Noting the pervasivness of this perception, they wondered about the standard against which this decline was being measured. When was the "golden age" of good spellers? In their research, they discovered that concerns about spelling are found throughout history. There was never a "golden age." Because surface features are the first things people see when they look at a piece of writing, they have always found them a quick measure of literacy—an easy way to distinguish the educated from the masses.

While much of the public hold the view that literacy is an acquired set of technical skills, many educators understand the issue to be more complex. They recognize that the social or cultural context often determines an individual's level of literacy. A person's inability to reach high standards of spelling accuracy may not be as important as other abilities when considering someone's level of literacy.

These viewpoints are at the center of issues affecting the teaching of spelling today and are reflected in concerns frequently voiced by teachers:

- Should my students use invented spelling?
- Should my students just learn to spell naturally as they read and write?
- Should I have a program to teach spelling?

Learning to spell is a developmental process, like learning to talk. As children learn to speak they make approximations, "muh" for "milk," and they are encouraged. Invented spellings are the approximations that writers make in an attempt to make sense of the spelling system. They, too, should be encouraged.

Before the process approach to writing was accepted in classrooms, it was thought that children should spell words correctly before they wrote. This view limited their writing and opportunities for them to create meanings for themselves. Using invented spelling for writing encourages ownership, risk taking, and problem solving. Children develop their own spelling strategies and use them to write for their own purposes. As Bean and Bouffler (1997) point out, "Children will only take responsibility for their own spelling if they are given meaningful and purposeful opportunities to write. They will learn to spell only when they have ample opportunities to write in a supportive environment" (p. 21).

Invented Spelling

Most of today's kindergarten and first-grade teachers feel little anxiety when their students use invented spellings. They note the children's growing fluency with writing and are encouraged by their increasing knowledge of sounds and letters. Even kindergarten teachers expect that their students will use some conventional spellings. However, teachers' and parents' anxiety increases as students move through the grades and invented spelling is still prevalent in their writing. When should children's invented spelling be replaced by conventional?

Research by Richard Gentry (Gentry & Gillet, 1993) helps us respond to that question. He identifies five stages of invented spelling that most children move through more or less sequentially: (a) precommunicative—describes writing before it can be read by others; (b) semiphonetic—spelling used represents some of the surface sound feature of the words; (c) phonetic—all essential sounds are represented; (d) transitional—many words are spelled conventionally, child attends to word's appearance as well as sounds; (e) conventional—most words are correct. Gentry believes that spelling instruction will have benefit for children who have entered the transitional and conventional stages. We can expect that children who engage in meaningful, consistent writing experiences will gradually move toward conventional spelling. Using these stages to assess children's progress can guide teachers' instruction and their communication with parents.

Is there an age when students should not be using invented spelling? All writers appreciate the convenience of invented spelling from time to time depending on the situation, and often those spellings are acceptable. Students should understand that correcting for spelling is a courtesy they extend their readers. Conventional spelling makes their writing more readable. Knowing one's audience, or the context for their writing, will determine if correct spelling is important and should guide students' attention to careful editing. Students also need to understand that conventional spelling or "book spelling" is their ultimate goal. By the time they have completed the primary grades, very few of their spellings should be invented.

The Natural Approach

So, if students are immersed in meaningful reading and writing opportunities, can teachers be confident they will acquire correct spellings on their own? Some schools, dissatisfied with traditional spelling programs, have eliminated spelling as a subject. While it is clear that extensive reading and writing are important in the acquisition of spelling knowledge (Smith, 1982), all children can benefit from a focus on the morphemic structure of words (Bolton & Snowball, 1993, p. 54).

Spelling Programs

Then what kind of spelling program should be used? Spelling books are common in elementary schools, but problematic. They focus on learning to spell lists of words (most of which students can already spell) and work with some specific spelling patterns, but they ignore learners' application of knowledge. Other criticisms include: they are boring, take too much time for the results they produce, repeat the same material year after year, and fragment the language arts (Wilde, 1992).

A balanced program anchored in the context of students' writing, where spelling is learned both informally and through instruction, is recommended. In a balanced program, children engage in invented spelling, learning a great many of the predictable consonant sounds on their own. Teachers often maintain a checklist to assess students' progress. As children read, informal learning about predicable spelling patterns also takes place.

In a balanced program, instruction centers on the spelling patterns used by students in their writing. Teachers plan whole class mini-lessons to focus on wide-range skills that benefit all students, such as discovering different ways to spell long *a* (see Decoding by Analogy, chapter 4). They form small instructional groups to meet students' specific needs and plan mini-lessons around skills such as forming plurals with *es*.

A balanced program may include spelling lists. Again, the words should have foundation in children's writing. Each week the students, perhaps with teacher assistance, can make personal lists of five words they need to learn to spell. They practice those words on their own time during the week and work with partners who test one another at the end of the week.

Concerns about spelling are lessened as teachers observe students' making independent discoveries during readers' and writers' workshops. Balanced with instruction focused on spelling patterns (see Decoding by Analogy, chapter 4) and strategies (see Spelling Strategies in this chapter) teachers can be assured that their students are developing into independent, skilled writers.

References

Bean, W., & Bouffler, C. (1997). *Read, write, spell.* Portsmouth, NH: Heinemann.

Bolton, F., & Snowball, D. (1993). *Ideas for spelling.* Portsmouth, NH: Heinemann.

Gentry, J. R., & Gillet, J. W. (1993). *Teaching kids to spell.* Portsmouth, NH: Heinemann.

Smith, F. (1982). *Writing and the writer.* New York: Holt, Rinehart, & Winston.

Wilde, S. (1992). *You kan red this!: Spelling and punctuation for whole language classrooms,* K–6. Portsmouth, NH: Heinemann.

Chapter 9

STUDENT-DIRECTED ACTIVITIES IN THE WRITERS' WORKSHOP

The Impact of Lucy Calkins: Notebooks

Lucy Calkins (1991, 1994) describes how writers keep notebooks that they fill with observations, questions, newspaper clippings, bits and pieces they have collected. Writers often do not know in advance just why these bits and pieces have attracted their attention. Gradually, as they explore these bits through writing, their thoughts begin to take form.

According to Calkins (1991), writers live wide-awake lives, having an alertness to the world around them. She cites the example of author Jean Little (1986), who recalled the exact moment in her childhood when she began to see the world as a writer. One day when Little was sick and at home in bed, her mother brought her a plate of orange slices. Little saw the slices as a fleet of bright boats, lined up behind one another. She was suddenly aware of the beauty of the moment, the wood of the window sill, the world outside. Little told herself that she would always remember how those orange boats looked. She felt for the first time that her world belonged to her, and she began making an effort to save precious memories so that she could always return to them.

"When people ask those of us who staff Teachers College Writing Project about our goals," Calkins (1991) writes, "we sometimes answer that our first goal is for young people to cherish the sight of orange slices lined up on a window sill" (p. 35). Calkins points out that we cannot give our students rich lives outside the classroom. However, we can help students to notice and appreciate the richness already present in their lives. In Calkins' view, notebooks become a lens through which students can view and reflect upon their lives. Calkins states,

> Notebooks validate a child's existence. Notebooks say, "Your thoughts, your
> noticings, your fleet of orange slices matter." (p. 35)

Capturing Significant Thoughts

Calkins sees notebooks as a way of helping students to live writers' lives and to write about what is most important to them. With notebooks students write down the thoughts that seem significant to them at the time, without the expectation that any

---

entry will immediately be extended and turned into a published piece. Instead, students write until they have created a collection of entries. They then go back through their notebooks, looking for themes in their entries or for a single entry that strikes them as particularly significant. Only then do they begin the work of developing a piece to be published.

Calkins (1991) gives the example of Luz, a young girl from Colombia. Luz read through the entries in her notebook, searching for language that seemed alive. She expanded some of these bits into entries and continued to read and reread, until she found a theme she felt strongly about. Luz chose an entry that described how, as a young boy, her father used to climb a tree and pretend that he was in an airplane flying to the United States. This entry was not among the best Luz had written, but it caught her attention. Luz began to write more about how her father left Colombia. This entry led to another about what she had loved about her own life in Colombia. Luz continued to live with her topic by writing more entries, among others, about packing her suitcase to leave Colombia and her fears of living in the United States. Gradually, Luz moved from writing notebook entries to writing rough drafts. In this example, Calkins conveys the sense of how students use notebooks to grow ideas for published pieces.

More Thoughtful Writing

Calkins' interest in notebooks grew from her concern that writing in many classrooms with writers' workshops was becoming routine. Students were moving pieces through the process—rehearsing or planning, drafting, revising, editing, and publishing—but their pieces showed a lack of spark. With notebooks, the writing of entries and the search for the topic may occupy as much, or more, of the time than the drafting and revising of the final piece. In classrooms with notebooks, students may publish fewer pieces in the course of a school year than in other writing process classrooms. However, the pieces they do publish are often written with more thought, feeling, and care.

Teachers who wish to teach writing with notebooks begin by keeping notebooks of their own. They share entries from their notebooks with students. They discuss how they chose their notebooks, perhaps by looking for a book of a certain size, with lined or unlined paper. Students purchase their own notebooks. Each day, students have time to write in their notebooks and to share their entries with others. Calkins (1991) points out that notebooks are not effective unless they leave the classroom. That is, students learn to carry their notebooks home and to record thoughts or observations when they are not in school. Writing, Calkins (1994) argues, is not desk work. It is life work.

References

Calkins, L. M. (1991). *Living between the lines.* Portsmouth, NH: Heinemann.

Calkins, L. M. (1994). *The art of teaching writing* (2nd ed.). Portsmouth, NH: Heinemann.

Little, J. (1987). *Hey world, her I am!* New York: Harper & Row.

Resource

Hindley, J. (1996). *In the company of children.* York, ME: Stenhouse.

Written by a teacher at the Manhanttan New School. Provides both inspiration and practical suggestions about the process approach to writing and the writers' workshop. Includes two chapters on notebooks.

Journals and Learning Logs

There are many different kinds of journals, but the personal journal is probably the form most commonly used in classrooms. The personal journal is usually a tablet in which students write diary entries or stories. Diary entries are often a simple recounting of events. This kind of journal writing may be valuable and enjoyable for students if it occurs once a week or so. For example, students can be asked to write about what happened over the weekend.

We do not recommend building the classroom writing program around personal journal writing because this practice may limit students' opportunities to grow as writers. Personal journal writing engages students in drafting, so they often develop some fluency as writers. However, it provides little or no opportunity for students to engage in the other four phases of the writing process: planning, revising, editing, and publishing.

Second-grade teacher Marcus Jamal expands personal journal writing beyond drafting. After students do their weekly journal writing about what they did over the weekend, they read their entry to a partner. Then the two work together to edit the draft.

Instead of relying exclusively on personal journals, you might consider trying the notebook approach developed by Calkins (see earlier article in this chapter). This approach encourages students to go beyond an accounting of events to reflect on the significance of events in their lives. Students review notebook entries to identify themes, and in this way entries can form the basis for longer pieces. Unlike personal journals, notebooks invite students to engage in all phases of the writing process, not just drafting. In our experience, notebooks offer more opportunity than personal journals for improving the quality of students' writing.

While we suggest limiting personal journal writing, we recommend extensive use of another form of journals—learning logs. Routman (1991) defines learning logs in this way:

> The student communicates how and what he has understood about a concept or unit of study. Students describe their learning processes—that is, "writing to learn." Some content area teachers take five to ten minutes at the beginning or end of a period for students to respond in their learning logs. Learning logs may be used in mathematics, science, music, art, foreign languages, or any subject area. (p. 229)

One tablet may become a math learning log, another a social studies learning log, and so on. Students may keep learning logs for only one content area subject or several, at the teacher's discretion.

Students may write at the beginning or end of the lesson. Writing at the beginning of the lesson may be a good choice when students are about to start a unit on a new topic. Writing beforehand may also be a good idea if the previous lesson in that content area occurred a while ago and students need to refresh their memories about the topic.

Usually, teachers have students write at the end of the lesson. The teacher's directions to the students are clear and simple. For example,

> Today we discussed different kinds of clouds, then went outside to see whether we could figure out what kinds of clouds were in the sky today. In your science learning logs, please write about what you learned today. This is a time for you to reflect on what you understood and what was unclear to you. Please be sure to include any questions you have at this time.

The teacher allows students about 10 minutes to jot down their thoughts. A brief sharing and discussion of learning log entries may occur if time permits. In any event, the teacher reads the students' learning logs before the next lesson to get an idea of concepts that were well understood and concepts that need to be retaught. Some teachers have students discuss their learning log entries as a way of starting the next lesson on the topic.

When working with learning logs, teachers help students feel comfortable about writing honestly about what they have and have not understood. This can be accomplished by complimenting students on their reflections, especially when they have struggled with the content in the lesson. However, having established this approach to learning logs, teachers should be prepared for some revelations about their teaching. Sometimes, students indicate that they have gained little understanding of the concepts we tried to teach, or they may have developed misconceptions. They may comment that the lesson was boring or too difficult for them. All of this is valuable feedback, if painful to read at times.

In short, learning logs are beneficial to students in two ways. First, they provide students with the opportunity to reflect upon and consolidate new content area learning. Second, if the feedback provided in the logs is taken seriously by the teacher, students will benefit from improved instruction.

References

Routman, R. (1991). *Invitations: Changing as teachers and learners.* Portsmouth, NH: Heinemann.

Peer Conferences

In peer conferences, students meet with other students to get responses to their writing and ideas about how to improve their writing. Peer conferences benefit student authors because, if they need help with their writing, they do not have to wait until the teacher is available. They also receive a wider range of responses than if their only conferences were with a teacher. Peers who conduct conferences benefit because they gain insights into the writing process and develop the social skills needed to communicate effectively and assist others.

Of course, most students do not automatically know how to help another writer. They need to learn from their teachers how to conduct conferences with peers (Graves, 1983). Thomason (1998) points out that the author's chair (see article in this chapter) is a good starting point for introducing students to the idea of peer conferences. In the author's chair, students are taught first to make positive comments about a peer's writing. Then they ask questions about the piece. Once students have learned this routine of praise followed by the asking of questions, they can transfer this knowledge to peer conferences.

Another step teachers can take to establish peer conferences is to demonstrate conferring skills by conducting conferences with small groups rather than with individual students. Small group conferences give students the opportunity to observe how the teacher helps others improve their writing, for example, by listening attentively, making notes, and phrasing questions and suggestions in a certain way.

Mini-lessons are a direct way to teach conferring skills. The teacher may use one of her own pieces of writing as the basis for a mini-lesson. After stating her own concerns about the piece and reading it aloud, the teacher invites students to make positive comments about the piece and offer suggestions for revision. Later mini-lessons may be centered on similar class revision conferences, but in response to pieces written by student volunteers.

Peer Conferences in Primary Grades

In kindergarten, first, and second grade, teachers often find it helpful to teach children exactly what to do and say in conferences. The recommended procedures and questions are posted on chart paper, providing children with a script to follow. The teacher designs questions to address goals she has for improving the children's writing. As children gain experience with conferences, they can respond spontaneously and will not need to refer to the chart.

In a first-grade classroom, most children were producing drafts of only two or three sentences. The teacher believed the children were ready to develop their ideas into stories, and she taught a mini-lesson showing how stories usually have a beginning, middle, and end. She encouraged students to extend their writing so that their pieces would have these three parts. To guide children during peer conferences, the teacher wrote the following on a sheet of chart paper:

Things to ask

- Does the story have a beginning?
- Does the story have a middle?
- Does the story have an ending?

During peer conferences, the author read the story. Then the peer asked the questions, which the author attempted to answer. The author and the peer tried to come to agreement about what the author should do to improve the piece. At the end of the conference, the peer wrote a comment on the back of the author's draft and signed his or her name. When it was time for a teacher conference, the teacher looked at the peer's comment and asked what the author had done to improve the piece before coming to see her. In this way the teacher showed that she valued peer conferences and encouraged the children to show initiative in making revisions.

As the year progressed, the teacher added other questions to the chart. At one point she felt that children were describing events but not discussing their feelings about those events. To meet this need, she added a question to the chart: *Does the story have feelings?* Other questions added to the chart included: *Does the story have a setting?* and *Does the story have interesting details?*

Procedures for Upper Grades

Teachers of older students, in the third grade on up, may find that their students also benefit from learning specific procedures for conducting a peer conference, but that these procedures can be more general and flexible than those for younger students. Here are questions and procedures that might be used in conferences with older students:

Peer:	Is there something you want me to think about while I'm listening to your piece?
Author:	Reads piece aloud.
Peer:	Makes a positive comments about the piece.
	Responds to author's concerns.
Author:	Responds to suggestions and raises other concerns.
Peer:	Helps author decide what to do next.

The author should take notes during the conference of suggestions made by the peer. Later, when making revisions, the author can refer to these notes.

Especially when peer conferences have just been introduced, teachers observe to see how they are going. Problems identified may be addressed either in mini-lessons or through individual coaching. For example, peers may need to be reminded that their first response to a piece should be to make positive comments. During a mini-lesson, the teacher can ask students for suggestions of positive comments they might make about an author's work, perhaps centering on their favorite part of the story, an interesting detail, or an engaging lead.

From Planning to Publishing

Peer conferences may take place during all phases of the writing process, from planning to publishing. Planning conferences may be used to give students a first experience with conferring. The teacher begins by conducting a mini-lesson in which she demonstrates how she thinks of topics for writing and makes a list of topics. The teacher asks the students to make up their own list of topics (see Topic Selection, chapter 8). The students then work in pairs. The first student (the author) discusses the topics on his list, while the second student asks questions and helps the author decide upon the topic he would like to write about first. Then the students switch roles. The teacher lets students know that, when they are not sure what to write about, they can always meet with a peer to discuss possibilities.

Conferences may occur while students are drafting. Sometimes students wonder whether the piece they have started is making sense or if it is interesting to other people. However, a prime time for conferences is when students have finished a first draft and want ideas for revision. The procedures and questions for primary- and upper-grade classrooms described above can be used effectively during revision conferences.

Editing conferences conducted by peers decrease teachers' responsibility and increase students' responsibility for correcting their own work. Most students know which other students can help them with spelling, grammar, and punctuation. In some classrooms, students take turns wearing visors that identify them as editors, and different students serve as editors on different days. A table may be reserved for editing conferences, with dictionaries kept on a nearby shelf. Teachers may wish to remind peer editors that their job is not to make corrections themselves but to guide the author in making corrections.

Blake (1992) studied a fourth-grade classroom in which native and non-native speakers of English participated together in peer conferences as part of the writers' workshop. She discovered that peer conferences benefitted students in at least four ways. First, conferences gave students a framework in which to interact and share ideas. Second, conferences helped students to revise and extend their first drafts. Third, conferences contributed to a sense of community in the classroom, as students came to know one another through their interactions around writing. Finally, conferences helped all students, native and non-native speakers of English alike, to write in a more clear and detailed fashion.

References

Blake, B. E. (1992). Talk in non-native English speakers' peer writing conferences: What's the difference? *Language Arts, 69* (8), 604–610.

Graves, D. (1983). *Writing: Teachers and children at work.* Exter, NH: Heinemann.

Thomason, T. (1998). *Writer to writer: How to conference young authors.* Norwood, MA: Christopher-Gordon.

Sharing and Publishing

Graves (1994) describes a scene in Ms. Pritchard's fourth-grade class in which Jennifer shared her writing with her classmates. Jennifer's piece described the birth of a baby lamb. Jennifer's classmates responded by telling her what they remembered about her piece, then asked questions and made suggestions for improvement. Ms. Pritchard had taught her students to respond in these ways to one another's writing. Graves observes,

> Writing is a social act. People write to affect the lives of others. If Jennifer's writing was addressed only to the teacher, the other children would not be able to participate in the excitement of her story or to ask questions to satisfy their curiosity. (p. 132)

Writing can be shared in many ways. Some ways of sharing, such as the author's chair (see article in this chapter) and teacher and peer conferences (see chapter 8 and this chapter) are rather formal. Other ways of sharing may be spontaneous and informal. For example, while drafting, Carlos found that his writing was going well, and he wanted to share his words with someone. He asked Jessica, seated across the table, to listen to what he had written.

Sharing benefits student authors by giving them an audience for their writing and the opportunity for response. Sharing contributes to the sense of community in the classroom by letting students learn about and support one another's writing.

Publishing is a form of sharing one's writing. In a broad sense, publishing is any means of making one's work public. Reading one's finished piece aloud may be considered a form of publishing. Publishing is also the last phase in the writing process, after revising and editing. In elementary classrooms, publishing often involves having students develop their revised and edited texts into illustrated books, wall charts, or other finished products.

Sharing Sessions

Successful sharing sessions do not just happen. Students must be guided to participate effectively. Graves (1994) begins with the premise that writers of all ages need attentive listeners. To encourage children to become attentive listeners, he suggests asking them to recall the author's exact words. Children respond to classmates' writing by (a) recalling the author's actual words, (b) making comments, and (c) posing questions. Comments may be reflections upon the author's piece. For example, Ms. Pritchard made the following comment about Jennifer's piece:

> I could see a good picture in the words you chose, Jennifer. It was messy and bloody. I had a kind of gooey picture although you didn't use the word *gooey*.
> (p. 132)

Teachers like Ms. Pritchard repeatedly model using comments to provide the author with feedback. After a time, students learn to generate comments of their own. This helps students in peer conferences. Graves sees advantages to having recall and comments occur before questions. He argues that good questions arise only after children have considered a text carefully.

Comments may also stem from the recollections of audience members, which arise as a result of having heard the author's piece. For example, if a child writes about her birthday party, other children may be reminded of their birthdays. Graves suggests letting only two children share their recollections, so that the discussion does not drift away from the author's piece.

Graves finds it helpful for children to learn this three-part format for responding. However, he cautions that the format should not be followed rigidly once it has become familiar to children, or responding may turn into an empty ritual.

Publishing

While publishing is the last phase in the writing process, its significance goes far beyond the finished product. "Publication matters," Calkins (1994) writes, "and it matters because it inducts us into the writerly life" (p. 266). Calkins describes how her own experience of being a published author made her feel that she had become an insider to the world of authors. In her view, publishing is significant because it marks the beginning of students' entry into authorship.

Teachers who conduct writers' workshops find that students do not have a clear picture of how the writing process works until they have published at least once. Before they publish, students have little sense of how the various phases—planning, drafting, revising, editing—fit together. Calkins believes that students should publish early in the school year, preferably by the sixth week, so that they gain a sense, early on, of what being an author is all about. Usually, teachers are not satisfied with the quality of students' writing at this point. However, after students have completed their first publication, they see that their writing will be going somewhere and they become more motivated to write. At this point teachers can focus on improving the quality of writing and raise the standards for publication. For example, in a first-grade class children might be allowed to publish their first book as soon as they have three sentences on the same topic. Later, children can be required to write more developed pieces, such as stories with a beginning, middle, and end.

In some classrooms teachers or parents take the major responsibility for publishing. After students have revised and edited their pieces, the adult enters the text on the computer and prints it out. The lines of the text are cut apart and pasted on pages to be accompanied by illustrations drawn by the students. The finished products are often quite impressive.

Calkins' (1994) takes a different perspective. She advocates leaving publishing in the hands of the students, even if the finished products are not as polished as they would be with adult assistance. She writes,

> I have come to believe, however, that it is better to put publication in its place—that is, into the hands of youngsters as they write. Young writers need to ask themselves, "Who will my readers be? What shall I make of this?" Writers need to imagine the form their texts will take, and most of all, writers need to imagine readers, perhaps opening their books as picture books and turning the pages, perhaps hearing the words as a toast at a family gathering. (p. 269)

Following Calkins' approach, teachers provide students with a variety of materials for publishing, such as paper of different sizes and colors, colored pens, paints, staplers, cardboard, and scraps of wallpaper or wrapping paper. Often, these supplies are kept at a publishing center, a large table with room for about 4 to 6 students. As students gather to publish their work, they gain ideas by observing the publishing efforts of their peers.

Teachers show students how to make different types of books, such as pop-up books and books with wallpaper covers (see Figures 9.1 and 9.2). Samples of publications, such as shape books, wall charts, and brochures, are available for students to consider. Students may have the choice of entering their text on the computer or of copying it by hand.

Teachers and peers guide students to consider the form of publishing that will best convey their ideas. Calkins gives the example of Becka, who wrote notebook entries about seeing a deer early in the morning. Becka was asked to consider what she could make of these entries, such as a collection of poems, a photo essay, or a picture book. Options for publishing can go beyond books and paper. For example, students might publish by reading their piece aloud on audiotape, or by recruiting classmates to perform their piece for videotaping.

Publishing, especially when students are doing illustrations, can be extremely time-consuming. To prevent students from spending more time drawing than writing, teachers set limits on the amount of time students can use to complete a book in class (although the student may spend more time on the book as homework). After students have completed their first publications, teachers may require that they complete a certain number of pieces (say, three) before choosing one to be published. This procedure helps students understand that the process of writing is as important as the finished product, and that not all pieces can or should be published.

FIGURE 9.1   MAKING A POP-UP BOOK

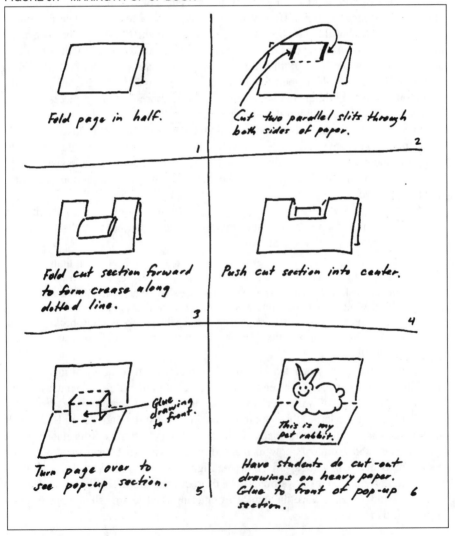

FIGURE 9.2   MAKING A WALLPAPER BOOK

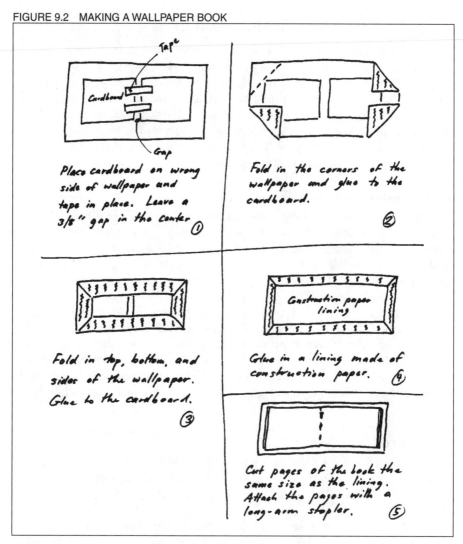

Place cardboard on wrong side of wallpaper and tape in place. Leave a 3/8" gap in the center ①

Fold in the corners of the wallpaper and glue to the cardboard. ②

Fold in top, bottom, and sides of the wallpaper. Glue to the cardboard. ③

Glue in a lining made of construction paper. ④

Cut pages of the book the same size as the lining. Attach the pages with a long-arm stapler. ⑤

References

Calkins, L. M. (1994). *The art of teaching writing* (2nd ed.). Portsmouth, NH: Heinemann.

Graves, D. (1994). *A fresh look at writing.* Portsmouth, NH: Heinemann.

Resources

Chihak, J. (1999). Success is in the details: Publishing to validate elementary authors. *Language Arts, 76* (6), 491–498.

Describes the Panther Paw Press, a successful schoolwide publishing program involving parent volunteers. Discusses benefits to students, parents, and teachers.

Johnson, P. (1990). *A book of one's own: Developing literacy through making books.* Portsmouth, NH: Heinemann.

Written for primary grade teachers but useful as a resource throughout the grades. Discusses book-making as an art form. Covers all steps in creating books, and provides instructions for making different types of books, from simple to elaborate.

Author's Chair

The author's chair is an essential part of the writers' workshop. The purpose of this approach is to allow students to share their writing and develop a sense of authorship, to learn what it means to be an author. Students sit before the class in a special chair, known as the author's chair, to read their work aloud and receive reactions from the audience—usually their classmates and the teacher. The author's chair is one way that students can publish or make their work public (see Sharing and Publishing, this chapter). The author's chair contributes to a sense of community in the classroom, as students come to appreciate one another's writing.

Background

The approach known as the author's chair was developed in Ellen Blackburn's first-grade classroom in Somersworth, New Hampshire, where it was studied by Don Graves and Jane Hansen (1983). In Blackburn's classroom, the teacher and children read aloud either trade books or their own published books. At present, the term author's chair usually refers to children's sharing of their own published books and drafts.

Graves and Hansen (1983) discovered three phases in the first graders' understanding of authorship. In the first phase, replication, their concept of authorship was vague. They knew that authors wrote books but did not have a sense of how this was accomplished. In the second phase, transition, the children came to see themselves as authors. They knew that they could choose their topics, and they become more proficient in the use of print to convey ideas. In the third phase, option-awareness, they became aware of what authors could do to make their writing more interesting, such as mixing fact and fiction.

Procedures

Many teachers have a special chair, such as an old rocker, that they place at the front of the classroom to serve as the author's chair. They introduce the approach through demonstrations in which they read aloud their own drafts or published pieces to the class.

Teachers have different ways of scheduling children to take their turn in the author's chair. Blackburn chose a child to be the author of the week, and she put the child's photo on the bulletin board along with a list of his published books. The author chose his favorite published books to read aloud to the class. She also let children sign up for the author's chair as soon as they had finished publishing their book. Other teachers encourage children to take a turn in the author's chair when they are working on a draft and want to get their classmates' ideas.

Teachers establish a procedure for the class to follow when an author finishes sharing a piece. First, the audience receives the piece. Students are taught to make statements about the content of the piece and what they liked about it, such as, "You wrote about visiting your cousins in Georgia, and I liked the part about going swimming in the river." Next, students ask the author questions, such as "When are you going there again?" If the author has read a draft and is trying to get ideas, the audience makes suggestions, such as "Maybe you could tell us what your sister did to make you so angry."

Teachers guide the students so that their responses are positive and helpful to the author. Because all students eventually take their turn in the author's chair, they soon learn to be considerate of one another's feelings. The author's chair has the additional benefit of preparing students to conduct peer conferences (see article in this section).

References

Graves, D., & Hansen, J. (1983). The author's chair. *Language Arts, 60* (2), 176–183.

Connections to Home and Community: Writing Backpacks

In writing process classrooms, most teachers want students to be motivated to write at home as well as at school. To find out whether students are already writing on their own at home, teachers may conduct interviews and ask students to bring in examples. Some of Ms. Parker's second-grade students brought in greeting cards, letters written to grandparents, and lists of phone numbers. One girl kept a diary at home. However, many of the students did not seem to be doing much writing at home.

Writing Backpacks

To strengthen students' writing at home, and to give parents an opportunity to help their children write, Ms. Parker introduced writing backpacks. Reutzel and Fawson (1990) developed a traveling backpack project, and Ms. Parker used a simplified version of their ideas. Given the schedule she intended to follow, Ms. Parker needed to purchase two backpacks. She filled the backpacks with all the materials students would need to draft and publish a short book. The materials were

- lined paper
- unlined (8 1/2 x 11) white paper
- colored pens
- construction paper for covers

- yarn and string
- hole punch
- student dictionary
- patterns for shape books

Ms. Parker sent a letter to parents to let them know that their child would be bringing a writing backpack home (see Figure 9.3). In the backpack, Ms. Parker included a laminated card with suggestions for parents (see Figure 9.4).

Ms. Parker followed the process approach to writing in her class, but she knew that many of her students' parents had rather traditional views about writing. A number of parents were more concerned with spelling than the messages conveyed in children's writing. Ms. Parker discussed the process approach to writing at the open house held in the fall and during parent conferences. However, with the writing backpacks, she asked only that parents work with their children in a manner comfortable for them, despite the fact that this might not be consistent with the process approach to writing.

Most of the children's parents responded enthusiastically to the writing backpacks. A few parents asked to have the backpacks come home more often. At conference time, Ms. Parker noticed that quite a few parents had specific questions about how to help their children grow as writers. Some children received help with publishing from a family member other than a parent, such as older brothers and sisters or grandparents. A handful of children reported that no one was available to help them, so they made books on their own. Most of the children brought their books to school to be shared. In short, writing backpacks seem to be an effective means of fostering students' writing at home with their families.

References

Reutzel, D. R., & Fawson, P. C. (1990). Traveling tales: Connecting parents and children through writing. *The Reading Teacher, 44* (3), 222–227.

Resource

Richgels, D. J., & Wold, L. S. (1999). Literacy on the road: Backpacking partnership between school and home. *The Reading Teacher, 52* (1), 18–29.

Another approach to using backpacks. This one focuses on sending books home to be read together by children and parents. Ideas for responding to the literature are included in the backpack.

FIGURE 9.3   PARENT LETTER

Dear Parents:

To encourage students to write at home, I'm introducing writing backpacks. These backpacks will be filled with the supplies your child needs to write and publish a simple book at home.

Beginning in October, your child will be bringing a writing backpack home once a month. If there is a certain day of the week that you prefer to have the backpack come home, please let me know by completing the form below.

When the backpack comes home, please take a few minutes to help your child think of a topic of interest and write and illustrate a simple book. There is no one right way of preparing the book. The important thing is that the writing experience be enjoyable for you and your child!

Please remind your child to put all the supplies back in the backpack and bring it back to school the next day. If your child would like to share the book you made together in class, please send the book along, too.

I hope you have fun with our new writing backpacks!
Sincerely yours,
Beth Parker

- -

I would like the writing backpack to come home on the following day of the week: _____.

_____

Parent's name

FIGURE 9.4   PARENT SUGGESTIONS

Suggestions for Parents

1. Have your child write his/her first draft on the unlined paper. Feel free to make suggestions. This draft can be messy!

2. Make the pages of the book by folding or cutting the unlined paper in half. Punch holes so you can use string or yarn to tie the pages together.

3. If you want to use other materials that you have at home, please feel free to do so. For example, you and your child might think of a way to make an interesting cover for the book.

4. Last year, parents came up with all kinds of ideas. In some families, each person did a page of the book. Go ahead and try new approaches!

5. Have fun!

Troubleshooting: What About Struggling Writers?

Most students flourish in the environment of the writers' workshop (Graves, 1983). However, teachers often find that there are a few students who struggle with writing. These students are supported through the structures of the writers' workshop, such as a regular time for writing, established classroom routines for writing, and teacher and peer conferences. These features are discussed in chapters 7 and 8. The importance of keeping these students motivated and involved in the writers' workshop cannot be over-emphasized. To keep students involved, teachers need to provide additional support for struggling writers.

Finding a Topic

One reason some children struggle with writing is that they cannot decide what to write about. These students often lack self-esteem, which leads them to believe that their lives are uninteresting in comparison to the lives of others. Melissa, a third grader, was an example of such a student. She did not seem able to identify a suitable topic. Day after day, she told her teacher, Mrs. Loew, that she just didn't know what to write about. Mrs. Loew had already demonstrated to the class how she identified topics (see Topic Selection, chapter 8), and now she held a writing conference with Melissa in which she asked her to talk about her life. Mrs. Loew soon learned that Melissa perceived her life as very uninteresting. She felt bored in school, and she professed to having no hobbies or interests outside of school. An only child, Melissa spent most of her time at her grandparents' home, because her mother worked at night as a nurse. As Melissa spoke, Mrs. Loew made notes. Then she had Melissa start a list of topics. She asked Melissa to write down these possiblities:

1. Staying at my grandparents' house
2. My mom's job as a nurse

Neither of these topics sparked Melissa's interest, and over the next few days Mrs. Loew continued to offer Melissa strategies for finding a topic. She had Melissa try the following,

- Confer with a friend, to find out what that person was writing about. Mrs. Loew suggested that Melissa might like to write about something similar.
- Write about everything noticed in the room and outside the window (Routman, 1991). Mrs. Loew had Melissa sit at her desk and write her observations, in the hope that an idea would be triggered.
- Think of a special memory, such as a family vacation or a birthday, and try to recall everything about that event (Routman, 1991).
- Think of a favorite book and write one similar in some ways, perhaps using the same characters or plot.

Mrs. Loew remained patient but persistent, letting Melissa know that she expected her to continue searching for a topic. Finally, Melissa approached Mrs. Loew with a draft. She had written about going to visit the hospital where her mother worked. In her conference with Melissa, Mrs. Loew learned that her mother had recently returned to work. Melissa missed having her mother at home but now understood what her mother's job involved.

Sometimes, as in Melissa's case, the student succeeds in finding a topic. However, if Melissa had not found a topic of her own, Mrs. Loew would have had her choose a topic from her list and spend several days writing about that topic (see Graves on nudges, chapter 6). Mrs. Loew wanted Melissa to know that she had something important to say, but she also made it clear that Melissa was expected to move forward with her writing.

A few struggling writers may not even be willing start a topic list or to identify any possible topics for writing. In these cases, after all other options have been exhausted, the teacher will take the initiative of assigning the student a topic. The teacher makes it clear that the topic has been assigned because the student has not come up with a topic, despite the time and options allowed. After the topic is assigned, the teacher monitors the student's progress to see that the piece is drafted. If the student decides on a new topic, that can be pursued next. By taking these steps, the teacher makes it clear that the student can and will be a productive writer. Not writing is not an available option.

Putting Words on Paper

Paul, another student in Mrs. Loew's class, represented another type of struggling writer. Paul had many ideas for topics, which he could discuss at length. However, he had great difficulty putting his ideas down on paper. Paul knew initial consonant sounds, but his spelling was poor. He spent most of his time during the writers' workshop making detailed drawings.

Paul wanted to write about going fishing with his father. Mrs. Loew began the conference by showing Paul how to make a web of the information to be included in his story: how he and his father got up early in the morning, how they drove to the harbor to meet his father's friends, how they went far out to sea in the boat, the kinds of fish they caught, and so on. Mrs. Loew recorded the information on the web, then turned the page over to Paul. She helped him to phrase the beginning of the story, turning his oral language into the words he would put down in writing. They decided that the story would begin with the sentence, *One morning I got up very early to go fishing with my dad.* Mrs. Loew wrote this first sentence of the draft for Paul. Then she helped him phrase his second sentence, *We put our poles and food in the car.* Mrs. Loew turned the paper and pencil over to Paul and helped him to start the sentence. She assured Paul that it was all right to use invented spelling in his draft, then left him alone for a few minutes. When Mrs. Loew returned, Paul had finished that sentence, and she helped him phrase and start writing the next sentence.

Mrs. Loew found that Paul would work well when she was close at hand and available to help, but he could not continue on his own for long. She taught three other students how to assist Paul by helping him to phrase the sentence he would be writing next, and by cueing him to say each word slowly and put down the sounds he could hear. These students took turns working alongside Paul as he drafted his piece. Mrs. Loew stressed to Paul that he was responsible for getting his words down on paper, that other people would help but would not write for him. Paul progressed slowly, but by the second semester he was able to draft on his own.

A struggling writer like Paul puts a lot of time and effort into completing a first draft. Such a student is often reluctant to do any revising and editing. To give these students a sense of revising and editing, without overwhelming them, teachers may take the following steps. First, students may be asked if there is a word or phrase they would like to add. Second, students can be shown how to circle a sentence and draw an arrow to show where it is to be moved. These two simple forms of revision do not require much effort and help to show students that revision need not be a painful process.

Editing may be daunting to these struggling writers because their drafts usually contain many words written in invented spelling. Teachers can make editing manageable for struggling writers by asking them to correct just a few of the words on their own. The words chosen for correction might be either words important in the students' piece (for example, the word *fishing* in Paul's piece) or common words likely to be useful to the student (for example, the word *with*). Or the teacher might ask the student which two or three words he or she would like to learn to spell correctly. After the words have been identified, the student is instructed to circle all examples of the words and to write their correct spelling above. The teacher or a peer editor takes the responsibility for correcting other misspelled words. The teacher then instructs the student to add the newly learned words to his or her personal dictionary. In the future, the student is expected to refer to the dictionary in order to spell these words correctly.

As these examples suggest, struggling writers can be helped to progress in the writers' workshop with help from both the teacher and peers. Struggling writers benefit when they understand that they have something meaningful to say and that they can learn to put their ideas down on paper. Teachers give students ways of getting their writing started, then work to build their confidence and independence as writers.

References

Graves, D. (1983). *Writing: Teachers and children at work.* Exeter, NH: Heinemann.

Routman, R. (1991). *Invitations: Changing as teachers and learners K–12.* Portsmouth, NH: Heinemann.

Resource

Ray, K. W. (1999). *Wondrous words: Writer and writing in the elementary classroom.* Urbana, IL: National Council of Teachers of English.

Practical ideas for motivating and assisting struggling writers, as well as strengthening the classroom writing program in general.

Section III:

Assessment and Evaluation

Chapter 10

OVERVIEW OF ASSESSMENT AND EVALUATION

Assessment and Evaluation in Mrs. Sally O'Brien's Kindergarten Class

It is nearly the end of the school year and Sally O'Brien is experiencing mixed feelings. She is looking forward to a vacation of rest and recuperation, yet she wishes she could continue working with this group of children. She knows them well, and appreciates the wonderful progress they have made. She would love to nurture their literacy development for another year. However, Mrs. O'Brien knows it is time to prepare her end-of-year reports, reflecting for a final time on what she has learned about these students. She draws upon a variety of resources to prepare her reports.

Each child in her classroom has a portfolio, a folder containing work products completed throughout the school year. The children have saved in their portfolios written responses to literature, audiotapes of their oral reading, lists of books they have read, and stories they have written. Their portfolios are housed in two plastic crates that sit atop a classroom bookshelf. The children have easy access to their portfolios and enjoy noting their own growth. For example, Melissa recently chose "My Pet" (see Figure 6.1 to place in her portfolio). She said she chose it because she loves her rabbit and because the kids liked her story.

In addition to the students' work products, Mrs. O'Brien has collected other evidence of student growth. She noted children's daily writing plans on a status of the class form (see Figure 11.5) and used a label grid to record anecdotal evidence of children's literacy development (see Figure 11.6). She also made notes when students read aloud to her which helped her monitor their use of various text cues to figure out that unknown words. When children placed entries in their portfolios, Mrs. O'Brien considered what each piece revealed about the students' growth as readers or writers. When Melissa selected "My Pet" for her portfolio, Mrs. O'Brien concurred with her choice. She noted that this was Melissa's most developed story. It had a definite beginning, middle, and end. Melissa added information to the story after a small group conference, she made good use of the class word charts, she was conscious of medial consonants and vowels, and she began using periods at the ends of sentences.

Earlier in the school year Mrs. O'Brien, another kindergarten teacher, and a first-grade teacher worked together to develop a set of benchmarks to reflect their learning expectations for typical students at the end of the school year. Mrs. O'Brien developed rubrics (see Figure 11.9) to show whether or not her students met the benchmarks.

Throughout the year the assessment data collected by Mrs. O'Brien and her students was used to complete the checklist. The checklist, along with its supporting evidence, formed the basis for Mrs. O'Brien's student progress reports, parent conferences, and her instructional planning.

Now, as the year is ending, Mrs. O'Brien will write progress reports in the form of narrative summaries (see Troubleshooting: What About Grading and Report Cards, in chapter 11) for each student, and she will place copies of the narratives into the portfolios for the children's new teachers. She will leave school knowing that the parents of her students have a good understanding of their children's literacy progress in kindergarten and knowledge of how to offer support in reading and writing during the vacation period at home and with community resources. She is confident that next year's teachers will have concrete information on which to plan a continuance of her students' literacy development.

Assessment and Evaluation in Mr. Marcus Jamal's Second-Grade Classroom

Toward the end of the first semester, Mr. Jamal sat down with his students' portfolios, writing folders, and literature response journals. He also had a folder containing status of the class sheets, anecdotal records, running records, and informal reading inventories on his students. He looked at the piles of papers and realized it was going to be a long afternoon, but one he felt would be well worth his time. He hoped by looking at the information he had, he would be able to accomplish three things: (a) finalize the recording of each student's achievement on the reading and writing benchmark checklist (see Figure 11.9) he and the other second-grade teachers had established when they met last spring, (b) complete his report cards, and (c) determine the specific skills and strategies he should focus on in second semester.

Mr. Jamal's task was made easier because he had already met individually with each student to review their portfolios and discuss their work thus far. He and his students were keeping evaluation portfolios. For this type of portfolio, the teacher establishes a set of "common tools" that every student must have in the portfolio. Some of this class's common tools were a book log, a photocopy of a page from a book the student read independently, a written response to literature, and a final draft of a writing piece taken to publication. His students also chose other items to show their growth and accomplishments as readers, writers, and learners. The students wrote a reflection about each item, telling why they chose it and what it revealed about them as a literacy learner.

When Mr. Jamal met with each student, they looked over the portfolio together and talked about how the student had grown as a literacy learner since their meeting the previous quarter. They used the class rubrics to examine the student's work and performance. They looked at the benchmark checklist to see which benchmarks they felt the student had achieved. This gave Mr. Jamal a head start on the benchmark checklists, most of which he tried to complete during the conference. He also asked the student to set one or two goals for the coming quarter.

Students also took their portfolios home to share with their parents, and most parents returned written comments on this experience and their feelings about their child's progress. Later, interested parents would meet with Mr. Jamal and their child for a conference.

At this point, Mr. Jamal could rely mostly on his notes and checklists from the individual student evaluation conferences. He glanced through portfolios, writing folders, responses to literature, and other information if he wasn't sure of an item for a particular student as he completed the report cards. He felt confident that he knew his students well, since he interacted with them daily in small groups and individually, made observations and took anecdotal records on each student monthly, and met with students for evaluation conferences quarterly.

When the checklists and report cards were completed, Mr. Jamal made a list of future plans based on the areas of need he saw. In the readers' workshop, for example, he saw evidence that all or nearly all of his students enjoyed reading, chose to read for their own purposes, and shared books with others, and about three-quarters participated well in reading discussions. In these areas he felt he was doing a good job. He planned to continue the same practices second semester he was using first semester, which included regularly scheduling time for independent reading, reading aloud, doing author and genre studies, giving book talks, asking students to give book talks and recommend books they thought others might like, and giving mini-lessons on how to talk about books in small group discussions.

However, only about half of his students wrote thoughtful aesthetic and efferent responses to literature. Some students still did not set important and realistic goals for their reading. And a few still needed instruction in cross checking to decode unfamiliar words. In these areas, Mr. Jamal knew he needed to provide more support for those who had not yet developed these skills. He decided to devote a series of mini-lessons on good written responses to literature, focusing on a different aspect each time. He would use good samples written by students from last year's class, and follow up during small group discussion time to see if the students were following these examples. He also decided to conduct individual mini-lessons for certain students to work on goal setting. In addition, he planned to convene flexible skills groups more often and to continue running records to monitor individual students' growth in cross checking.

Mr. Jamal developed a list of plans for the writers' workshop after a similar process of review and reflection. He noted that all of his students chose their own topics; nearly all planned their pieces before drafting; and most could draft, confer, and revise with support from him and each other. He planned to continue working on helping students understand how to organize their ideas clearly, which he felt could best be accomplished in individual and small group conferences as students considered pieces in progress. He also planned to do more whole-class mini-lessons on editing for punctuation, perhaps using one or two students' pieces as examples (with their permission) on the overhead.

Assessment and Evaluation in Ms. Brenda DeRego's Fourth-Grade Classroom

Ms. DeRego's fourth-grade students have been working on research projects in second quarter. Now that the quarter is nearly at an end, Ms. DeRego has been meeting with each student individually to review their goals, the work in their portfolios, and their reflections.

At the start of the quarter, Ms. DeRego's students were introduced to "I Can" statements concerning research writing. They already knew that good writers try to make their writing interesting to their audience, organize their ideas so the reader can follow the story line, put their own voice into their writing, and use proper punctuation and capitalization to help the reader along. Most students felt that they did these things when writing personal narratives, which were the focus for the first quarter's writing. In second quarter, Ms. DeRego asked the class what they thought was important to do in research writing. Together, they came up with items such as: include enough information so the reader learns something they didn't already know about the topic, write accurately so the reader won't learn false information, and explain hard vocabulary so the reader won't get confused. They agreed that the items for personal narratives were still important for research writing. The new ideas were written as "I Can" statements and added to the classroom "I Can" chart.

When Ms. DeRego sat down to meet with Paul, she was glad to see his finished research report in his portfolio (see Figure 6.3 for part of Paul's report). He also had included his research notes, drafts, conference forms, and self-evaluation form. In his reflection, Paul stated that he had learned a lot about his topic—wolves—and he thought his classmates had too. He liked the way he decided to speak from the wolf's perspective in his report. He felt it gave the report a lot of voice while still relating the facts he had discovered.

During their conference, Ms. DeRego and Paul talked about the skills Paul had learned, the goals and benchmarks he had met this quarter, and the evidence of his accomplishments. Paul said he thought the organizational form he used for his wolf report helped him with paragraphing, and Ms. DeRego agreed that his paragraphs were well organized in that piece. Using the benchmark checklists (see Figure 11.9) and Paul's own goals, Ms. DeRego and Paul discussed other achievements and noted specific pieces of evidence from the portfolio. Paul had already identified many of these and marked them with post-its. He and his classmates were learning to find their own evidence to show that they were meeting specific benchmarks. Ms. DeRego also shared with Paul evidence from her anecdotal notes that showed how well he used his time on this project. Paul agreed that he was very focused, because he loved his topic.

Paul also discussed his plans for next quarter's writing projects. He wanted to continue writing about wolves and thought he would try a poem next. He also wanted to work more on one of the class "I Can" statements: "I can use new words and interesting language in my writing." He said that, even though it was on the class chart, he didn't think he was very good at it yet. Ms. DeRego told him poetry would be an excellent format for working on that goal. She made herself a note to talk about the use of language in an upcoming mini-lesson she was planning on poetry and to look for some nature poems to share with the class.

From her observations, conferences, and reflections about Paul's progress, Ms. DeRego felt that Paul had developed a firm, beginning understanding of the research process. She saw evidence that he used a variety of resources to find the information he wanted, generated good research questions throughout his investigation, and engaged in many conferences with classmates that resulted in improvements to his work.

Along with his classmates, Paul was learning to conduct a conference about his portfolio for his parents. He organized the work samples and other data in his portfolio and completed a reflection for each piece. He presented his portfolio to another student, just as he would for his parents in the conference. His partner asked him questions and made comments about his work. The partners then reversed roles. Afterward, they talked together about what each could do to improve their presentations or make their portfolios better.

Participating in student-teacher conferences and preparing for three-way conferences helped Ms. DeRego's students consider the quality of their work, not just whether or not they had completed it. Students reviewed their work with the same critical eye their teacher used to determine what they were learning, how they were learning it, and how well they were learning. Through these activities, Paul and his classmates were increasing their ability to take responsibility for their learning.

The Impact of P. David Pearson: Standards for Language Arts

P. David Pearson (1993) is a leading literacy researcher noted especially for his work on comprehension instruction. As the standards movement has gained momentum in the United States, Pearson has been at the forefront of researchers working with language arts standards and writing thoughtfully about the standards movement and new forms of assessment.

Standards are generally seen as the expectations we have for students' learning in different content areas such as the language arts. The standards movement is considered to date from 1989, when the concept of high, rigorous standards was endorsed by the nation's governors. The standards movement has proven to be a long-term trend with real impact on teachers and students. By 2000, 49 of the 50 states had administered tests based on their own standards (Scherer, 1999).

Pearson (1993) reminds us that standards are not a simple matter, beginning with the idea that standards can be defined in different ways. Standards may encompass the idea of identity, priorities, or core values. They may connote direction or momentum, or they may specify a level of performance. Finally, they may be related to concepts such as responsibility, rights, and opportunities. Pearson's point is that the term standards has a range of meanings. In any discussion of standards, it is important to establish what meaning is being assigned to this term.

In this chapter we speak of standards primarily in the first sense, as representing core values or important aspects of learning. Standards of this kind are known as *content standards*. According to Pearson (1993), content standards answer the question, "What should students know and be able to do?" The following are examples of possible content standards:

- Students will have the habit of daily reading.
- Students will read both fiction and nonfiction texts with understanding.
- Students will understand and apply all phases of the writing process: planning, drafting, revising, editing, and publishing.
- Students will edit their writing, showing knowledge of conventions such as spelling, punctuation, and grammar.

Content standards in the English language arts were established at the national level by the field's two leading professional organizations, the National Council of Teachers of English (NCTE) and the International Reading Association (IRA) (National Council of Teachers of English and International Reading Association, 1996). States have their own language arts standards, which are usually aligned with the national standards. Many districts have their own language arts standards, aligned with those of their state.

Pearson (1993) notes that there are other kinds of standards, in addition to content standards. *Performance standards* answer the question, "How much is good enough?" They describe the level of performance students must achieve to meet the standard. For example, suppose that the content standard is "Students will be able to read both fiction and nonfiction texts with understanding." A performance standard might indicate the following:

- The fiction and nonfiction texts must be written at that grade level. That is, third graders must read texts written at the 3.2 (third grade, second semester) level of difficulty.

- To show understanding, students must write a summary.
  - For fiction, the summary must include the following story elements: characters, setting, problem, solution, and theme.
  - For nonfiction, the summary must include at least three important ideas.

Delivery standards refer to the material conditions that must be met in schools before students can (or should) be assessed on the standards. Funding for consultants may be needed to provide teachers with professional development, for example, in literature-based instruction or the process approach to writing. Or the school may need to purchase multiple copies of novels so that students can read and respond to authentic works of literature. The idea behind delivery standards is that teachers and students cannot be held to higher standards until the system has provided adequate resources to support the higher level of achievement sought.

Opportunity standards refer to the learning opportunities afforded to students. While related to delivery standards, they refer more to issues of curriculum than to material resources. According to Pearson (1993), opportunity standards address the extent to which students have had the opportunity to participate in a curriculum that has helped them develop the attitudes, knowledge, and skills needed to meet the standards. Opportunity standards are an especially important consideration in the case of groups that typically have not been well served in schools, such as students of diverse cultural and linguistic backgrounds, struggling readers and writers, and those in special education.

In short, the standards movement raises many complex issues. As Pearson implies, student learning does not improve simply because higher expectations have been set. Rather, student learning will improve when educators, parents, and the public have a clear understanding of standards, and when the system provides schools, teachers, and students with the necessary resources to reach the standards. Furthermore, new forms of literacy assessment must be developed that will capture in a fair and authentic manner the complex forms of reading and writing specified by high standards (Bisesi, Brenner, McVee, Pearson, & Sarroub, 1998).

References

Bisesi, T., Brenner, D., McVee, M., Pearson, P. D., & Sarroub, L. K. (1998). Assessment in literature-based reading programs: Have we kept our promises? In T. E. Raphael & K. H. Au (Eds.), *Literature-based instruction: Reshaping the curriculum* (pp. 239–259). Norwood, MA: Christopher-Gordon.

National Council of Teachers of English and International Reading Association. (1996). *Standards for the English language arts*. Urbana, IL and Newark, DE: NCTE and IRA.

Pearson, P. D. (1993). Standards for the English language arts: A policy perspective. *Journal of Reading Behavior, 25* (4), 457–475.

Scherer, M. (1999). Perspectives: Measures and mismeasures. *Educational Leadership, 56* (6), 5.

Chapter 11

EVALUATING PROGRESS

The Impact of Sheila Valencia: Portfolio Assessment

Sheila Valencia, an expert in literacy assessment, conducted a long-term collaborative research project with teachers in the Bellevue Public Schools, Bellevue, Washington. As a result of this project, Valencia and her colleagues gained many insights about portfolios and their use in the classroom (Valencia, 1998). Valencia defines a portfolio as "a purposeful collection of a range of student work and records of progress collected over time" (p. 23).

The first key concept in this definition is "purposeful collection." Any teacher who has worked with portfolios knows that there is nothing easier than to simply collect work in a folder. The problem occurs when the time comes to make sense of that random collection of paper. This is why Valencia emphasizes collecting work only for specific purposes. A good starting point for the portfolio is the teacher's goals for student learning. If you are clear about what you want students to learn, you can structure your students' portfolios around those goals (see article on Establishing Grade-Level Benchmarks in this chapter). Then only evidence that relates to those goals will go into the portfolios. For example, suppose that one of your goals is that students will make personal connections to literature. You might ask students to find an entry in their literature response journals showing that they have written about a personal connection to their novels. This entry (or a copy of it) is placed in the student's portfolio as evidence of progress toward this goal.

The second key concept is "a range of student work and records." This concept emphasizes having multiple forms of evidence that show the students' achievement from a variety of perspectives. For example, in terms of the goal of having students make personal connections to literature, you might include observations you have made of students' participation in book clubs. This means that you will not have to rely only on students' written responses for evidence of progress toward this goal. Notice that both forms of evidence—written responses and teacher observations—are authentic to the classroom, in the sense that they reflect the ongoing work of the teacher and students with literature-based instruction. Portfolio evidence can be obtained without the need for a separate test to evaluate student learning.

The third key concept is "of progress collected over time," which refers to the importance of gathering assessment information in an ongoing manner. Obviously, nothing can be known about students' growth over time if evidence is only collected at the end of the school year. Instead, evidence should be collected systematically, at regular intervals throughout the year, in order to document progress. For example, you might collect students' written responses to literature, showing the making of personal connections, at the end of each quarter of the school year.

Valencia (1998) points out that portfolios represent a process and not just a product. In this sense she suggests thinking of portfolio is a verb as well as a noun. Portfolios are an ongoing, collaborative process involving teachers, students, and parents as well. Once goals for student learning are made clear, teachers and parents can help students move toward those goals. Perhaps once a quarter, the teacher sets aside time for students to work on their portfolios. Students collect evidence and they prepare written reflections on what the evidence shows about their growth as readers and writers (see article on Collecting Evidence in this chapter). As part of the reflection process, students can set learning goals for the next quarter, with the guidance of the teacher and their parents.

In this chapter we highlight evaluation portfolios, which have the purpose of evaluating students with respect to standards or grade-level benchmarks. However, portfolios can take a number of different forms, depending on purpose. Valencia describes four other kinds of portfolios. Showcase portfolios may be used if the purpose is to highlight the best work that students have done. Documentation portfolios seek to show how students have grown over time, on their own terms, without respect to external standards. These portfolios also inform instruction. Process portfolios show the steps students have followed in completing a certain product. For example, a process portfolio might show the outline, notes, and rough drafts that students created while preparing a research report. Finally, composite portfolios may combine a number of these purposes. In reality, most portfolios used in classrooms serve multiple purposes and so are composite portfolios.

Valencia (1998) suggests that the following features will be in place in classrooms showing the sound use of portfolios and classroom assessment. As you work with portfolios, you might want to use these features as a mental checklist.

- Contains evidence that resembles authentic reading and writing
- Uses direct evidence/demonstrations of what students can do
- Is integrated with and grows out of high-quality literacy instruction
- Provides evidence that is collected over time
- Values and distinguishes between individual growth and performance against a standard
- Is used by teachers for instructional decision making
- Is understood by parents
- Represents students' abilities across a variety of tasks and contexts
- Requires students to reflect on their learning
- Requires teachers to reflect on their teaching
- Is a collaborative effort among teachers, students, and parents (pp. 21–22)

References

Valencia, S. W. (1998). *Literacy portfolios in action.* Fort Worth, TX: Harcourt Brace College Publishers.

Establishing Grade-Level Benchmarks

Grade-level benchmarks are goals for student learning established for a particular grade. Grade-level benchmarks refer to the expected achievement of the hypothetical average student at the end of the school year. The following is an example of one grade-level benchmark that teachers might set:

> Students will engage in all aspects of the writing process: planning, drafting, revising, editing, and publishing.

Grade-level benchmarks provide a foundation for standards-based assessment and may be its most important element. Although reading and writing are closely intertwined processes, we recommend that work with grade-level benchmarks focus first on either reading or writing.

We believe the starting point for setting grade-level benchmarks should be the philosophy, knowledge, and experience of teachers at a particular school, not external sources such as national and state standards. If your whole school is working on establishing grade-level benchmarks, there should first be a discussion by the whole faculty about teachers' philosophies of teaching, learning, and literacy.

This discussion of philosophy leads into the formulation of a vision statement. The vision statement describes the kind of reader or writer (depending on the focus chosen) you would like the hypothetical average student to become by the time she graduates from your school. Suppose that yours is a K–6 school. The teachers at your school meet by grade levels. Each grade level produces its own vision statement for the sixth-grade reader. These vision statements are shared, and teachers discuss common themes as well as points of difference. At the end of the discussion, a committee is chosen to combine the best features of the various statements into one vision statement for the school. The following is an example of a completed vision statement:

When sixth-graders leave Oak Forest Elementary School, they

- will be able to comprehend and critically evaluate both fiction and nonfiction texts,
- understand the importance of reading both in and out of school, and
- have a life-long love of reading.

Once the vision statement for the excellent reader or writer has been written, you are ready to begin establishing grade-level benchmarks. Grade-level benchmarks describe the contribution to students' learning that teachers at each grade level expect to make, in order to achieve the school's vision of the excellent reader or writer.

Teachers at each grade level can begin by choosing just two benchmarks in each of three areas. If the focus is reading, the three areas are attitudes, comprehension, and strategies and skills. If the focus is writing, the three areas are attitudes, writing process, and strategies and skills. A think sheet teachers can use for establishing grade-level benchmarks in reading is shown in Figure 11.1.

The reason for limiting the number of benchmarks is to keep things clear and manageable for both teachers and students. Having five or six benchmarks, and no more than seven, means that teachers and students can remember all the benchmarks. Also, since evidence will be collected and analyzed for each benchmark (see articles later in this chapter), having too many benchmarks will make the assessment process unwieldy.

You will soon discover that writing grade-level benchmarks can be quite a challenge. Benchmarks must be specific, yet they cannot be too narrow. For example, at kindergarten, separate benchmarks cannot be used to list each of the letter-sound corre-spondences children are expected to learn, because there will be far too many bench-marks. However, a benchmark like the following might be appropriate:

> Students will show knowledge of initial consonant sounds and sight words
> when they read.

An important point to remember is that the benchmarks will not cover your entire curriculum. Benchmarks represent the major goals for student learning, the ones you feel it is important to measure. An example of benchmarks suitable for fourth grade is shown in Figure 11.2.

Once you have a first draft of your grade-level benchmarks, the time has come to examine the relevant standards for your state. Read your state's standards over care-fully to make sure that your benchmarks cover all the areas they address. If there is an area that you have not addressed, revise the draft of your grade-level benchmarks to include it. For example, suppose that the state standards refer to students' making per-sonal connections to text and that your draft has not addressed this stance. You will rewrite your benchmarks to include personal connections to text. This process is called alignment. You are making sure that your grade-level benchmarks address all the areas covered in your state's standards.

A question that often arises has to do with the consistency of benchmarks across grade levels. For example, what if the fifth-grade teachers come up with benchmarks easier than those proposed for fourth grade? What if the second-grade teachers have an important benchmark that is not built upon in third grade? While these are significant concerns, our experience suggests that consistency should not be the first priority. Rather, the first priority should be to make sure that each grade level has had the time and opportunity to think its own thoughts and draft its own benchmarks. Once each grade level has drafted its benchmarks, the process of sharing and gradual revision can begin. Because they have had time to think their own thoughts, the teachers at each grade level will then be better prepared to engage in the revision process in a thoughtful and confi-dent manner.

In many schools, teachers are asked to work directly from the state standards. They are asked simply to take the state standards, make the necessary adjustments for their grade level, and work with these slightly adjusted standards. We have not found this process to be effective in giving teachers a thorough understanding of standards or ownership over the process of standards-based assessment. In our experience, using external standards as a starting point separates the process of standards-based assess-ment from teachers' own best thinking about how reading and writing achievement can be improved. Teachers then perceive standards-based assessment as something imposed on them from the outside, instead of as a tool they can use to assess students' learning and improve instruction.

That is why we recommend the process for developing grade-level benchmarks described in this article. Although this process requires much time and thought on the part of teachers, we have found it to provide a firm foundation for standards-based assessment. While we have described the process of establishing grade-level bench-marks in terms of a whole-school effort, the same steps can be followed by a small group of teachers or even by a teacher working alone.

FIGURE 11.1   THINK SHEET FOR DRAFTING GRADE-LEVEL BENCHMARKS

Grade-Level Benchmarks

Attitudes

- _____

  _____

- _____

  _____

Comprehension

- _____

  _____

- _____

  _____

Strategies and Skills

- _____

  _____

- _____

  _____

FIGURE 11.2   EXAMPLE OF BENCHMARKS FOR FOURTH GRADE

Reading Benchmarks for Grade 4

Attitudes

- Students read books daily during sustained silent reading.
- Students have favorite books and recommend books to others.

Comprehension

- Students identify the theme (fiction) or main idea (nonfiction), supporting their ideas with information from the text.
- Students make personal connections to the text.

Strategies and Skills

- Students use context and word parts (root words, affixes) to infer the meaning of new vocabulary when they read.
- Students locate information from different sources, including the internet, encyclopedia, nonfiction books, and periodicals.

"I Can" Statements

You have just finished reading about how to establish grade-level benchmarks. These benchmarks are the goals you are trying to achieve for your students' learning. "I Can" statements are one means by which grade-level benchmarks become understandable to students. (Note that some authors prefer to call these We Can statements (Cleland, 1999)). It is essential to the assessment process that students have a good understanding of the goals we have for their learning at a particular grade level. We want students to be actively involved in standards-based assessment and to feel that they are at the center of a process that is supporting their learning. Ultimately, our goal is for students to be able to set their own learning goals and to assess their own progress as literacy learners.

Here are some steps you can take to move from grade-level benchmarks to "I Can" statements and to involve students actively in the process of assessment. The following description assumes that you are focusing on reading, but the same steps are applicable to a focus on writing.

You can start by having a whole-class discussion centered on the question, "What do good readers do?" As the students make suggestions, make a web organizing their ideas. A web based on the responses of third graders is shown in Figure 11.3 (Wong-Kam, 1998). If your students have not had much previous experience with the readers' workshop, you may find that their concepts about reading could use quite a bit of expansion. For example, students might be aware that reading involves answering literal questions, but they may not associate reading with thinking about the theme of a novel. If this is the case, you may want to have further discussions of what good readers do after you have had time to expand students' thinking. As new ideas emerge, these can be added to the web.

Once you are satisfied that students are developing a sense of what good readers do, you can begin introducing the "I Can" statements. "I Can" statements are developed by adjusting the wording of the grade-level benchmarks so that they are readily understandable to the students. For example, a kindergarten grade-level benchmark might be:

Students have the habit of daily reading.

This language is not likely to be readily understandable to kindergarten children. Thus, the "I Can" statement for this benchmark might be:

I can read a book every day.

Figure 11.4 shows the "I Can" statements for the Reading Benchmarks presented earlier in Figure 11.2. You will notice that some of these grade-level benchmarks did not need much rewording. Of course, more rewording will be required with younger children.

Teachers who have used "I Can" statements for a while know that students may be overwhelmed if all the "I Can" statement are introduced at once. Instead, it works well to introduce a few "I Can" statements each quarter. For example, consider the fourth grade "I Can" statements shown in Figure 11.4. The teacher might decide to introduce the two attitude "I Cans" early in the first quarter, because she believes that her students will have the best chance of becoming good readers if they develop positive attitudes towards books and reading. She might introduce the two comprehension "I Cans" in the second quarter, and the two strategies and skills "I Cans" in the third quarter. The teacher will be providing students with instruction and guidance in all of the benchmarks/"I Cans" throughout the year, but it is in these quarters that she will focus on assessment of these particular benchmarks. This gradual introduction keeps the assessment process focused and manageable for both teacher and students.

When you introduce the first "I Can" statements to students, begin by reminding them that there are different things to be learned each year they are in school. Right now, you will be discussing what they will be learning as readers at this grade level. Then introduce the "I Can" statements and make sure that students understand that these are the goals for their learning for the end of the year. Have students discuss what each of the "I Can" statements means. You may want to make a chart for each "I Can" statement, listing students' ideas. Sometimes the wording students use is more effective than the teacher's wording in communicating the meaning of an "I Can" statement to other students.

FIGURE 11.3   GOOD READER CHART, THIRD-GRADE CLASS

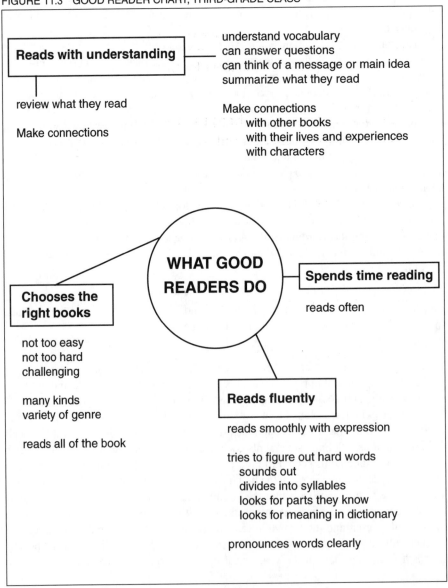

The grade-level benchmarks and the "I Can" statements provide the structure for creating evaluation portfolios to provide evidence that students are meeting state or district standards. In the next article, on collecting evidence, you will learn how to decide what goes into an evaluation portfolio.

References

Cleland, J. V. (1999). We Can charts: Building blocks for student-led conferences. *The Reading Teacher 52* (6), 588–595.

Wong-Kam, J. A. (1998). Sharing responsibility for assessment and evaluation with our students. In T. E. Raphael & K. H. Au (Eds.), *Literature-based instruction: Reshaping the curriculum* (pp. 305–329). Norwood, MA: Christopher-Gordon.

FIGURE 11.4 EXAMPLE OF "I CAN" STATEMENTS FOR FOURTH GRADE

"I Can" Statements for Grade 4

Attitudes

- I can read a book every day during sustained silent reading.
- I can name my favorite books and recommend books to others.

Comprehension

- I can identify the theme or main idea and back up my thinking by referring to the text.
- I can see connections between what I read and my own life.

Strategies and Skills

- I can figure out the meaning of a new word by using context and word parts.
- I can locate information from different sources, including the internet, encyclopedia, nonfiction books, and periodicals.

Collecting Evidence

In order to successfully document students' progress relative to the benchmarks, it is necessary to have specific evidence reflecting each child's performance. This evidence will include student work products, student reflections, and records of teacher observations.

It is important that there be enough evidence for teachers and students to confidently assess performance at a given level. Also, to make the process more efficient, teachers will want to consider their students' work products as offering opportunities for assessing multiple aspects of a benchmark or more than one benchmark within each product. Portfolios are usually the receptacles for much of this evidence (see The Impact of Sheila Valencia: Portfolio Assessment, this chapter).

Background

Sheila Valencia's (1998) definition of a portfolio is, in part "a purposeful collection of a range of student work and records of progress collected over time" (p. 23). She suggests that teachers within a school work together to determine what evidence will be collected and when. One way to do this is to consider each benchmark and determine which instructional or assessment tasks could provide evidence related to the benchmark. Teachers are likely to discover that there are certain tasks common across all classrooms: for example, book logs on which students list the books they have read, writing folders, and running records or informal reading inventories. These items, which Valencia terms "common tools," would be collected as evidence by all teachers for every child. Teachers and students then have the option to include other tasks, specific to their classrooms, for evidence as well. Valencia suggests that teachers determine how frequently the common tools will be collected (perhaps three or four times per year) so that sufficient evidence is available for each student. As teachers examine their regular readers' and writers' workshop activities they will discover that most of the evidence needed for assessing the benchmarks are to be found within a limited number of student work products and teacher records of progress.

Procedure

Within the readers' workshop, students' responses to literature will provide important evidence of progress. The work may be written (e.g., response journals, lists of books read, research notes), created in an art medium (e.g., drawings or paintings, student-designed book jackets), or audio or videotaped (e.g., tapes of discussions, dramatic performances, reading aloud). Teachers' observations will include evidence such as informal reading inventories, various diagnostic tests and surveys (e.g., knowledge of letters and sounds), and running records (see The Impact of Marie Clay: Cue Systems chapter 4).

The full range of written work done within writers' workshop offers a wealth of evidence. Teachers will want to be sure that planning notes and edited drafts are collected along with final drafts and published pieces. Students' writing folders can provide evidence of conferences, knowledge of editing skills, and lists of publications (see Materials, chapter 7). There may be audio or videotapes and computer discs of special presentations. Teachers' observations will include diagnostic tests and surveys (e.g., spelling) and notes made during writing conferences (see Teacher Conferences, chapter 8).

Many teachers find that taking a status of the class (see Figure 11.5) prior to each writers' workshop provides a valuable record of students' writing growth and development. Nancie Atwell (1998) has used this procedure for many years in her middle school writers' workshops, and it has been adopted and adapted by many elementary school teachers. Each day, before the children go off to write independently, each child states his or her plans. Mini-lessons early in the year help children understand how they might respond (e.g., "I will continue to draft my story about the zoo." "I am publishing 'Traveling with Granny.'") In two or three minutes the teacher has recorded a contract with each child, students have heard options they may want to try, and the writing community has been furthered. By keeping the records over time, teachers are able to note patterns for individuals and for groups of students that help to guide their instruction and assessment.

FIGURE 11.5   A TEACHER'S STATUS OF THE CLASS SHEET

CLASS STATUS SHEET: WRITING WORKSHOP

NP—New Piece D—Drafting R—Revising C—Conferencing E—Editing P—Publishing

Week of __2/5__

Student	M	T	W	T	F
Sam	NP "Fishing"	D.	D	D/Cw/Matt	R
Arketta	P Computer	P Illustration	Share pub. NP	D-Birthday Party	D
Ramón	ab.	C w/Tony D Irish...	R	R	E
Mindy	EC w/Patti	C w/me marks	EC W/Patti	Final E Con.P	D
Leslie	P	P Share P	NP (couple) C w/Dari	D Angy	D
Cindi	NP ?	NP -sister	ab	N.P. dog	Cw/me
Edward	E	EC w/Jamie	Final E Brain P	P	P
Matt	R Museum visit	R	E	Cw/Sam	E
Eric	D Baseball	D	R	NP abandoned book	ab.
Patti	EC w/Mindy D-B.party	R adding dialogue	EC w/Mindy D	D	E
Jackson	ab.	Final E Con.P.	D	D fixing Short P	D
Nicole	Finish P read to kids	NP- Piano lessons	D	C w/Jame D	D
Mistry	NP-poem	D poem	D	R	R
Lurita	D Baby Bro	D	D.	Try story as a poem	D-poem
Steven	P Dinner at Home	ab.	P	P Share ?	NP -? Jane
Tony	Final E Con.D	P	P Share P	NP-poem	D-poem Words C
Jamie	D Gram...	EC w/Ed D	D	C w/Nicole D	D
Lisa	D Volcano	D	D	C w/Mindy to add dia.	R
Dari	D football game	D	C w/Leslie R-football game	R	E
Karl	P- will share today	NP ?	D Snail Fight	D	D C(?)

Important evidence for both readers' and writers' workshops are anecdotal records. These are brief, informal notes that teachers make as they move around the room observing independent or group work. Because time for note taking within a busy classroom is limited, teachers need to be selective about what they record. They will want to review their benchmarks and note what information is not available elsewhere. This information should be the focus for their anecdotal records. Dated notes, accumulated over time, help teachers make sense of what their students do as readers and writers and provide a basis for discussing progress and setting instructional goals.

Teachers also need to be efficient in how they record information and have discovered a variety of means for recording their observations. Post-its and peel-off labels work well as they can be carried easily and later placed on students' individual record forms (see Figure 11.6). Assessment checklists like the one for ownership (see Figure 5.1) can yield important evidence about students' developing attitudes toward literacy. During readers' workshop teachers may also find a checklist useful for recording student behaviors (see Figure 11.7). These notes and checklists help teachers determine which skills and strategies need to be addressed with the group in coming meetings and provide a way to monitor individual student's progress and needs. The status of the class form might also double as a note taking form for observations made during writers' workshop.

Students' reflections give both teachers and students insights into the processes of learning and assessment. One way to include this is to schedule a weekly class discussion during which students reflect on their learning experiences, and the teacher makes a record of their responses. The teacher may want to prompt students by asking one or two of the following questions until students are comfortable with the process:

- What went well for you this week? What didn't go well? Why?
- What new and interesting things did you learn?
- What did you learn about yourself? For example, did you discover strengths, new skills, growing interests, definite dislikes? How can this information be useful to you?
- Did anything help you learn better? If so, what was it, and why do you think it helped?
- Did anything make it harder for you to learn? If so, do you have ideas for making learning easier for yourself in the future?

Reflections on specific pieces of work also are valuable. Students can fill in an entry slip (see Figure 11.8 for an example) for each item they put in their portfolios. Another possibility is to have students fill in a reflection sheet occasionally for a special work product. Questions on the reflection sheet might ask,

1. Why did you choose this item? What does it show about you as a learner?
2. What do you feel you learned by doing this piece of work (about the topic and about yourself)?
3. Did you try something new in this piece of work? How did it come out?
4. If you did a similar piece of work in the future, what would you do differently, and why? What would you do the same way, and why?

An important part of self-reflection is goal setting. As students begin to look at what they can do, they can begin to set goals for what they want to learn next and how they will try to accomplish them. Student goals can be recorded on a separate sheet and kept with their portfolios or in a separate folder. When students review their portfolios, they can write reflections on their goals and what they can do now that they weren't able to do before.

After collecting student products and teacher observations, it is possible to look

FIGURE 11.6   A LABEL GRID FOR ANECDOTAL RECORDS

Name_____

Notes:

Reading	Writing

For for use with computer mailing labels.

at the collection and wonder, "Now, what do we do with all this stuff?" When our instruction is aligned with our benchmarks, we can feel confident we have enough of the right information to assess students' performance. Our portfolios will include the pertinent evidence needed by us, our students, and their parents to clearly evaluate literacy learning.

FIGURE 11.7 ANECDOTAL RECORD FORM

Discussion Group

Book ___ Stone Fox _____

Date ___ Nov. 18 _____

Names	Prepared for discussion	Participation in discussion	Comments
Jana	—	✓	Absent 2 days but able to add to discussion.
Lester	✓	✓+	validated answers by going back to book on own.
Sharon	✓	✓–	Needed to be redirected and prompted.
Brandon	✓–	—	Didn't finish reading? said little.
Yukio	✓	+	Asked "why do you think..." & "what would happen if..." questions and gave own ideas

Other observations: several children shared personal feelings about willie's grandfather not wanting to live anymore and made connections to own family members who are elderly and don't have much money.

FIGURE 11.8   ENTRY SLIP FOR PORTFOLIO ITEMS

Entry Slip

*Name*_____ *Date* _____

Description of item _____

I chose this item for my portfolio because _____

_____

_____

_____

References

Atwell, N. (1998). *In the middle: New understandings about writing, reading, and learning.* Portsmouth, NH: Heinemann.

Valencia. S. (1998). *Literacy portfolios in action.* Fort Worth, TX: Harcourt Brace College.

Resources

Harp, B. (2000). *The handbook of literacy assessment and evaluation.* Norwood, MA: Christopher-Gordon.

Reviews a wide variety of teacher-made and published assessment and evaluation tools. Teachers are encouraged to try the black-line masters in their classrooms and modify them to fit their needs.

Hill, B. C., Ruptic, C., & Norwick, L. (1998). *Classroom based assessment.* Norwood, MA: Christopher-Gordon.

Provides manageable and practical ways to collect information about young learners. Book offers 135 pages of assessment forms that can be copied for classroom use plus a CD-Rom for modification of the forms.

Analyzing Evidence with Rubrics

When students follow the writing process to produce a personal narrative or a story, or when they participate in a literature discussion group, there are no "right answers." However, we know that some responses reflect better thinking and processing. How do we evaluate so that we understand more clearly what each student knows and doesn't yet know about reading and writing processes? And how do we use this information to guide our teaching? These concerns have helped fuel the move to develop rubrics as classroom tools for assessment.

Background

A rubric is a set of criteria used to help determine the level of competence a student has reached on a given benchmark. Rubrics give teachers specific descriptors for assessing student products and performance, and they provide a detailed road map for where to go next in instruction. One reason rubrics appeal to teachers and students is that "instructional rubrics provide students with more informative feedback about their strengths and areas in need of improvement than traditional forms of assessment do" (Goodrich, 2000, p. 14). Using rubrics as a guide for evaluating student work makes the teacher's expectations clear to students, and helps both teachers and students become better judges of quality.

However, Popham (1997) cautions us about some potential problems with rubrics. One, if the evaluative criteria are task-specific, rather than skill-specific, they will not be much use to teachers in further instructional planning. This is because the next task a teacher uses to evaluate how well students have acquired the skill may be completely different from the first task. Two, if the criteria are extremely general, they will not give teachers worthwhile information about what is truly significant in a student's response. These kinds of criteria tend to tell us only that a good piece of work is good, and a bad one is bad. Three, if a rubric is overly detailed, most teachers will not choose to use it. Although more detail may make the rubric clearer, most teachers will not choose to use something that is extremely time consuming. And four, a rubric should not equate the test of the skill with the skill itself. Therefore, teachers need to be careful they are not relying on a single performance to evaluate whether or not a student has mastered a particular skill.

Procedure

There are many sources for rubrics, so teachers do not need to start from scratch unless they choose to. Some states have developed rubrics in conjunction with their state's standards. Educational publishers have put together rubrics for particular subject areas. Software programs are available to help develop rubrics on computer that can be used with electronic portfolios. Students and teachers can also create rubrics together. The resources list at the end of this article will give you some places to start looking (see Figure 11.10).

If you are going to develop your own rubrics or modify existing ones, it is helpful to determine how many levels of descriptors you need. For some benchmarks, it may be enough to define what is proficient and what is not. For other benchmarks, you may want more levels to describe growing competence with a skill. A three-point scale might define the levels as: (a) does not yet meet the benchmark, (b) meets the benchmark, and (c) exceeds the benchmark. An example of a five-point scale is: (a) not yet, (b) emerging, (c) developing, (d) maturing, and (e) strong. For whatever scale you use, you should identify the expected level of performance for a given benchmark, or what you are aiming for. Figure 11.9 provides examples of reading and writing rubrics using a three-point scale (*Meets* defines the expected level).

FIGURE 11.9   EXAMPLES OF RUBRICS FOR READING AND WRITING BENCHMARKS

Benchmark (Reading)	Exceeds	Meets	Not Yet
Makes personal connections to the text.	• Personal response made with extensive explanation. • Includes meaningful connections to own life and/or other texts.	• Personal response made with some explanation. • Includes some connection to own life and/or other texts.	• Personal response doesn't include any explanation. • Personal response doesn't make sense.
Benchmark (Writing)	Exceeds	Meets	Not Yet
Organizes writing logically.	• Structure moves reader through writing. • Writing is cohesive, focused, holds together.	• Structure generally supports meaning. • Easy to follow, but may have some bumpy spots. • A few parts may need rearranging.	• Connections are confusing or missing. • Lacks sense of completeness. • Wandering, lost.

Rubrics are often clearer and easier to score when accompanied by anchor pieces—work or performance samples exemplifying the qualities defined by the rubric. If your rubrics do not have anchor pieces, you can work with others at your grade level to identify student samples to serve as anchor pieces. This is a good step in helping you get clearer about what you are looking for in students' work. Since there are usually multiple qualities and several levels of performance defined in a rubric, you may need more than one anchor piece for each rubric. You may want one anchor piece to show a proficient level of performance on the rubric, and another anchor piece that shows a superior level.

Next, try using your rubrics and anchor pieces to see whether you can determine if students have met a particular benchmark. One way to begin is by working with a partner at your grade level. Score a few pieces of student work, trade with your partner and score her samples, and compare your scores. Discuss your differences and try to resolve them so that you understand how each of you interpreted the wording of the benchmarks and rubrics. At this point, you may need to revise the wording of the rubrics or add information to the descriptors to make them clearer.

Once you have your rubrics, anchor pieces, and scoring procedures, you will need to decide how often to use them. Some teachers use their rubrics for each writing piece that is taken to publication (which works out to once or twice a quarter). When students begin reading chapter books or novels, teachers may use their rubrics after the reading group completes a book. Other teachers score benchmark evidence at the end of each quarter, using the information to help them complete report cards (rubric descriptors are especially helpful for the narrative or comment section to describe what a student has accomplished and still needs to do).

In order to make rubrics a useful guide for instruction, you probably will want to check on student progress half way through the quarter as well as at the end of the quarter. At mid-quarter, you can assess just a few of your students instead of the whole class. Be sure to include some high, middle, and low achievers in your sample to give yourself a better idea of how students of different abilities are doing. Alternatively, you may want to assess samples of work from all your students, but on just a few benchmarks. This is especially valuable when you want to assess how well students are achieving benchmarks you have been working on in that time frame. At the end of the quarter, you will want to assess all your students on the set of benchmarks you are using for readers' and writers' workshops.

What does the information tell you? Look for patterns across the class. A fourth-grade teacher noticed that most of her students were meeting her writing benchmark "uses effective language to convey the message," but none were exceeding it. Examining the rubric, she realized that she was not teaching her students how to do the things that would help them exceed. She added mini-lessons for the whole class with examples of student writing that used precise nouns, powerful verbs, clear images, and natural-sounding dialogue. She also worked with groups of students as they completed their first drafts to help them apply what she taught in the mini-lessons. By the time the students completed their second piece of writing, some had reached the "exceeds" level on this benchmark.

In addition to class patterns, look for patterns for individual students. After examining his data, a second-grade teacher noted that three of his students who were low readers had not met the benchmarks "shows interest in reading" and "selects appropriate books," benchmarks all the rest of the class had met by the end of first quarter. Since he had focused on these benchmarks all first quarter, he realized he needed to work more closely with these three students. He decided to check with them each day and to recommend books at their level and of high interest. He also kept a record of their book choices. With more guidance, these students soon were able to select books at their reading levels and of interest to them. Consequently, they showed more interest in reading.

If your students are older, they can use the benchmarks and rubrics to evaluate themselves. Some teachers post the anchor pieces on a chart next to the rubric descriptors so students can see examples of high, average, and low quality work. (Of course, posted samples, especially the low-quality example, need to come from a classroom other than your own and be anonymous.) As students write reflections on their writing pieces, book projects, and so forth, they can include their reasons for the rubric scores they gave themselves. When you meet for individual end-of-quarter conferences, you have the opportunity to help the student assess his or her progress on the benchmark and set goals to improve specific skills described in the rubric.

References

Goodrich, H. (2000). Using rubrics to promote thinking and learning. *Educational Leadership, 57* (5), 13–18.

Popham, W. J. (1997). What's wrong—and what's right—with rubrics. *Educational Leadership, 55* (2), 72–75.

FIGURE 11.10   SUGGESTED RESOURCES FOR DEVELOPING RUBRICS

Resources for Developing Rubrics

- *Classroom Assessment: Principles and Practices for Effective Instruction.* James H. McMillan. Allyn & Bacon, 1997. Includes information on how to develop rating scales and scoring criteria to evaluate student work.

- *Classroom Based Assessment.* Bonnie Campbell Hill, Cynthia Ruptic, & Lisa Norwick. Christopher-Gordon, 1998. Contains rubrics for writing (folktales, fiction, nonfiction), reading (discussion, response to literature, response project), oral presentations, and science logs.

- *Developing Educational Standards.* (http://putwest.boces.org/standards.html). Web site with an annotated list of Internet sites with K–12 educational standards and curriculum framework documents, including rubrics.

- *Designing Performance Assessments.* (http://scrtec.org/track/tracks/f00133.html). Web site article has links describing ways to implement performance assessment, including the use of rubrics, with different student populations in different subject areas.

- *Designing Rubrics for K–6 Classroom Assessment*, Debbie Rickards & Earl Cheek, Jr. Christoper-Gordon, 1999. Explains how to develop rubrics, introduce them to students, and use them for evaluating student work and performance in reading, writing, social studies, science, and math. Also includes information on accommodations for students with special needs.

- *MidLink Magazine's Rubrics & Handouts.* (www.ncsu.edu/midlink/ho.html). Web site with rubrics for reading, writing, social studies, and technology.

- *Northwest Regional Educational Laboratory.* (www.nwrel.org/eval/writing/). Web site with rubrics for writing traits (ideas, organization, voice, word choice, sentence fluency, conventions) and presentations.

- *Open-Ended Questioning: A Handbook for Educators.* Robin Lee Harris Freedman. Addison-Wesley, 1994. Explains how to use open-ended questions for assessing writing, reading, and speaking activities, and includes the use of rubrics. Offers rubrics for assessing different types of writing: analysis, comparison, description, evaluation, fiction, problem-solving, and writing about mathematics.

- *The Role of Rubrics in Classroom Assessment.* Video. IOX Assessment Associates (5301 Beethoven St., Suite 190, Los Angeles, CA 90066). Explains what a rubric is and how to judge what makes a good rubric. Sample rubrics are included.

- *Writing Assessment: Training in Analytic Scoring.* Northwest Regional Educational Laboratory. Video. IOX Assessment Associates (5301 Beethoven St., Suite 190, Los Angeles, CA 90066). Describes a six-trait model (ideas and content, organization, voice, word choice, sentence fluency, conventions) for scoring writing and how to use the model for classroom instruction and assessment.

Evaluation Portfolios

A major purpose of evaluation portfolios is to provide evidence of students' progress in meeting standards. Throughout this chapter, we have presented you with different parts of the process for creating evaluation portfolios. Now let's put the pieces of the puzzle together, so you can get an overview of how to set up and maintain evaluation portfolios with your students.

As described in the article on grade-level benchmarks, the starting point for evaluation portfolios is establishing clear goals for student learning. You will develop grade level benchmarks and align them with the relevant set of standards, perhaps established by the state or district. It is important to keep to a small number of benchmarks, perhaps just 5 to 7 for reading and the same number for writing. In the beginning, it is wise to focus either on reading or writing and not to try to do too much. A focus on writing provides the more convenient starting point, because evidence of writing performance is easier to gather than evidence of reading performance.

You will translate the grade-level benchmarks into language understandable to students, in the form of "I Can" statements. So that students will better understand the "I Can" statements, you will hold discussions with them about what good readers or writers do. Then you will share the "I Can" statements with students, making the connection that working toward the "I Can" statements will help them to become better readers and writers. Most experienced teachers do not introduce the "I Can" statements to students all at once but add a few each quarter.

Suppose that you have decided to introduce two attitude "I Can" statements near the beginning of the first quarter. Throughout the quarter, you remind students about the "I Can" statements and make connections between classroom activities and progress in meeting the goals set through the "I Can" statements. For example, if the "I Can" statement has to do with reading books of one's own choice, students can be reminded during sustained silent reading that they are working on this "I Can" statement.

At the end of the quarter, you tell students that you will be helping them to create individual evaluation portfolios. These portfolios may consist of manila folders, three-ring binders, or similar holders. You begin by reminding students of the attitude "I Can" statement: I can read a book every day during sustained silent reading. You ask them what evidence they might provide to show that they have made progress on this "I Can" statement. Students suggest that they can use the logs in which they write down the titles of the books they read each day. You agree that the logs can serve as evidence. You have students select a recent log sheet. You hand each student a reflection sheet (see Figure 11.8 and article on Collecting Evidence earlier in this chapter) to attach to the log sheet. On the reflection sheet, the student records the "I Can" statement addressed by this piece of evidence, tells why he chose this piece of evidence, and reflects on what it shows about him as a writer. The reflection sheet is then stapled to the piece of evidence, and these materials are put into the evaluation portfolio.

You will need to develop a schedule or system for having the students add evidence to their evaluation portfolios as the year goes on. Many teachers set aside time at the end of each quarter for the whole class to work on collecting evidence and preparing written reflections. The teacher may want to confer with individuals, although small-group conferences often work nearly as well. At this time you can guide students to write down the reading and writing goals they will be working on during the next quarter. These goals will include the "I Can" statements but should extend to individual goals that may not be addressed by the grade-level benchmarks.

Evaluation portfolios are structured for a specific purpose—to provide evidence that students are progressing toward the grade-level benchmarks. This means that the portfolios must be organized to make it easy to track students' progress. The portfolios might have index tabs so that evidence can be put into four sections, one for each quarter of the school year. Or the portfolio may be organized by areas. For example, there might be one section for attitude "I Cans," one for comprehension "I Cans," and one for skill and strategy "I Cans."

Each quarter, you can use rubrics to score the evidence students have put into their portfolios (see article on Analyzing Evidence with Rubrics earlier in this chapter). If reliability of scoring is a concern (for example, if scores are to be combined across classes in a grade level or reported to the district), the rubrics should be based on just three levels of performance. Reliability of scoring can almost always be achieved with three levels but not with four or more levels. The terms to be applied to the three levels might be,

- Exceeding the benchmark or standard (performance above grade level)
- Meeting the benchmark or standard (performance at grade level)
- Working on the benchmark or standard (performance below grade level)

The results obtained by scoring the students' evidence with the rubrics can then be summarized in the form of bar graphs. A sample bar graph for a classroom with 27 students, covering results for the four quarters of the school year, is shown in Figure 11.11. This graph shows that in the first quarter, 22 of the students were working at or below grade level, with respect to comprehension benchmark #1. This is the expected result in the first quarter, because benchmarks are goals for student learning set for the end of the school year. In the second quarter, the number of students meeting the benchmark increased, but 18 students were still below grade level. In the third quarter, for the first time, two students exceeded the benchmark, and almost half the class had met the benchmark. By the fourth quarter, six students had exceeded the benchmark, 14 had met it, and 7 were still working on it. As you can see, bar graphs of this type can be very useful in giving an overview of students' progress toward meeting benchmarks over the course of the year.

In short, evaluation portfolios are a sound approach for meeting accountability concerns through standards-based assessment. Through evaluation portfolios, classroom evidence that reflects the day-to-day accomplishments of students and teachers can be summarized in the form of bar graphs. The information provided through students' portfolios, and summarized in these graphs, is likely to present a view of student achievement much more detailed and accurate than that obtained through large-scale testing.

FIGURE 11.11 EXAMPLE OF BAR GRAPH SHOWING STUDENT RESULTS

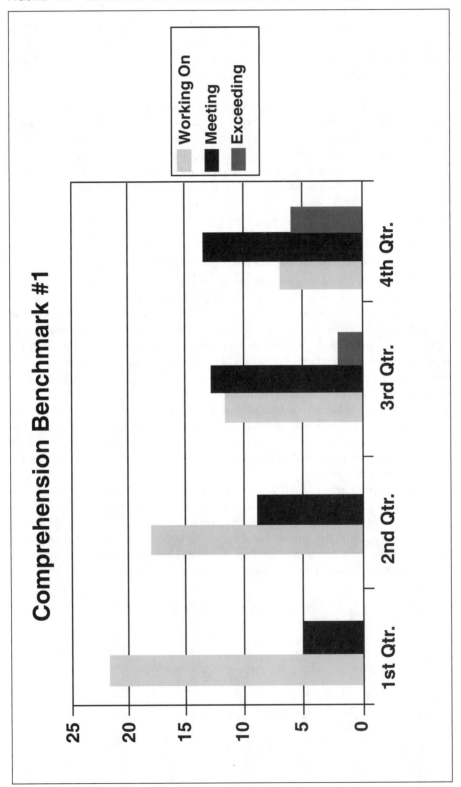

Connections to Home and Community:
Three-Way Conferences

Teachers using a balanced literacy approach may find it challenging to communicate with parents about students' growth in reading and writing abilities. Parents unfamiliar with literature-based instruction and the process approach to writing may assess progress differently than teachers do. For example, parents may focus on activities such as listening for decoding errors as their child reads aloud, or looking at written work for neat handwriting and correct spelling. Parents may place a great deal of importance on report card grades and standardized test results.

While these things are not unimportant, teachers of readers' and writers' workshops need to give parents additional information they can use to evaluate their child's achievements. One way to do this is by showing parents their child's portfolio. This is even more powerful when the child takes the lead in preparing the portfolio and presenting the information.

Background

Davies, Cameron, Politano, and Gregory (1992) developed the idea of three-way conferences to give students a more equal voice in communicating their learning to their parents. Instead of the traditional parent-teacher conference where the teacher provides information about the student, sometimes in the student's absence, three-way conferences give students equal responsibility for explaining what they are doing in school and how they are progressing. Students take responsibility for explaining their goals, plans, work, and accomplishments to their parents. Parents can ask questions and discuss concerns with their child and the teacher so that everyone has a clear picture of progress to date and next steps. Parents, students, and the teacher can then work together to develop the child's goals and plans for the next term.

Procedure

Having students take the lead in sharing what they've learned with parents requires preparation in the classroom. Third-grade teacher Jo Ann Wong-Kam (1998) worked on this process throughout the school year. She began by helping her students set goals and make plans for themselves in specific areas of reading and writing they wanted to improve. The students used ideas from their class chart What Good Readers Do to choose one thing they could do to help themselves be a better reader (e.g., spend more time reading) and write a plan (e.g., read every night with my dad, record what I read on my reading log). They followed the same process for writing. The students saved responses to literature, writing pieces, reading logs, projects, and artwork as evidence of working toward and meeting their goals.

Each quarter, Mrs. Wong-Kam gave her students time to review their work and select work samples for their progress folios (Davies & Politano, 1994). Progress folios are a type of portfolio where quarterly samples of work are laid out side-by-side to show progress over time. Mrs. Wong-Kam's students wrote reflections to link each work sample to their goals and personal progress. The teacher met with each student to review the contents of the progress folio and discuss what it showed. Students explained what they thought they were doing well and identified areas where they felt they needed more help. With their teacher's help, they determined how they could turn their needs into new or modified goals.

The students used a conference planning form (see Figure 11.12) to organize their thoughts about their strengths, identify two areas of need, decide on evidence to show their strengths and needs, and set a goal for the next quarter. The teacher guide (see Figure 11.13) was used to record the same information, with room to add parent's comments during the actual conference. There also was space to set up an action plan and identify what the student, teacher, and parent would do to support the plan. To prepare parents for this new experience, Mrs. Wong-Kam sent out a letter ahead of time that detailed how the time would be structured and what to expect. She reasoned that parents would not be prepared for a conference where their child, rather than the teacher, explained the child's progress. She wanted parents to be ready to "think and act in new ways" (Wong-Kam (1998), p. 326).

Finally, students were ready to present their progress folios to their parents. Although the students took the lead in presenting their work and reflections, Mrs. Wong-Kam was there to provide additional information and answer questions as needed. She served as facilitator, encouraging open and honest dialogue about successes and challenges and keeping the tone positive. After the child's presentation and teacher input, parents were invited to ask questions and make comments. Then the parents, the child, and the teacher set goals and formed a plan of action for the next quarter. The family took the progress folio home for parents to review more fully. Mrs. Wong-Kam also sent home a feedback form so that parents could let her know how they felt about the conference and the information shared.

References

Davies, A., Cameron, C., Politano, C., & Gregory, K. (1992). *Together is better: Collaborative assessment, evaluation and reporting.* Winnipeg, Canada: Peguis Publishers.

Davies, A., & Politano, C. (1994). *Multiage and more.* Winnipeg, Canada: Peguis Publishers.

Wong-Kam, J. A. (1998). Sharing responsibility for assessment and evaluation with our students. In T. E. Raphael & K. H. Au (Eds.), *Literature-based instruction: Reshaping the curriculum* (pp. 305–329). Norwood, MA: Christopher-Gordon.

FIGURE 11.12 CONFERENCE GUIDE FOR STUDENTS.

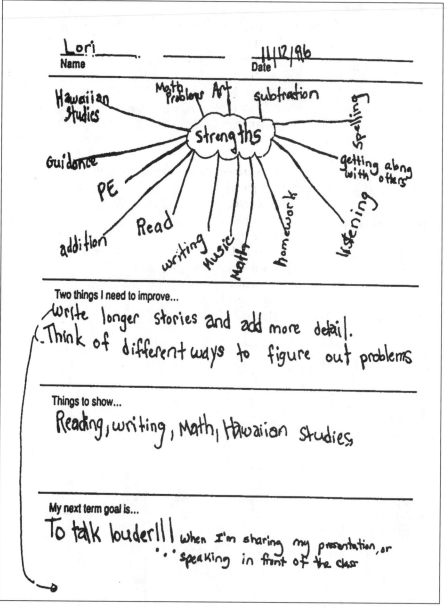

From *Together is Better* by Davies/Cameron/Politano/Gregory © Peguis Publishers, 1992.
This page may be reproduced for clasroom use.
Printed with permission.

FIGURE 11.13   CONFERENCE GUIDE FOR TEACHERS

Three-Way Conference Guide for Teachers

Student's name _____   Date _____

Areas of strength	Areas needing improvement

Notes for the conference	Additional notes

Action Plan
Goal:

Student will...	Teacher will...	Parent will...

Other notes:

From *Together is Better* by Davies/Cameron/Politano/Gregory © Peguis Publishers, 1992.
This page may be reproduced for clasroom use.
Printed with permission.

Troubleshooting: What About Standardized Tests?

Assessment provides information to different groups, or stakeholders, concerned with children's reading progress (Farr, 1992). The portfolio assessment process we described in this chapter is important to teachers as it informs their daily decisions about instruction. It is important to students because they must understand their own strengths and needs if their literacy skills are to improve. Parents are interested in portfolio assessment, because they want to monitor their children's progress and take an active part in their education. Administrators look to these measures to compare students' performance with the school's curriculum.

Another group, members of the general public, usually require broader means of assessing student achievement. These are the people who judge school's effectiveness and determine if education dollars are wisely spent. This group usually turns to norm-reference, standardized tests for information. Standardized tests are of interest to school administrators, parents, and teachers who use the results to compare their children's performance with others across the nation.

Unfortunately, standardized tests have been ascribed an increasingly prominent role in our schools, often becoming the only tests that "count." The sole measure of many schools are their test scores. Often, because of this emphasis, teachers find themselves following a narrowly defined curriculum created by district offices or textbook publishers, rather than a curriculum based upon the diverse needs of their particular students.

Typically, standardized tests are administered to large groups of students, have a multiple-choice format with only one correct answer, and are machine scored. The raw scores from these tests are interpreted into percentile ranks, stanines, and grade equivalents. Reading tests usually contain subtests of decoding, comprehension, and vocabulary.

Criticism of Standardized Tests

In recent years standardized tests have come under a high degree of criticism from educators. Tierney, Carter, and Desai and colleagues (1991) discuss four problems with these kinds of tests:

1. *They reflect an outdated view of classrooms and restricted goals for learning.* Reading programs of the past contained text passages with artificial controls on vocabulary. Accompanying workbooks required marking correct answers or responding with a few words. Today's programs are literature based and students work together to discuss books and construct meanings. Extended written responses have replaced workbooks. Standardized tests are not consistent with current practices.

2. *They reflect a limited view of reading and writing.* Most test publishers have not responded to the current perspective that reading is a meaning-constructing process in which skills are integrated, not isolated. They overlook the complexities of reading abilities, reducing them to a total score.

3. *They disenfranchise teachers and constrain instructional possibilities.* When too much importance is given standardized tests, teachers may loose faith in their abilities to make instructional decisions based on the needs of their students. Teachers' instructional time may be guided by someone else's test, limiting students' learning and decision-making opportunities.

4. *They do not engage students in self-assessment.* Instead of empowering learn-
    ing and teaching, the tests are detached from it. Students' views of progress are
    not considered.

Problems with our current standardized tests are obvious, yet we are encouraged
by cooperative efforts currently underway that should lead to an improvement in future
reading assessment measures. As examples, The National Council of Teachers of English has produced standards that are reflected in the New Standards tests, criterion-
referenced assessments. Each state, too, is currently working to develop consensus on
standards; and there is a call for national exams based on the curriculum frameworks of
the National Assessment of Educational Progress (NAEP). But at present, many teachers still must deal with an annually administered test that reflects the problems noted
above. An important segment of the community may use results from the tests to judge
students and their reading. This is a group that often makes decisions which affect
classroom curriculum and materials.

A Sensible Approach

Calkins, Montgomery, Santman, with Falk (1998) offer a "survival guide to standardized reading tests," suggesting that teachers provide students with strategies for
dealing with standardized tests. They believe it important for students to do as well as
possible on these tests because:

- Unless students score well, teachers may lose the freedom to teach in ways they
  believe best for children.

- If students do well on tests, teachers are in a stronger position to be critical of
  those tests. It is easier, politically, to disclaim or discard a test on which a large
  number of students perform well than one on which they do poorly.

- Test scores have importance for students because they are used for identification
  and tracking.

- If student's home language is different from test language, an introduction to
  test language and format can help alleviate their disadvantage.

- If students learn ways to approach tests, they can apply their knowledge to other
  types of standardized tests they are likely to encounter throughout life.

- When test preparation is condensed, powerful, and timely, teachers can regulate
  the process in a sensible way (pp. 7–8).

In order to help students develop powerful test-taking strategies, Calkins et. al.
(1998) believe that teachers need to provide active and assertive instruction. In order to
determine effective instruction, Calkins' group studied tests, took tests themselves, talked
about their own strategies, watched students taking practice tests, and talked with students about their strategies. As a result of their research they developed teaching techniques based upon their observations and discussions. Then they presented their mini-
lessons to students and observed the impact of their teaching. When the impact of a
lesson wasn't productive, they discussed possible reasons and altered the approach.

After working with many students in many classrooms, Calkins et al. (1998) offer
mini-lessons that their students seemed to find useful (p. 93). The goal is to help children develop an approach to test taking that is different from their approach to everyday reading.

1. Have students first read the questions and then the passage. To demonstrate
    this strategy the teacher first explains to students that this is similar to going on

a scavenger hunt where you have a list of things to look for. For example, after reading the first question, she thinks, "OK. I'll be looking for what made Adam feel sad. The next question wants me to look for the kind of dog Adam owned." After the teacher reads a few questions, she says, "This is probably enough for me to keep in mind." Then she reads the passage aloud, exclaiming, "There it is!" when she finds an answer.

2. Help students discover how many questions they can hold in their minds as they read the passages. As children practice test-taking, they will recognize how many questions they can remember. Calkins' group found this "scavenger-hunt" strategy helpful even for students who could recall as few as two questions. Besides having a list of items to look for, their stance changed from one of pleasure reader to test taker.

3. When answer sheets are separate from the test booklets, have students first fill in the all answers for a passage in the booklets and then mark the corresponding bubbles on their answer sheets. When children assume a "scavenger hunt" approach, it is unlikely that they will find answers in the passages in the same order they are listed on the test. As the researchers observed students they found this sometimes caused them to mark the wrong bubble. Because the "scavenger-hunt" strategy had such a positive payoff for students, the researchers worked to solve the problem by suggesting that children first fill in the answers on the test booklet. This approach worked for the students and, because the test booklets were not reused, it did not matter that marks had been made on them.

4. Teach students ways to mark the passage so it will be easier for them to go back to find or check specific parts. While reading a passage students might write key words in the margins, circle or underline important words or phrases. Again, because the booklets were not reused, the researchers encouraged students to mark the test booklets while reading. In mini-lessons teachers demonstrated by underlining dates or places saying, "I'll bet they'll ask about this fact. Now, I can come back here if they do." Children may need to learn, too, that it is all right to return to the passage once they have begun answering the questions. Knowing this, they will understand that jotting "lost" in the margin by the paragraph where the dog became lost will allow them to more quickly access information about a related question.

5. Have students use an index card to hold their place or block out distracting print. Seeing only one passage or section at a time helped some students see the text as less overwhelming.

6. Provide test-taking practice on easy or familiar text by retyping it in the same format as the test passages. Because the dense format of test passages appeared overwhelming to some children, their teachers took stories they could easily read and retyped them to look like test passages. This gave children confidence and experience in reading text of this kind and helped students see that a story can look difficult, yet not be that demanding.

Moving Forward

These ideas should serve as a starting point for teachers. While exploring a test-taking curriculum with students, teachers will develop other strategies based upon their own findings and the needs of their particular children.

It is also important that teachers discover the limitations of the current standardized tests and work to influence change. Accountability is important, but teachers and students should know what they are accountable for. As teachers, we can support the development of standardized forms of assessment aligned with our standards for student learning, our curriculum frameworks, and the beliefs of our professional organizations. A relevant standardized test, placed alongside classroom-based assessments, can provide all stakeholders with a richer, more balanced understanding of student progress.

References

Farr, R. (1992). Putting it all together: Solving the reading assessment puzzle. *The Reading Teache*r, 46, 26–37.

Calkins, L., Montgomery, K., Santman, D. with Falk, B. (1998). *A teacher's guide to standardized reading tests: Knowledge is power*. Portsmouth N.H.: Heinemann.

Tierney, R. J., Carter, M. A., & Desai, L. E. (1991). *Portfolio assessment in the reading-writing classroom*. Norwood MA: Christopher-Gordon.

Resource

Popham, W. J. (1999, March). Why standardized tests don't measure educational quality. *Educational Leadership*, 56, 8–16.

Troubleshooting: What About Grading and Report Cards?

Teachers of readers' and writers' workshops may wonder about how to deal with grades and report cards. What do grades and report cards reflect about a student, and is the information they tell us what we need to know? How do we report in a meaningful way a student's successes and challenges in literacy learning?

The Traditional Role of Grades

Grades have been used for three main purposes (Trumbull, 2000). One is to communicate students' performance to the students, their families, others involved in the educational system, and the teachers themselves. A second purpose is to motivate students, so that students with lower grades will be inspired to earn higher grades and students with higher grades will work to keep them. A third purpose is to sort students—for class placement, for admission to a private school, to determine if a student can be promoted or can graduate.

One problem with grading to communicate or motivate is that sometimes students and parents do not truly understand why a particular grade was given and how to go about improving it. In these circumstances, students are not motivated by grades, but merely labeled by them. In reviewing studies on the effects of grading, Guskey (1994) found that students who receive low grades might withdraw from learning in order to protect their self-image.

Another problem, researchers and teachers Spandel and Stiggins (1990) remind us, is that, "In the final analysis, grades are a form of personal response and cannot be more. If we're going to use them at all, we should be very honest with students about this. At the same time, it's also honest to acknowledge that in the real world, evaluations, even when they're subjective, sometimes do count" (pp. 115–116).

Making Grades More Meaningful

When grades are given, they should be based on clear and important learning criteria that can be explained to students, parents, and others. Spandel and Stiggins (1990) recommend that effort and attitudes not be included in the same grade as achievement. They feel this gives students the message that they do not have to perform well as long as they appear to be trying hard and enjoying what they do. In addition, they feel that taking into account ability or aptitude shortchanges both "high ability" students by holding them to a higher standard and "low ability" students by failing to expect enough of them. Research indicates that students work up to the level others expect them to achieve.

Grades should be used sparingly. Some teachers feel compelled to grade every piece of work a student does, fearing perhaps that students will not be motivated to complete assignments otherwise. Even if this is true, grades as motivation will not inspire students to become lifelong learners. In classrooms where readers' and writers' workshops are at the heart of literacy learning, students can find personal motivations that are more compelling. Since learning is a social act (see The Impact of Lev Vygotsky, chapter 1), social motivators such as sharing ideas about a book you have read or reading your writing to someone else for feedback can be more meaningful than earning a grade for a reading or writing activity.

Teachers and students can work together to determine how many and which writing pieces or reading activities will be graded. With this knowledge, students may spend extra time on those examples. This means that teachers will grade the best products students can produce, which is a better evaluation of a student's performance than a composite grade based on every piece of work produced. For example, if students know only certain writing samples will be graded and they have some say in which ones are chosen, they may be willing to take more risks in their writing. These risky efforts may or may not work out, but students will certainly learn more from them than they would from producing another safe, predictable piece. And regardless of whether students receive a grade for a piece of work, they should receive some form of response to it.

The Changing Report Card

A year-long study of evaluation (Harste, 1996) found that parents wanted the following things from report cards:

- information about classroom expectations
- information about classroom activities during the grading period
- descriptions of how well their child did, overall and in specific activities
- ideas about what parents could do to support their child's learning

The teachers in this study created a narrative report card to address these four expectations. They identified the major components of their curriculum, wrote about specific activities that occurred for that component, and described how the child did, identifying both strengths and weaknesses. In addition, the students wrote letters to their parents to assess how well they felt they were doing during the grading period.

A student's performance on standards or benchmarks can be attached to the traditional report card, used to compute grades, or used in place of grades. Teacher and researcher Regie Routman's (1996, 2000) school system replaced their report card with a benchmark checklist and supporting narrative comments. Items such as *chooses to write regularly and uses details and interesting words* are keyed as C—is *consistently* achieving objectives, E—is progressing toward objectives as *expected*, or P—needs more *practice* and experience to meet objectives. Student portfolios and conferences are used to document the information in the checklist.

Testing coordinator Linda Elman (in Busick, 2000) suggested a method to turn rubric scores into grades. First, you need to develop a rule for assigning a grade to a single piece of work. It could be that a certain percentage of rubric scores need to be in a certain range; for example, on a five-point writing rubric with six traits (e.g., meaning, voice, organization, language, sentence fluency, and conventions), half the scores need to be at 5 with no scores below 4 to get an A on the piece. Or you could decide that mostly 4s and 5s equal an A, 3s and 4s equal a B, and so forth. Once you have your rule, you need to determine a system for weighing the pieces in your grade book to come up with a final grade for the report card.

Even if traditional report cards are used, accompanying narratives can be based on descriptors from "I Can" statements and rubrics. This can be helpful in communicating to students and parents what students can do, and what they still need to learn. In addition, portfolios can be sent home with the report card. The portfolio is an excellent means for teachers and students to communicate a student's growth and accomplishments to parents (see The Impact of Sheila Valencia: Portfolio Assessment, as well as Connections to the Home and Community: Three-Way Conferences, both in this chapter).

References

Busick, K. (2000). Grading and standards-based assessment. In Trumbull, E., & Farr, B. (Eds.). *Grading and reporting student progress in an age of standards.* Norwood, MA: Christopher-Gordon.

Harste, J. (1996). Using a narrative report card. *School Talk, 3* (3), 3.

Guskey, T. R. (1994). Making the grade: What benefits students? *Educational Leadership, 52* (2), 14–20.

Routman, R. (1996). Curriculum fuels changes. *School Talk, 3* (3), 2.

Routman, R. (2000). *Conversations: Strategies for teaching, learning, and evaluating.* Portsmouth, NH: Heinemann.

Spandel, V., & Stiggins, R. J. (1990). *Creating writers: Linking assessment and writing instruction.* New York: Longman.

Trumbull, E. (2000). Why do we grade—and should we? In Trumbull, E., & Farr, B. (Eds.). *Grading and reporting student progress in an age of standards.* Norwood, MA: Christopher-Gordon.

SECTION IV:

CONCLUSION

Chapter 12

KEEPING IT GOING

Teachers Engaged in Learning

The following vignettes give examples of how teachers may go through the process of change in order to make balanced literacy instruction a reality in their classrooms. Both cases show the importance of colleagues in supporting the process of change.

A New Teacher Focuses on the Writers' Workshop

Marilyn Smith was starting her second year in the classroom. She had found her first year quite a struggle, although she had managed in the second semester to introduce a writers' workshop to her sixth graders. This year Marilyn wanted to start her writers' workshop right away. She made plans to work with Alison Lee, a resource teacher at her school. When Marilyn approached her, Alison said she would be happy to come to the classroom to observe, to assist with writing conferences, and to offer suggestions. Alison's schedule allowed her to visit Marilyn's classroom once every two weeks.

Alison and Marilyn sat down to go over a copy of the implementation checklists for the writers' workshop shown in Figure 12.1 (Figure 12.2 presents the parallel implementation checklist for the readers' workshop). Marilyn felt that all the items were appropriate for her classroom, and that she would like to use the checklist to help her set goals. Marilyn went over the checklist and marked the items that she felt she already had in place. These had mainly to do with scheduling and the physical arrangement of her classroom. For the first month, Marilyn decided, her goal would be to give mini-lessons on classroom procedures. These would include teaching the students how to conduct peer conferences. Alison agreed that this was a good place to start.

The following Wednesday, Alison came to observe Marilyn's writers' workshop. Marilyn had planned her mini-lesson well, but it lasted nearly 20 minutes. When the time came for the students to begin writing, they had difficulty settling down. Alison and Marilyn both circulated around the room, conducting brief conferences. Alison noticed that Marilyn had excellent rapport with her students. Just as all the students seemed to be getting involved in their writing, the recess bell rang.

At recess, Alison asked Marilyn how she felt the writers' workshop had gone that morning. Marilyn replied that she thought the students had gotten restless because her lesson had gone on too long. Once they started writing, the students seemed noisy and restless. Alison agreed with these observations. Marilyn said she would work on keeping her mini-lessons brief, no longer than 10 minutes, so that the students could begin writing sooner. Alison suggested that, after the mini-lesson, Marilyn have five minutes of sustained silent writing, in order to help the students calm down and focus. Marilyn liked this idea and said she would give it a try.

The next time Alison observed, Marilyn kept her mini-lesson to 10 minutes. Then Marilyn had her students engage in sustained silent writing for five minutes. She circulated around the room to keep the students focused, and her approach seemed to help the students concentrate. After sustained silent writing, the students were free to confer with one another, continue drafting, revise, or edit. Marilyn and Alison stationed themselves in different parts of the room and held conferences with individual students. Marilyn told Alison she felt her workshop was running more smoothly. The peer conferences needed polishing, but many of the students were getting the idea.

At the end of the month, Alison and Marilyn met after school, and Marilyn completed the reflection and goal-setting form shown in Figure 12.3. Marilyn felt her goals for the past month had been accomplished, and that she wanted to move toward the goals of writing with her students and sharing her own writing. Marilyn thought that, instead of circulating around the room during sustained silent writing, she could sit down and write in her own notebook. She could also begin to share her notebook entries with the class. These two steps would help her to reach the goal of writing with her students. Alison suggested that Marilyn sit with a different table of students each day, so everyone in the class would have a chance to see her write.

Experienced Teachers Focus on the Readers' Workshop

Angie Diaz had been a teacher for 18 years. She had tried various grade levels but had found that first grade was her favorite. Angie had the reputation for being an innovative teacher and was regarded as a leader at her school. This year, Angie's goal was to conduct an excellent readers' workshop. Angie's district favored literature-based instruction, as did her principal. However, unlike Marilyn, Angie did not have a resource teacher to work with her. Furthermore, due to budget cuts, the district was not offering any workshops on literature-based instruction.

Another first-grade teacher, Gail Heinrich, and a second-grade teacher, Donna Fleming, shared Angie's interest in the readers' workshop. Together, they decided to map out plans for their own professional development. The group decided to meet once a week after school. The time shifted from week to week, and sometimes the group was not able to meet at all. However, they kept in touch through brief conversations and evening phone calls.

At their first meeting, the members of the group discussed their concerns. Angie began by saying that she felt she was successful with most of her first graders but needed to find ways to promote the decoding ability of the struggling readers. She wanted to develop a schedule that would allow her to provide more small group instruction during her readers' workshop. Gail said she shared Angie's concerns but was not as far along in her understanding of the readers' workshop. She wanted to learn more about shared reading from Angie, in particular, how to teach phonics lessons with big books. Donna described her main concern as meeting the needs of all her students. She had some students whose literacy was still emergent and others who could read at the fourth-grade level. She wanted ideas for organizing her readers' workshop to address this wide range. She said she too would be interested in learning more about shared reading, since her class included four emergent readers. After further discussion, the group decided that their first goal would be to work on the overall organization of their readers' workshops. After that, they would turn to the question of small group instruction and shared reading in particular.

Angie had copies of a number of checklists for the readers' workshop, including the ones shown in Figure 12.2. The teachers decided to devise their own checklist, using the ones in Figure 12.2 as a model. Donna, a computer whiz, offered to produce clean copies of the checklist. At the next meeting, each of the teachers sat down with a copy of the checklist and marked off the items she felt were already in place in her classroom. Each also identified the items in the classroom organization section of the checklist that she wanted to focus on for the coming month. The teachers then discussed their goals with one another.

The teachers did not have the opportunity to observe in one another's classrooms, but they decided that they would move their meetings around to different classrooms. This would enable them to gain a better sense of what the others were doing. Since they were in Angie's room, Angie offered to share the schedule she was trying for her readers' workshop. She also gave a guided tour of her room, including the classroom library, computer area, and center for small group instruction. On subsequent occasions the group met in Gail's room and Donna's room, then returned to Angie's room again.

At the beginning of each month, the teachers took the first 10 minutes of the meeting to complete their reflection and goal setting forms (see Figure 12.3). Sometimes they had the same goals, and sometimes they pursued individual goals.

The teachers had somewhat different systems for tracking their professional development. Angie had a large three-ring binder in which she kept her checklist, reflection forms, and articles on literature-based instruction and related topics. Angie took notes during the meetings, and she kept these notes in her binder. Gail kept a manila folder for the meetings and also brought along her writers' notebook. Her notebook included reflections on her teaching as well as other reflections. She often copied quotations from professional books and articles into her notebook. Donna, too, kept her materials in a manila folder. She preferred to write on the computer, and she sometimes read printouts of her electronic journal entries to the group.

A School Focuses on Evaluation Portfolios

Steve Wong was excited about starting work at his new school. In his interview with the principal, he learned that the whole school was going to be working on evaluation portfolios. Steve had only one year of teaching experience. He was well aware of the importance of standards-based education, but he had not yet had the opportunity to learn how to use portfolios in his classroom. Now he would have that chance with his fourth graders.

Steve arrived early for the all-day staff orientation meeting held on the first duty day for teachers. The day began with a brief round of introductions, and then the principal launched right into the business at hand—the school's goal of improving writing achievement and measuring that improvement through evaluation portfolios for each and every student. The principal reviewed the teachers' belief statements, generated the previous spring, that defined the school's philosophy of teaching, learning, and literacy. Then she reviewed the vision statement for the excellent sixth-grade writer. The task that morning was for the teachers at each grade level to work on drafting their grade level benchmarks and "I Can" statements: two for attitudes, two for the writing process, and two for strategies and skills. Steve soon found himself deep in discussion with the other three fourth-grade teachers. The principal, a resource teacher, and a consultant from the district office circulated around the room to assist the teachers with the task.

Steve soon learned that he was indeed fortunate to be at this school. Through a grant, the principal had obtained funding to hire substitutes, so the teachers had four days, one each quarter, set aside to work on the evaluation portfolios. Steve enjoyed listening to the speakers, some of them classroom teachers like himself, who came to provide ideas about writing instruction and evaluation portfolios. But what he appreciated most was the time to work with the other teachers at his grade level. As the least experienced teacher in the group, he benefitted from knowing how the others handled different issues.

Steve and the other fourth-grade teachers all made use of the writers' workshop implementation checklists (see Figure 12.1a-d). But because the other teachers had considerable experience with the writers' workshop, they could focus mainly on integrating evaluation portfolios into this structure. Steve had to first learn how to implement a writers' workshop, so that he would have good instruction in place, before he began to use evaluation portfolios. He found himself scrambling to collect data each quarter, because there was so much that he was still figuring out how to do. He did manage to implement evaluation portfolios in his classroom, but he knew he could not have done so without the help of his colleagues.

Steve liked the idea that all the teachers in the school were committed to working toward a common goal. Although it would take several years and a great deal of hard work before all the details of using the evaluation portfolios would be worked out, Steve knew that the process would get easier as time went on. He and the other teachers felt confident they would reach their goal of improving students' writing achievement and documenting that progress through evaluation portfolios.

The Process of Change

A paradigm shift involves a change from one world view to another. Such a shift is currently taking place in the field of literacy instruction, as educators move from a focus on the transmission of skills to a focus on meaningful activities with embedded skill instruction (Au & Carroll, 1997; Carroll, Wilson, & Au, 1996). The process of moving toward balanced literacy instruction—including the writers' workshop, the readers' workshop, and portfolio assessment—can be lengthy and often involves a good deal of soul-searching.

One constraint on change is that not everyone is ready to change at the same time. Lea Ridley (1990) worked as a reading and writing consultant helping teachers move toward whole language. She encountered teachers with three different stances toward change: (a) proponents of the whole language philosophy, (b) those interested primarily in applications of whole language, and (c) those interested neither in philosophy nor applications. As Ridley learned, teachers in a given school seldom have the same readiness for change, whether they are moving toward whole language, balanced literacy instruction, or another philosophy. At the outset participants should recognize that people will be at various places along a continuum of change, and that different kinds of professional development activities will be appropriate for different groups.

In some schools, such as that in the vignette with second-year teacher Steve Wong, the principal provides strong, focused leadership and the resources to enable the whole faculty to move forward together. Teachers in such schools receive ongoing opportunities for professional development and time to work together on curriculum and assessment. They have the support they need to improve their instruction and evaluation procedures. These are the ideal conditions for implementing balanced literacy instruction. Excellent accounts of the school change process include those by Lois Bridges Bird (1989) and Kelly Chandler and the Mapleton Teacher-Research Group (1999). The latter provides an excellent introduction to teacher research (Hubbard & Power, 1999), which can be a logical extension of the change process.

Many teachers, however, do not have the good fortune to find themselves in a school like Steve Wong's. They may be in situations like that of Marilyn Smith or Angie Diaz, where there is no whole-school system for moving toward balanced literacy instruction. These teachers are "goers" and must take the initiative to create their own professional support group by finding other "goers" to work with.

Initial Discussions

Suppose that a group of "goers" has been identified. What steps might members of this group take to move forward? A first step might be to begin with discussions of philosophy and the reasons for making changes. Questions for structuring the discussions include the following:

• What beliefs do members of the group hold about literacy, teaching, and learning?

• What do they hope to accomplish by bringing about change in their classrooms?

Members of the group do not have to come to consensus about these issues. Rather, the purpose of the discussion is to give individuals the chance to make their beliefs, assumptions, and goals explicit. If notes are taken at each meeting, the group can gradually refine its goals and instructional philosophy.

The four articles in chapter 1 will prove useful as background reading during these discussions. Each article is short enough to be read and discussed in the course of an after-school meeting. Participants may also follow a jigsaw approach. The group counts off from one to four. All the "ones" read the article on Strickland, the "twos" read the article on Vygotsky, and so on. After reading, the participants form jigsaw groups, with a one, two, three, and four in each group. Participants share the key ideas they gained from their reading with those who read different articles.

Choosing a Focus

Once the "goers" have discussed their beliefs and goals, they are ready for the next step, which is to select a focus for change. Teachers should choose to focus either on the writers' workshop and the process approach to writing, or on the readers' workshop and literature-based instruction. All teachers in the group need not choose the same focus. Au and Scheu (1996) found that teachers were more likely to be successful if they concentrated on one workshop at a time. Most teachers in their study chose to begin with the writers' workshop. The teachers did not neglect reading or other curriculum areas, but continued to teach these subjects in much the same way as they had before. Making the decision to keep their teaching in other areas the same freed them to concentrate on making changes in the writers' workshop. Having a focus on just one of the workshops helped teachers to keep from feeling overwhelmed and allowed them to develop a thorough knowledge of their chosen workshop.

At this point, teachers whose states, districts, or schools are focusing on standards or benchmarks may wish to identify their major goals for student learning, either in reading or writing. Developing five to seven broad goals for student learning (provides a good start (for ideas, refer to the article on establishing grade-level benchmarks in chapter 11).

Participants who choose to focus on the readers' workshop will find it helpful to read and discuss chapters 2 through 5. Those who choose to focus on the writers' workshop will find chapters 6 through 9 informative. None of the chapters needs to be read straight through. Rather, participants should feel free to pick and choose among the articles, depending on the issues they find themselves facing in their classrooms. The articles featuring the work of a particular educator—such as Violet Harris, Marie Clay, Donald Graves, or Lucy Calkins—provide background on theory and research. Other articles, while alluding to the research, address practical concerns, such as classroom organization and scheduling, or describe instructional strategies and activities.

In most cases, chapters 10 and 11, on evaluating students' progress in the readers' and writers' workshops, will prove useful after changes in instruction have been made. It is important to be clear about goals for student learning. However, introducing an elaborate assessment or evaluation system, without first improving students' learning opportunities through changes in instruction, generally does not lead to the desired increases in students' literacy achievement (Au, 1994).

Teacher as Reader, Writer, and Self-Evaluator

Most teachers, while they were students themselves, did not have the opportunity to participate in a readers' or writers' workshop or to create their own evaluation portfolios. Thus, a good experience for preparing to conduct a readers' workshop is to participate in a teachers' book club (see article in chapter 4 on The Impact of Shelley Harwayne and teachers as readers). Similarly, a good experience for preparing to conduct a writers' workshop is to participate in a teachers' writing group and become a writer yourself (see article in Chapter 8 on The Impact of Donald Graves and teachers as writers).

Creating a professional portfolio is an excellent way to learn more about the process of setting goals and evaluating one's own learning (McLaughlin et al., 1998). Professional portfolios may be used to document teachers' achievements, just as evaluation portfolios may be used to document students' achievements.

Working Toward Full Implementation

Once the change process is underway, it is essential for teachers to keep on track and work toward full implementation of their chosen workshop. Au and Scheu (1996) found that improvements in student learning did not occur until teachers had fully implemented their chosen focus. Their findings point to the importance of staying with a particular focus for a least a year and possibly two or three years.

Teachers need to define what will constitute full implementation in the context of their particular classroom and school. Often, full implementation is best described in terms of a checklist, such as those presented in Figures 12.1 and 12.2. As shown in the vignettes earlier in this chapter, teachers may refer to these and other checklists, such as those developed by Johnson and Wilder (1992) and Vogt (1991). The checklists shown here were used by experienced teachers to evaluate their own practices. They liked these checklists because of the specificity of the items. However, other teachers may find these checklists too detailed and lengthy.

Most teachers probably will not want to adopt an existing checklist in its entirety. Instead, they will develop their own checklist for the writers' workshop or readers' workshop while borrowing ideas from existing sources. Teacher-developed checklists can be tailored to the situation in particular schools and classrooms.

Once the checklist has been devised, teachers sit down and evaluate their teaching practices, noting which items are already in place in their classrooms and which items are not. At this point, they may find it helpful to use the reflection and goal-setting form shown in Figure 12.3. As illustrated in the vignettes, they set goals for the coming month by identifying the items they would like to work on. In our experience, one of the keys to success is setting clear goals as well as a deadline by which those goals will be accomplished. New goals are set and pursued until teachers feel that all checklist items are in place in their classrooms. At this point, teachers may decide to add on to the checklist or to move on to another area (for example, from the writers' workshop to the readers' workshop).

A pair or small group of teachers may choose to work on the same items together, providing one another with ideas, and teachers may arrange to visit or observe one another. Peer coaching may prove to be a valuable means for teachers to give and receive feedback (Robbins, 1991). At this point the key to sustaining change may be the formation of formal and informal networks of teachers assisting one another.

In conclusion, while the process of change is always challenging, it can be made manageable if teachers keep a clear focus. The change process is facilitated if teachers can count on their colleagues for support through discussion groups and networks. Patience is required, as the change to new forms of literacy instruction and assessment is often a matter of years rather than months. Yet the benefits experienced by teachers and students can make all the hard work worthwhile. Teachers report new enthusiasm for teaching and a commitment to continue with innovative forms of instruction and assessment. Best of all, teachers see that they are able to develop students' ownership of literacy, as well as their ability to read and write.

References

Au, K. H. (1994). Portfolio assessment: Experiences at the Kamehameha Elementary Education Program. In S. W. Valencia, E. H. Heibert, & P. P. Afflebach (Eds.), *Authentic reading assessment: Practices and possibilities* (pp. 103–126). Newark, DE: International Reading Association.

Au, K. H. & Carroll, J. H. (1997). Improving literacy achievement through a constructivist approach: The KEEP Demonstration Classroom Project. *Elementary School Journal, 97* (3), 203–221.

Au, K. H., & Scheu, J. A. (1996). Journey toward holistic instruction. *The Reading Teacher, 49* (6), 468–477.

Bird, L. B. (1989). *Becoming a whole language school: The Fair Oaks Story.* Katonah, NY: Richard C. Owen.

Carroll, J. H., Wilson, R. A., & Au, K. H. (1996). Explicit instruction in the context of the readers' and writers' workshops. In E. McIntyre & M. Pressley (Eds.), *Balanced instruction: Skills and strategies in whole language* (pp. 39–63). Norwood, MA: Christopher-Gordon.

Chandler, K., & Mapleton Teacher-Researcher Group. (1999). *Spelling inquiry: How one elementary school caught the mnemonic plague.* York, ME: Stenhouse.

Hubbard, R. S., & Power, B. M. (1999). *Living the questions: A guide for teacher-researchers.* York, ME: Stenhouse.

Johnson, J. S., & Wilder, S. L. (1992). Changing reading and writing programs through staff development. *The Reading Teacher, 45* (8), 626–631.

McLaughlin, M., Vogt, M. E., Anderson, J. A., DuMez, J., Peter, M. G., & Hunter, A. (1998). *Portfolio models: Reflections across the teaching profession.* Norwood, MA: Christopher-Gordon.

Ridley, L. (1990). Enacting change in elementary school programs: Implementing a whole language perspective. *The Reading Teacher, 43* (9), 640–646.

Vogt, M. (1991). An observation guide for supervisors and administrators: Moving toward integrated reading/language arts instruction. *The Reading Teacher, 45* (3), 206–211.

FIGURE 12.1   WRITER'S WORKSHOP: CLASSROOM ORGANIZATION

	Oct.	Nov.	Dec.	Jan.	Feb.	Mar.	Apr.	May
1. **Frequency** (avg. 4-5 times/week)								
2. **Length** (minimum 45 min./day)								
Workshop rules/procedures:								
3. Collaborative decisions								
4. Clarity and consistency								
Materials:								
5. Accessibility								
6. Amount								
7. Variety								
References and resources:								
8. Accessibility								
9. Variety of types								
Regular location for:								
10. Large group sharing								
11. Conferring								
12. Quiet work								
13. Editing								
14. Publishing								
15. Promoting collaboration								
Student publications:								
16. Variety of genres								
17. Variety of formats								
18. Regularly published								
19. Accessible								
20. Use in instruction								
Writing folders/notebooks:								
21. Contain work in progress								
22. Record keeping forms								
23. Items show organization								
Filing system:								
24. Drafts								
25. Published with drafts								
Systems/schedules:								
26. Conferring								
27. Sharing								
28. Editing								
29. Publishing								

FIGURE 12.1 cont.   WRITER'S WORKSHOP: INSTRUCTIONAL PRACTICES

		Oct.	Nov.	Dec.	Jan.	Feb.	Mar.	Apr.	May
Teacher as writer:									
1.	Demonstrations								
2.	Writes with students								
3.	Shares own writing								
4.	Shares experience with writing process								
Teacher's mini-lessons:									
	Audience:								
5.	Whole class								
6.	Small group								
7.	Individual								
	Types:								
8.	Classroom procedures								
9.	Author's craft								
10.	Mechanics								
	Content (list):								
11.	Student writing used for instruction								
12.	Takes advantage of teachable moments								
13.	Makes connections to literature								
14.	Language/vocabulary development								
Teacher/student conferences:									
15.	Procedures								
	Content (list):								

FIGURE 12.1 cont.   WRITER'S WORKSHOP: STUDENT OPPORTUNITIES FOR LEARNING

(Has the teacher created an environment where most students can...?)

		Oct.	Nov.	Dec.	Jan.	Feb.	Mar.	Apr.	May
	Ownership of process:								
1.	Enjoy writing								
2.	Show confidence & pride								
3.	Value the writing process								
4.	Have a sense of audience								
	Knowledge of process:								
5.	Select own topics								
6.	Plan								
7.	Draft								
8.	Revise								
9.	Edit								
10.	Publish								
11.	Share								
12.	Confer								
13.	Understand reasons behind process								
14.	Show independence as writers								

FIGURE 12.1 cont.   WRITER'S WORKSHOP: ASSESSMENT

		Oct.	Nov.	Dec.	Jan.	Feb.	Mar.	Apr.	May
Student portfolios:									
1.	Contain writing samples								
2.	Record keeping forms								
3.	Student-teacher meetings								
Knowledge of benchmarks:									
4.	Teacher								
5.	Students								
Teacher monitoring:									
6.	Status of the class								
7.	Portfolios								
8.	Other forms								
9.	Data informs instruction								
Goals:									
10.	Teacher has system for goal setting								
11.	Students set goals								
12.	Students reflect on goals								
13.	Students evaluate own progress								

FIGURE 12.2   READER'S WORKSHOP: CLASSROOM ORGANIZATION

		Oct.		Nov.		Dec.		Jan.		Feb.		Mar.		Apr.		May	
1.	**Frequency** (avg. 4-5 times/week)																
2.	**Length** (minimum 60 min./day)																
	Workshop rules/procedures:																
3.	Collaborative decisions																
4.	Clarity and consistency																
	Materials:																
5.	Accessibility																
6.	Amount																
7.	Variety																
	References and resources:																
8.	Accessibility																
9.	Variety of types																
	Regular location for:																
10.	Large group sharing																
11.	Small group instruction																
12.	Peer group meetings																
13.	Individual work																
14.	Library																
	Student response to literature:																
15.	Written/drawn/drama																
16.	Connected to benchmarks																
17.	Aesthetic and efferent																
18.	Regularly assigned																
	Systems/schedules:																
19.	Small group instruction																
20.	Peer instruction																
21.	Sharing																
22.	Voluntary reading																

FIGURE 12.2 cont.   READER'S WORKSHOP: INSTRUCTIONAL PRACTICES

	Oct.	Nov.	Dec.	Jan.	Feb.	Mar.	Apr.	May
Teacher as reader:								
1. Demonstrations/read aloud								
2. Reads with students								
3. Shares own reading								
4. Shares experience with reading process								
Small group instruction:								
5. Varies grouping for different purposes (ability, interest, skills)								
6. Instruction frequency (minimum 3 times/week)								
7. Length (minimum 15 min./group)								
8. Lesson structure (e.g., ETR, DRTA, CTA)								
9. Talk-story structure								
10. Vocabulary strategies								
11. Authentic literature								
12. Other resources (e.g., dictionary)								
Teacher's mini-lessons:								
Audience:								
13. Whole class								
14. Small group								
15. Individual								
Content (list):								
16. Student responses used for instruction								
17. Takes advantage of teachable moments								
18. Makes connections to writing								
19. Word reading strategies								
20. Language/vocabulary development								
21. Connections to voluntary reading								

FIGURE 12.2 cont.   READERS' WORKSHOP: STUDENT OPPORTUNITIES FOR LEARNING

(Has the teacher created an environment where most students can...?)

		Oct.	Nov.	Dec.	Jan.	Feb.	Mar.	Apr.	May
	Ownership of process:								
1.	Enjoy reading								
2.	Show confidence & pride								
3.	Value the reading process								
	Reading community member:								
4.	Join teacher-led discussion								
5.	Discuss reading with peers								
	Knowledge of process:								
6.	Read for a purpose								
7.	Use word reading strategies								
8.	Use vocabulary development strategies								
9.	Show personal response to literature								
10.	Comprehend story elements								
11.	Construct themes								
12.	Make life connections								
13.	Understand reasons behind process								
14.	Show independence as readers								

FIGURE 12.2 cont   READER'S WORKSHOP: ASSESSMENT

		Oct.	Nov.	Dec.	Jan.	Feb.	Mar.	Apr.	May
	Student portfolios:								
1.	Contain written responses to literature								
2.	Record keeping forms								
3.	Student-teacher meetings								
	Knowledge of benchmarks:								
4.	Teacher								
5.	Students								
	Teacher monitoring:								
6.	Monitoring individual students								
7.	Systematic data collection								
8.	Observations inform instruction								
	Goals:								
9.	Teacher has system for goal setting								
10.	Students set goals								
11.	Students reflect on goals								
12.	Students evaluate own progress								

FIGURE 12.3   PROFESSIONAL DEVELOPMENT REFLECTION AND GOAL-SETTING FORM

**Professional Development
Reflection and Goal-Setting Form**

Name_____

Date_____

1. I feel the following are going well in my classroom:

2. I have accomplished the following goals:

3. My current goals (continued from last time or new this time) are:

4. The kinds of support I could use to reach my current goals are:

Reflections:

Author Bios

Dr. Kathryn Au

Kathryn H. Au is a professor in the College of Education at the University of Hawai'i. Previously, she worked as a researcher, curriculum developer, teacher educator, and classroom teacher at the Kamehameha Elementary Education Program (KEEP) in Honolulu. Her research interest is the school literacy learning of students of diverse cultural and linguistic backgrounds, and she has published over 70 articles on this topic. A member of the Board of Directors of the International Reading Association, Kathy has been president of the National Reading Conference and vice president of the American Educational Research Association. She received the Causey Award for outstanding contributions to reading research and is a member of the Reading Hall of Fame.

Judith A. Scheu

Judith A. Scheu currently teaches first grade at the Kamehameha Elementary School in Honolulu. She has also taught preschoolers and second graders and worked as a primary grades remedial reading teacher in a federally funded program. Judy was a curriculum developer for 13 years with the Kamehameha Elementary Education Program (KEEP), where her work centered on enhancing the literacy growth of native Hawaiian children.

Jacquelin H. Carroll

Jacquelin H. Carroll is an independent curriculum developer, researcher, and evaluator in Honolulu, working with public schools and non-profit organizations on a variety of curriculum and assessment projects. She also supervises student teachers for the University of Hawai'i College of Education. Previously, Jackie was a curriculum researcher and developer for the Kamehameha Elementary Education Program (KEEP), where she worked on literacy development in the upper-elementary grades. She has been a classroom teacher at the elementary, intermediate, and high school levels, teaching regular and special education with a focus on reading.

INDEX

Author Index

Title Index